THE NOVEL OF
HUMAN RIGHTS

THE NOVEL OF
HUMAN RIGHTS

James Dawes

 Harvard University Press

Cambridge, Massachusetts
London, England   2018

First printing

Library of Congress Cataloging-in-Publication Data
Names: Dawes, James, 1969– author.
Title: The novel of human rights / James Dawes.
Description: Cambridge, Massachusetts : Harvard University Press,
    2018. | Includes bibliographical references and index.
Identifiers: LCCN 2018001853 | ISBN 9780674986442 (alk. paper)
Subjects: LCSH: Discourse analysis, Literary—United States. |
    Human rights in literature. | Literature and morals—United States. |
    Fiction genres. | Aesthetics.
Classification: LCC P302 .D33 2018 | DDC 809.3/93582—dc23
LC record available at https://lccn.loc.gov/2018001853

For David and Suzanne

Contents

Introduction

THE CONCEPT OF HUMAN RIGHTS is not new to US political culture. Frederick Douglass was among the first US activists to consistently use the phrase in his work. Franklin Roosevelt's 1941 Four Freedoms address called for the "supremacy of human rights everywhere." And Jimmy Carter called for an "absolute" commitment to human rights in his 1977 inaugural address.[1] But despite this long history, human rights has only ever been a "guest language" in the United States, to use Mark Bradley's phrase.[2] It never achieved widespread cultural legitimacy, neither as movement nor as rhetoric—that is, until only very recently.

What is happening in the United States today is unlike anything that has happened before. A globally articulated human rights movement has infused US ethics, language, and thought. A wide array of diverse internal populations and institutions are speaking in overlapping vocabularies and self-consciously forming alliances around the rhetoric of universal human rights.[3] Large organizations like Amnesty International have achieved an almost universal iconic status. And lesser-known human rights nongovernmental organizations (NGOs) have proliferated around the nation to address regional, local, and even neighborhood needs. In the United States we are, for the first time, living in a popular culture of human rights. Even the dramatic setbacks to human rights policy in the most recent moments of US politics are, to my mind, best understood as a sign of the pervasiveness of human rights as a movement. Its power has helped trigger a frightened, revanchist ethno-nationalism.

For the purposes of this book, what is most important about this rise of a popular culture of human rights is the corresponding increase in institutional intersections between human rights and literature. "Literature and human rights" is not only a name for an academic subfield, but also a descriptor of increasingly deliberate institutional relationships and collaborations. In 2008, Dave Eggers's book series Voice of Witness became a registered nonprofit dedicated to changing US conceptions of human rights through storytelling. In 2009, Amnesty International commissioned leading writers from around the world to write short stories prompted by individual articles of the Universal Declaration of Human Rights. That same year, it published a similar book for young adult readers.

Literary scholarship both reflects and contributes to this increased threading of intersections. Scholars are teaching literature and human rights courses in colleges and universities across the country. Leading institutions like the National Humanities Center and the University of Chicago are developing online syllabi banks for faculty to consult. The Modern Language Association (MLA) and American Comparative Literature Association regularly convene literature and human rights panels, and academics are organizing literature and human rights conferences around the world.

This upsurge of interest within literary studies is changing human rights research and pedagogy across disciplines. Once dominated by philosophy, history, and political science, human rights journals increasingly include literary research. Graduate and undergraduate human rights programs are following the lead of early innovators like Bard College and Macalester College in treating the arts as central to their curriculum rather than as ornamental. In 2012 the National Humanities Center held the first of three planned interdisciplinary conferences on human rights. At that inaugural meeting, literature professors were in the majority. In all the interdisciplinary conferences I had ever attended on human rights in the previous decade, this was a first by a very wide margin.

Literature and human rights emerged as a subfield of literary studies in 2006–2007, with the publication of a special issue of *PMLA* on human rights and four simultaneous monographs that mapped out the historical and ethical parameters of the interdiscipline: Joseph Slaughter's *Human Rights, Inc.: The World Novel, Narrative Form, and International Law* (2007); Elizabeth Swanson Goldberg's *Beyond Terror: Gender, Narrative, Human Rights* (2007); my own *That the World May Know: Bearing Witness to Atrocity* (2007); and Lynn Hunt's *Inventing Human Rights: A History* (2007). But as Swanson and Alexandra Schultheis Moore aptly note, the roots of the subfield extend back several decades. Pathbreaking works like Elaine Scarry's *The Body in Pain* and Kay Schaffer and Sidonie Smith's *Human Rights and Narrated Lives* laid the foundation of the subfield, as did the collective work of a range of disciplinary movements, including law and literature, trauma theory, queer theory, Holocaust studies, and postcolonial studies.[4]

Partly as a result of these diverse theoretical precursors, literature and human rights as a subfield does not align neatly with preexisting literary periods or national groupings. Its scholars come from a range of backgrounds and engage topics that can be bewilderingly diverse for manuscript reviewers and editors. There is, however, one unifying fact about the subfield that can be asserted with clarity: it is dominated today almost entirely by scholars who do not self-identify as Americanists.[5] Here's a minor but telling example. *American Literary History*'s 2011 review article on human rights and literature consisted of four display cases. Notably, three were not works of literary criticism and the one literary-critical work was not Americanist. The essay concluded by citing the need for a broad survey of scholarship committed to the "wholesale discrediting of human rights."[6]

With this book, I hope better to connect Americanist literary studies with the new subfield of literature and human rights. I will argue for the importance of an explicitly articulated human rights framework to Americanist literary criticism, and for the importance

of Americanist literary criticism to that same human rights framework. In particular, I hope to connect the origin narratives of the
literature and human rights subfield to the urgent work on ethics,
rights, and aesthetics produced over decades in Americanist literary
studies. Key fields of interest here include ethnic American literary
studies, regional and hemispheric American literary studies, and scholarship on sites regularly targeted by reports from Amnesty International and Human Rights Watch, such as US prisons.[7]

I hope to contribute further to literature and human rights by
addressing an increasingly felt critical imbalance internal to the subfield itself. Since literature and human rights has deep roots in the
"ethical turn" of 1990s literary studies, a great deal of its theory has
focused on ideology critique and moral normativization. Critics have
framed texts by way of ethical paradoxes inherent to the broader
human rights movement itself. They have argued, for instance, that
representations of atrocity are both principled interventions and acts
of voyeurism; that human rights protects the dignity of the human
by juridically restricting what counts as human; and that it grounds
itself in the integrity of the unviolated body even as its theoretical
dualism denigrates bodily experience. Considerations of aesthetic
form have received significantly less attention. However, there are
key exceptions, including a 2015 volume in MLA's Options for
Teaching book series and, most notably, Slaughter's *Human Rights,
Inc.: The World Novel, Narrative Form, and International Law*. The
latter magisterially tracks the centuries-long ideological overlap
between the rise of human rights and the narrative functions of the
bildungsroman, from Goethe's *Wilhelm Meister's Apprenticeship* (1795)
to contemporary first-person postcolonial bildungsromane.

My ambitions for contributing to the underdeveloped scholarship
on form and human rights are narrower in scope than Slaughter's.
In this book, I identify the centers of aesthetic gravity that pull texts
together into what I have come to think of as a genre of the contemporary American novel: namely, the novel of human rights. I
write in response to the felt need among literary scholars for an articulation of the genre of human rights. Scholars, writers, and readers
alike have found it useful to conceptually group literary works narratively organized around human rights concerns. These groupings

range from Elizabeth Anker's academic analysis of "human rights bestsellers" to the human rights booklists on Goodreads and the human rights book clubs of Amnesty International and the Advocates for Human Rights. Using a human rights lens is by now an established method of reading a novel. But nobody has yet attempted to clearly name and articulate the novel of human rights as a contemporary genre. This book argues that the human rights novel, just like the mystery novel or the novel of manners, exists as a form that affects both reader and writer expectations. It also claims that thinking about the novel of human rights as a genre adds an aesthetic and conceptual depth to our readings not fully provided by the human rights interpretive method. As Claudio Guillén writes: "A genre is a descriptive statement, but, rather often, a declaration of faith as well. Looking toward the future, then, the conception of a particular genre may not only incite or make possible the writing of a new work; it may provoke, later on, the critic's search for the total form of the same work."[8]

As I elaborate on some of the genre's formal features over the chapters that follow, I will take up a series of related questions. What connective structures and recurring concerns can be discerned at this early stage in the development of the genre? How do its ethical pressures generate formal patterns and, in turn, how do its formal patterns generate ethical pressures? And finally, since both the textual and political forms are rapidly evolving, what can this rising genre teach us about the near futures of literature and literary studies in the United States?[9]

To begin, I will argue that the novel of human rights is both a contemporary and a US genre. This is an important but not obviously true claim, and both of its terms require examination. Let me start with the idea that the genre is contemporary. At the highest level of abstraction, there are two primary and opposed narratives for thinking about the history of human rights: the continuity and discontinuity models. The continuity model includes the work of historians like Hunt, Paul Gordon Lauren, and Micheline Ishay. These scholars argue that the history of human rights as a movement can be traced back at least to the French Revolution and the Declaration of the Rights of Man and of the Citizen, and possibly much further,

as far back as Greek and Roman Stoic formulations of the cosmo-
politan. This model presents human rights as a historical telos
grounded in philosophical reason and the historical expansion of empathy. Political movements and religious ideas about human dignity
from centuries ago and across cultures are best understood as ante-
cedents that have established the basic conceptual groundwork of our
contemporary moment. The history of human rights is the history
of a messy and complicated but nonetheless continuous progress.

On the other end of the spectrum is the discontinuity model. The
most visible spokesperson of this model, Samuel Moyn, argues that
the human rights movement is just what happens to be left over, now
that history's other utopias have all failed. For Moyn, the historical
story offered by scholars like Lauren is a basic mistake. The story of
the march of history toward our contemporary moment of human
rights is a teleological story that should be considered suspect. It is a
grand narrative that makes us the end point of history, that looks for
deep historical foundations for our contingent modern values. It
treats wildly different political, religious, and utopian traditions as
if they were all inevitably pointing to and building upon each other.

The truth of the matter, Moyn says, is that human rights in the
way we think about it today in the United States is essentially a post–
Jimmy Carter phenomenon. Figures from the past who have been
depicted as fighting for human rights—even those who used the
phrase "human rights"—were either historically marginal or they
were thinking about something fundamentally different from what
we currently think of as "human rights." They were talking about
citizenship or membership rights rather than the rights due to us
simply by virtue of being human. The closest we can get to a plausible origin point, Moyn believes, is 1977. In that year, Amnesty International received the Nobel Prize, Jimmy Carter used the phrase
"human rights" in his inaugural address and made it a modern buzz-
word, and the *New York Times* quintupled its use of the phrase over
all previous years that we can trace.[10]

The debates between these two factions (in conferences, books,
journals, and magazines) are fierce—much more fierce than usual for
academic arguments about historical end zones and goalposts. They
are fierce because each story is based upon a powerful, if implicit,

moral claim. Continuists believe that their story supports the urgent work of human rights today. It does so by providing historical and philosophical authority to new, fragile organizational forms that are vulnerable to delegitimization not only by way of political force but also by way of intellectual and cultural arguments. The discontinuist story, which seeks to break the link between the history of empathy and the development of human rights, has a different but equally compelling moral motivation. It objects to the continuist claim that when we study social justice movements from the past, we are studying particular points along the long arc of the history of human rights. If we accept this claim, discontinuists worry, we accept that the concept of human rights is the only relevant framework for understanding empathy and political organization. In other words, human rights continuism constrains what we can imagine as justice.

For my purposes, what is important about this debate is not the primary point of contention but rather the primary point of agreement. However and whenever the human rights movement began, all parties agree that it has achieved an unprecedented cultural saturation, political comprehensiveness, and clarity of articulation in the United States only in the past thirty years. Emerging alongside this consolidation of rights culture in the United States, I argue, are a range of new narrative patterns that are beginning to cohere. These patterns develop from and draw on related genres like the contemporary expatriate novel and earlier traditions of justice writing, including slave narrative, Holocaust literature, and even the war novel.

Now let's turn to my claim that the novel of human rights is a specifically US genre. This is an equally contentious matter. I want first to emphasize that my basic claim is a minimalist one. I simply argue that among US-based texts there is a pattern emerging that can be usefully understood as a new genre of the novel. The pattern may or may not be distinct to particular literary markets, histories, and geographies; similar or dissimilar patterns may be emerging across the globe. Hopefully, framing a specifically US novel of human rights will not implicitly reinforce a Western-centric model of human rights precisely because it is premised upon the limited particularity, rather than the assumed universality, of political discourse in the

United States. And as I hope to show in the pages that follow, the choice to restrict myself to a narrow, US-based framework can bring focus to debates and trends that might otherwise be lost in a larger comparative or world literature framework. Perhaps most important as a matter of method, the US frame offers a good opportunity to think through debates about the "American" in American studies that have vexed the discipline for decades.[11]

In broad brushstrokes, the critical conversation has moved through three primary stages. First, with the ascendance of New Historicism in American literary studies in the 1980s, scholars positioned themselves against earlier work that organized cultural and literary imagination around a reified notion of the nation-state. Deconstructing notions of American exceptionalism, challenging homogenizing cultural narratives, and unmasking the ideological function of the idea of the United States, scholars like Sacvan Bercovitch participated in an opening of the field that was both methodological and archival. As many have pointed out since, however, relentless debunking of the "myth of America" nonetheless served to reinforce US centripetalism. Scholars refigured the United States as a site of dissent rather than consensus, but, as Peter Carafiol puts it, they also continued to privilege the same field-defining question: "how to unite the disparate and fragmentary facts of experience in the New World into a coherent account about the national culture."[12]

In response, a range of scholars began to articulate models of US pluralism resistant to unifying narrative reductions of culture and ideology. These scholars started to formulate a trans-American imaginary that refigured "American" fiction anew as a heterogeneous grouping of overlapping but distinct regional, hemispheric, and even global discourses. As Paul Giles prompted: "American literature should be seen as no longer bound to the inner workings of any particular country or imagined organic community but instead as interwoven systematically with traversals between territory and intercontinental space."[13] Debunking what might be thought of as literary epistemologies of territory, Carolyn Porter argued that a new American studies should comprise "a quadruple set of relations between (1) Europe and Latin America; (2) Latin America and North America; (3) North America and Europe; and (4) Africa and both Americas." The point, she emphasized, was not mere hemispheric expansion, "but rather to grasp how the cultural, political, and economic relations between and within the Americas might work to reconstellate the field itself, reinflecting its questions in accord with a larger frame."[14]

Finally, in our current moment, scholarship seeks to construct methodologies that can address key institutional and ideological challenges that the "hemispheric turn" faces. First, how can hemispheric American studies cohere as a field when populated by entrenched departments defined by national, linguistic, or regional frameworks? And second, how can the expansion of American studies avoid reproducing colonializing, US-centric principles for organizing knowledge? As Sophia McClennen writes in her provocatively titled essay, "Inter-American Studies or Imperial American Studies?," the hemispheric turn assumes that

> inter-American studies does not already exist, that it is a field available for exploration and development and that the members of the American Studies Association could simply rename themselves inter-Americanists . . . What would an inter-American studies housed in English and History departments in the United States and taught by monolingual faculty be, if not an example of US intellectual expansionism?[15]

It is in this broad and conflicted context that I call for thinking of a novel of human rights that is specifically US-based. The idea of the genre I am proposing embodies the paradoxes of the hemispheric in American studies no less than the political work of human rights itself does. There is no morally or conceptually durable resting point between the particular and the universal in literary or political forms. Nationalism is both the primary obstacle to newly theorized cosmopolitanisms and also a key mechanism for their realization. And any perceived necessary localization is also always, to some degree, only a temporary construct.[16] Nonetheless, I believe there are benefits to temporarily narrowing our scope of analysis from analyzing literature and human rights as a matter of world systems—as the subtitles of Slaughter's and Anker's defining studies emblematically characterize it—to viewing it in more narrow frames.

There is no such thing as a single US human rights movement. Instead, there is a crisscrossing series of human rights movements operating across multiple borders and under various umbrella organizations, national languages, and categories. Nonetheless, it is true that, at the broadest level, the political, rhetorical, and ideological function of human rights in the United States has not only operated in distinction from but also often in direct contradiction to the practices and conceptions of human rights across the Americas, Europe, Asia, and Africa. As Eleni Coundouriotis has demonstrated in her discussion of African war novels, the concept of human rights signifies differently and generates distinctive literary patterns depending upon the primary nation-specific audience for which it is articulated.[17]

Specifically, human rights as a rhetoric produced by and for US-based audiences must be understood in its complicated relation (sometimes collaborative, sometimes antagonistic) not only to US civil rights movements but also to totalizing historical narratives of US exceptionalism, interventionism, and expansionism. Indeed, human rights as a cultural commodity occupies a market space in US literary publishing that authors inside and outside its borders write toward—a point illuminated brilliantly in Anker's case study of US-based post-9/11 "human rights bestsellers." In her view, these bestsellers consoled "narcissistic fears about the growing instability of Western hegemony" by imaginatively distancing the reader from antithetically figured "violated, anarchic postcolonial bodies."[18]

Unlike the selected best sellers Anker focuses on, the US novel of human rights as a more comprehensive genre is less easy to theoretically encapsulate. It is, moreover, both inward- and outward-looking, taking not only atrocity abroad as its narrative focus but also atrocity at home. Indeed, many US rights novels are quite deliberate about subverting the ideological distinction between rights inside and rights outside national borders. Dave Eggers's *What Is the What* (2006)—a book about "rights outside"—is self-consciously emblematic in its strategy of detailing atrocities committed in Sudan within the narrative framework of race relations in the United States.[19] Just so, Ana Castillo's *The Guardians* (2008)—a book about "rights inside"—insistently contextualizes the comprehensive effects of racism in a New Mexican border town through a global human rights frame, invoking the Berlin Wall, the School of the Americas, and Human Rights Watch.

Part of what makes it important to theorize a specifically "US" novel of human rights, then, is the urgency of the following question: What is gained and what is lost when we import the terms and methods of universal human rights both to ethnic American literary studies and to the specific historical and contemporary justice movements it analyzes?

While the case studies in the chapters that follow are my deepest answer to that question, I also want to offer more direct answers now to frame my readings. The question for us as literary critics about the losses and gains of the human rights frame is a specific instantiation of a larger question about the relationship between human rights and civil rights in the United States. I believe this question helps contextualize much of the Americanist distancing from literature and human rights as a subfield. The activist Dorothy Thomas recalls the discouraging moment when her most respected professional mentor told her that "the idea of reintegrating human rights into U.S. social justice activism 'was a loser' and its potential 'minuscule.'"[20] I have experienced similar discouraging moments of resistance when helping colleges implement human rights curricula at the undergraduate level. Colleagues in legal studies in particular have declined to include African American literature courses that focus on civil rights. Some oppose translation of civil rights into human rights because they believe the latter's universalizing discourse flattens out the urgent historical specificities of race relations in the United States. Others argue that the concept of civil rights is a constitutional matter that invokes the idea of the "citizen" rather than the "human," and that the civil rights movement developed largely independently of the post–World War II human rights legal regime.

Indeed, it could be argued that the history of US civil rights is a history of a traumatic split from and disillusionment with human rights. In 1947, W. E. B. Du Bois and the NAACP petitioned the newly created United Nations Commission on Human Rights to investigate the systematic violation of the human rights of African

Americans. But the petition, *An Appeal to the World*, outraged
Eleanor Roosevelt, who was the chair of the Universal Declaration
of Human Rights drafting committee. Roosevelt was also a prominent member of the NAACP board of directors. In response to the
petition, she threatened to resign from the NAACP, arguing that
the rights of the "colored people in the United States" were not an
appropriate matter for the human rights commission. She insisted
that the petition only played into the hands of the Soviet Union,
which was eager to support investigations that might embarrass
the United States. NAACP leader Walter White ultimately balked,
appealing to Roosevelt to remain on the board and, later, announcing
that the NAACP would never again bring a case to the United
Nations.[21]

While I understand the strength of these arguments against the
utility of human rights in a US context, I side with those who today
see more potential gains than losses. After all, it was precisely the
perceived seriousness of the threat that human rights treaties posed
to Jim Crow legislation—specifically, the fear that the 1948 Genocide Convention could boost federal antilynching efforts—that
prompted southern senators to push for the extremist Bricker
Amendment. This stealth rewriting of the Constitution would have
effectively annulled the executive branch's capacity to make international treaties.[22] Moreover, in my opinion there is a disquieting
proximity between the legalist view that the only relevant vocabulary for understanding US racism is the language of civil rights and
the exceptionalist view that human rights violations are things that
occur in other countries. Just as significantly, new theoretical work
in human rights provides powerful counterarguments to the long-
standing criticism that human rights is a universalizing discourse
that flattens out local realities. Domna Stanton's work on "new" or
"critical" universalism in human rights is exemplary in this respect.[23]
Moreover, in my experience, local activists around the world are
much less likely to endorse this criticism than academics.

Finally, I am persuaded by the legal scholar Cynthia Soohoo, who
argues that collaboration between civil rights and human rights
organizations within the United States has in recent years gained
critical momentum and offers unique opportunities. "The wall be-

tween domestic social justice and international human rights work is crumbling," she writes, citing three key causes:

> (1) globalization and increased receptiveness on the part of at least some US judges and lawyers to international and foreign law; (2) a decline in the effectiveness of traditional civil rights legal strategies, opening the way for new strategies; and (3) the growth and development of the international human rights advocacy model, which is now being adapted for the U.S. context.[24]

There is, of course, the further question of the utility that the human rights framework offers specifically to literary scholarship. Does it newly link texts and help us see them individually anew? Does it bring understudied texts to more prominent attention? To begin the work of answering these questions, I start with a claim: where both authors and activists are going, literary critics should follow.

Before I turn to the novels themselves, let me finish this introduction with a definition, three caveats, and a map of the arguments in the chapters that follow. First, the definition. I have for several pages now been using the phrase "human rights" as if it is a clear and uncontested concept. From one angle, that is a fair thing to do. The claim of human rights is simple. We all have rights that are due to us simply because we are human, not because we are citizens of a particular state or members of a particular religion. We can also clearly distinguish human rights from other social justice movements by identifying a particular legal background and set of institutions. These include the Universal Declaration of Human Rights, the United Nations Human Rights Council, and the nine core human rights conventions, each with its own monitoring body.[25]

Clear enough so far, but that is only a small part of what "human rights" means. It is difficult to keep track of the proliferating number of organizations around the world that self-describe as dedicated to the promotion of human rights. But what we do know is that their goals do not coalesce around a simple, agreed-upon concept, and many make no explicit connections to the instruments and bodies described above. The concept of human rights is not owned by international lawyers or the United Nations. Many groups invoke its moral authority even as human rights legalists deny the legitimacy of their claims—typically by arguing that the claims are a matter of citizenship or constitutional protections rather than human rights.

But even within circles restricted to legalist purists, there is often contentious disagreement about what human rights are. Much more on this later, but for now: many embrace human rights minimalism, emphasizing a core set of protections necessary for basic human dignity; and many embrace human rights maximalism, pushing for ever more inclusive conceptions of human flourishing. Significantly, each group sees the other as a threat to the project of human rights.

The concept of human rights has yet another tangle. It is often conceptually blended with humanitarianism, even though the two traditions have distinct missions and legal histories. The historical path of international humanitarian law is more or less unrelated to the major human rights touchstones of the French Revolution, Nuremberg, and the Universal Declaration of Human Rights (UDHR). It starts instead in 1864 with the Geneva Conventions, which were drafted to provide protection during wartime to persons considered "hors de combat," including soldiers wounded on the battlefield, soldiers shipwrecked at sea, prisoners of war, and civilians. And the primary organizational guardian of humanitarian law is not the UN but rather the International Committee of the Red Cross (ICRC).

The core principles of humanitarianism are neutrality, independence, and impartiality: respectively, aid workers do not take sides in any conflict; aid organizations remain independent of governments; and aid is given on the basis of need alone, not nationality, race, gender, religion, or political affiliation. In other words, humanitarianism assiduously avoids the political so that it can be more effective in its primary work: alleviating suffering.

Human rights, by contrast, is nothing if not political. Its ultimate aim is not to mitigate suffering but to confront and disable the systems causing suffering. As it is sometimes explained, humanitarianism is a matter of providing "a bed for the night," whereas human rights is a matter of "naming and shaming." Take Guantánamo Bay as a clarifying contrast. In 2016, Human Rights Watch was still petitioning for full access to prisoners at Guantánamo Bay, more than a decade after the ICRC's first intensive on-site investigations.[26] The

ICRC is granted unique and critically important access to detention centers around the world so that it can improve conditions for prisoners. It is permitted to do so precisely because it promises not to share information about what it discovers and not to bring international pressure to bear on perpetrator regimes. Human Rights Watch—a sharer and shamer—has nothing like the ICRC's access, but it is also not constrained by confidentiality agreements and can therefore take immediate and public action to pressure governments.

These key differences aside, however, human rights and humanitarianism have significantly overlapping goals. Indeed, they are frequently taught in combined programs at universities because of curricular synergies. In the example above, human rights and humanitarianism are both dedicated to protecting the same rights of the same prisoners. And post-9/11, the treaties most often invoked in US political discussion of human rights were the Geneva Conventions rather than the UDHR. Moreover, some notable organizations have begun explicitly combining the distinct approaches. Michael Barnett's aptly titled lecture, "Human Rights and Humanitarianism: Distinctions with or without a Difference?," draws attention to a rising "rights-based" orientation in the humanitarian sector, emphasizing the serious concerns this shift has raised over the integrity of humanitarian missions.[27] Médecins Sans Frontières (MSF), most famously, is a humanitarian organization that has sometimes taken public political stances more like those of Human Rights Watch than those of the ICRC. MSF was, indeed, founded by doctors who broke with the ICRC in Biafra because they could not remain politically silent while the Nigerian government slaughtered and starved civilians. At the same time, however, MSF has also reacted strongly against the increased blending of humanitarianism and development (another overlapping field) because of the latter's nonemergency focus along with its explicitly political dimensions.[28]

Even if one emerges from all of the above with a clear sense of what we mean when we say human rights, there are still *at least* five distinct models of what human rights actually are—or rather, how they function. For the benefit of clarity, but at the risk of cartooning, I will describe them as simply as possible.

One group I have already alluded to might best be described as human rights teleologists. They conceptualize global history, sometimes loosely and sometimes strictly, as a movement toward the moral end point of human rights—an end point that is foundationally grounded in religion or philosophical reason. They believe human rights are universal in the sense that they are true and apply independently of whether or not any particular set of people believe in them.

Human rights pragmatists, by contrast, believe that the concept of human rights is a flawed and temporary historical construct that nevertheless provides the most effective set of institutions and vocabularies available today for promoting human flourishing. They believe human rights are provisionally universal in the sense that we have reasons to argue for enforcing them even in the face of cultural relativism. In response to any particular challenge to a human rights claim, pragmatists can say one of two things. First, however theoretically contestable a claim may be, it can be defended empirically if similar claims or conceptions are evident in local values and traditions. Second, if human rights "gets it wrong" empirically, one can still defend it on procedural grounds. Human rights as an overall system merits support because it is a self-revising, always-in-process aspiration to universality rather than a substantively closed worldview. The affect of pragmatists is often similar to that of teleologists, in that they are ardent defenders of the movement. However, pragmatists believe the concepts deserve protection not because they are atemporal moral universals but rather because they are, as regulating ideals, as fragile as they are essential.

A third group, what are often called "realists," view human rights law as an unenforceable set of contingent norms that are minimally relevant to the real world of power politics. The concept of human rights is advantageous only insofar as it can be used to politically pressure those with competing interests. It is disadvantageous insofar as it undermines "our" state sovereignty (whoever "our" is).

A fourth group, human rights skeptics, comprises scholars and political actors trained in ideology critique, anti-colonialism, and anti-foundationalism. Such thinkers tend to characterize human rights as a system of values infiltrated by Western and, in particular, US imperialism. They warn that the human rights movement consolidates political and cultural visions of the individualized liberal subject at the expense of competing visions of human flourishing based on, for instance, the values of community and duty.

And finally, what might be thought of as human rights rejectionists view the human rights movement as a reformist project that aims to preserve the status quo. They reject the concept of human rights because it is a mechanism designed to make unjust neoliberal systems tolerable enough to stave off radical movements demanding substantive change.

For my purposes, it is not necessary to pick a team. In fact, as I will argue at the end of this book, I think it is best not to pick a team. At any given place and at any given time, one, some, all, or none of the above descriptions may be useful. Purists who insist upon a single stance seem to me, quite simply, wrong—that is, unless they are using their purism as a way of diluting the purism of others.

In this book I will not be advancing a singular thesis about human rights or about how the novel of rights relates to the movement. Some novels, as we shall see, implicitly critique Westernized conceptions of human rights by highlighting the damaging effects of the United States' Cold War demotion of economic and social rights. Others implicitly endorse such Westernized conceptions by modeling a liberal subjectivity constituted by individualism and citizenship and by fetishizing the violation of privacy, in the form of either private property or bodily integrity. Some novels depict human rights work as an urgent ethical necessity, and some as an ineffectual bureaucratic structure dedicated to its own operational self-preservation. The novels—like the movement—are not singular.

Now for the three caveats. First, my argument for the novel of human rights as a genre, and for the inclusion of any particular book within that genre, does not depend upon the intent of the author. It is a critical platitude to distinguish between what an author intends and how a text functions. Nonetheless, I contend that in many and perhaps even most cases authors are writing within what might be called an aesthetic awareness of human rights and humanitarian discourse. Chang-rae Lee, for instance, makes Henri Dunant's *Un Souvenir de Solférino* (the world's seminal humanitarian text) a symbolic center for his own humanitarian novel *The Surrendered*. Similarly, Ann Patchett makes the International Committee of the Red Cross (the world's most important humanitarian organization, which was brought into being by *Un Souvenir de Solférino*) a symbolic center for her humanitarian novel *Bel Canto*. Of course, when authors like Lee discuss the moral inspiration of their work, they are often quick to clarify that their ambitions are aesthetic rather than didactic. Such disclaimers testify to the continuing aesthetic influence of modernism, which rejected the morally edifying premises of the nineteenth-century humanitarian narrative or social problem novel. Nonetheless, I contend that most authors who write contemporary rights novels do so with an ambient sense of moral purpose, and some even with an explicit and specific social mission.

National Book Award finalist Patricia McCormick and best-selling author Corban Addison, to cite two of the more overt examples, are clear about the rights-oriented ambition of their novels, making the front edge of their marketing ethical rather than aesthetic. Addison's web page bio underscores that he is a "supporter of numerous humanitarian causes" and that he uses the novel to "address some of today's most pressing human rights issues."[29] And McCormick explains that she writes "to give voice to experiences that might not otherwise be spoken about . . . to bring attention to issues people might not otherwise know about and . . . to change attitudes."[30]

Second, as the first work that attempts to identify and map out the US novel of human rights, this book will have significant limits, necessarily raising as many questions as it answers. Does the search for patterns across regional foci—for instance, linking literature of Central American displacement with eastern European war crimes—reproduce the pernicious flattening out of context attributed to human rights legal universalism? Do the narrative patterns I have identified draw primarily from rights practice as it entered US cultural consciousness in the late 1970s through the 1980s, through representations of transitional justice in Latin America (for instance, Ariel Dorfman's *Death and the Maiden*)? Or from Soviet dissidents (Aleksandr Solzhenitsyn's *The Gulag Archipelago*)? Or South African anti-apartheid activism (the work of Nadine Gordimer)? And to what extent do they draw on works across African American literary traditions, from the *Narrative of the Life of Frederick Douglass* to Richard Wright's *Native Son* to Ernest Gaines's *A Lesson before Dying?*[31] Indeed, what is the relationship between the novel of human rights and not only slave narrative but also what is often called neo–slave narrative— for instance, Octavia Butler's *Kindred* or Charles Johnson's *Middle Passage?*

Finally, at what point does framing the project by way of distinctive US cultures of rights and US literary markets become a constraint in understanding developing patterns in Anglophone or even global literatures and rights cultures? Do we also, and simultaneously, need broader regional or global frames for bringing together novels like, for instance, Michael Ondaatje's *Anil's Ghost*, Chimamanda Ngozi Adichie's *Half of a Yellow Sun*, and even the speculative fiction of China Miéville?

The answer to that last question is almost certainly yes. The effort to organize initial genre analysis by way of US-based texts is meant to inspire rather than close off comparative analyses of rights fiction around the world. Indeed, even as I frame my arguments by way of Americanist literary study, I will throughout this book occasionally reference non-US-based texts. I will do so both to highlight connections between this work and scholarship in global literary studies, and to reinforce the idea that the national frame I am using as a construct is, so to speak, only useful as long as it is useful.

Third, while genres are useful forms of pattern recognition, they have what can only be described as seriously fuzzy borders. Just as there are books about crime that we would not call crime novels, there are novels manifestly about human rights, as we currently understand them, that I would not call human rights novels. Examples include Émile Zola's *Germinal*, which has political and ethical aspirations that, as Moyn would argue, should not be teleologically subsumed into human rights, and Vince Flynn's *Memorial Day*, in which torture figures prominently, but as a celebrated political tool. Just so, there are novels that have the formal features of detective fiction— murder, red herrings, English country estates, and the unraveling of mysteries through ratiocination—that we would not call detective fiction: for instance, Kazuo Ishiguro's *Never Let Me Go*. In the same way, there are books that have what I will identify as the formal features of the human rights novel—a justice or escape plot, with a cluster focus on violated homes, mobility crises, and damaged families—that I would not call human rights novels: P. D. James's *Children of Men*, for instance, or some of the *Harry Potter* novels (although, of course, one could read both James and Rowling from a human rights perspective, emphasizing allegories of authoritarianism and discrimination—but that's a different matter from analyzing human rights as a genre).

In the end, it is every reader's judgment whether or not a particular novel passes a threshold for "counting" as part of a genre, just as it is their judgment whether or not thinking of genre adds anything to our experience of reading. I hope you will agree that the novels I have selected in this book count. And I hope that my genre-based readings will persuade you that the novel of human rights is a useful addition to our contemporary critical vocabulary.

Finally, the map. In the pages that follow, I will provide a broad sense of the thematic concerns and aesthetic properties cohering in the novel of human rights, and also highlight the wide range of texts one might fruitfully analyze under this conception of genre.

In Chapter 1, I will focus on two primary narrative patterns in human rights novels as they relate to one primary ideological conflict in the human rights movement. I will do so through close analysis of emblematic examples rather than through catalogs. First, I will identify two distinct plot structures that characterize contemporary novels that take human rights as an explicit and dominant concern: the escape plot and the justice plot. Second, I will focus my readings upon the creative tensions generated within each text by the most fundamental division in the contemporary human rights movement: the ideological split between the "generations" of rights. Authors I will focus on include John Edgar Wideman, Karen Tei Yamashita, Francisco Goldman, and Isabel Allende.

In Chapter 2, I will examine a much wider range of texts to map out what I see as the defining topoi of the novel of human rights. Following a conceptual framework for prioritizing rights that is embedded in the Universal Declaration of Human Rights, I will track how the genre organizes itself around the recurring concerns of privacy, mobility, and family. While the key texts in Chapter 1 use plot patterns to deliberately challenge US-centric, liberal conceptions of human rights, the texts in Chapter 2, I will argue, tend implicitly to reinforce such values because of their reliance upon perceived normative thematics.

In Chapter 3, I will return to a shorter list of narrative case studies, focusing on the work of Richard Powers, Chang-rae Lee, and a small cluster of lesser-known novelists. My primary aim here will be to investigate more deeply the role of gender in human rights representation, particularly as it relates to conceptions of nationhood and human rights internationalism. More specifically, I will focus on power asymmetries and voyeurism in human rights representations, linking these to what I see as the contemporary, rights-based reconfiguration of Fredric Jameson's controversial concept of "national allegory."

Finally, in Chapter 4, I will close with an in-depth examination of atrocity—not from the perspective of survivors, witnesses, or fieldworkers, but rather from the perspective of the perpetrators themselves. While I will consider a range of works, including Chris Abani's *The Secret History of Las Vegas*, I will focus most extensively upon Jonathan Littell's *The Kindly Ones*. I will argue that Littell's novel presents two different models of perpetrators: perpetrators as moral monsters, and perpetrators as "ordinary men," in Christopher Browning's phrase. I will contextualize the latter model by using principles from organizational sociology, analyzing what Littell sees as the "bureaucratic" roots of evil. The opportunities and challenges of representing the perpetrator, which might be considered the boundary case for human rights representation, will allow me in the closing section to circle back to some of the questions broached in this introduction about the conceptually precarious and, sometimes, politically self-consuming nature of our contemporary human rights movement.

CHAPTER 1

The US Novel of Human Rights

OVER THE NEXT four chapters, I will try to persuade you that the novel of human rights exists as a genre and that it is aesthetically and intellectually vital. Each of the texts I will discuss could be illuminated through the prisms of existing, well-understood genres: the thriller, the war novel, the romance, or even the mystery. It is my hope that reading these texts differently, as examples of a newly developing genre of the novel, will help us better understand not only the texts themselves, but also the ethico-political contexts in which they are being written. Like all genres—but especially those in the process of aesthetically cohering—the novel of human rights is a complicated, multilayered formal construct, resistant to simple definitions. By the end of this book, I hope I will have provided a satisfying and even comprehensive account of that complicated layering. To begin, I want to offer a starting point that is both clear and helpfully generalizable. The novel of human rights as a genre tells myriad stories. But in the end, it is almost always defined by one of two different kinds of plots: the justice plot or the escape plot.

In the justice plot, the central narrative is a narrative of return, of violation and its investigation, of the pull of past crime and attempts to repair it. In the escape plot, the central narrative is a narrative of departure, of accumulating, forward-pushing violations, of escape as opposed to repair. The justice plot looks to the detective novel, while the escape plot looks to the picaresque. The justice plot is centripetal, spiraling inward to a single point, while the escape plot is centrifugal, arcing outward into ever wider space. I will return to the latter in the second half of the chapter. For now, I want to focus on the justice plot.

Justice as a concept is normally read in one of two ways: distribution or restitution. That is, justice is either about the fair or unfair distribution of wealth and opportunities in an ordered society, or it is about the attempt to provide closure after wrongdoing, either through compensation or punishment. In US novels of human rights, justice plot protagonists are agents of restitution. This structural tendency, I will argue, is critical to understanding how US-based authors affirm or challenge the US vernacular of human rights. Typically, justice plot protagonists are estranged from the land they once inhabited. They reconcile themselves to their past by returning home to investigate a single crime that stands in for systematic human rights abuses. They are transitional figures for the reader, entering a place that is both alien and intimate, a place they must come to terms with and, finally, claim as their own to promote their vision of justice.

Discussing Camus's allegorical exploration of the Holocaust in *The Plague*, Shoshana Felman argues that the task of the literature of witness is to impart knowledge: "a first-hand, carnal knowledge of victimization, of what it means to be 'from here' (from quarantine), wherever one is from . . . knowledge of the way in which 'this history concerns us all,' in which 'this business' of the Plague 'is everybody's business.'"[1] In novels of human rights, this task is urgent and pervasive. Justice plots cling to a remarkably consistent narrative framework, whether depicting atrocities in Argentina, Chechnya, Sri Lanka, or Philadelphia. Tremorous from the moral hazards of proxy advocacy and, equally, what Viet Thanh Nguyen has called "the emblematic victim," they focus on protagonists who see themselves as morally compromised.[2] In Anthony Marra's *A Constellation of Vital Phenomena* (2013), for instance, the protagonist returns to her home in Chechnya to rescue from sex traffickers the sister she left behind.

In Sylvia Sellers-García's *When the Ground Turns in Its Sleep* (2007), the protagonist returns to his birthplace in Guatemala under false pretenses to investigate his parents' history, only to discover his family's culpability in an abduction orchestrated during civil unrest. And in Sara Nović's *Girl at War* (2015), a former child soldier, sole survivor of a Serbian massacre, returns to her village in Croatia to learn the fate of all those she abandoned.

Sometimes the investigating protagonist is not a guilty expatriate but rather an alienated internal exile. Examples include Nathan Englander's novel about disappearances in the Dirty War, *The Ministry of Special Cases* (2007), and Aminatta Forna's *The Hired Man* (2013), in which the "returnee" function is split between the Croatian protagonist, Duro, and the British outsider whose arrival triggers a reinvestigation of his village's tortured past. Whatever the variation, across justice plots the dominant characterological feature is displacement. In Isabel Allende's *Of Love and Shadows* (1987), the protagonist investigates abuses in the unfamiliar interior of her own nation, a new land for her that is both familiar and foreign, hers and not hers. Debbie Ogedemgbe of Buchi Emecheta's *Destination Biafra* returns to Nigeria after her education abroad at Oxford, participating in the Nigerian Civil War and working to imagine a new Nigeria. The protagonist of Hong Ying's *Summer of Betrayal* flees from the state crime at Tiananmen Square (and its mirror crimes of informing and betrayal) to find her personal liberation in an underground subculture whose hedonistic defiance makes it both alien and truly hers. In Demetria Martínez's *Mother Tongue* (1994), the protagonist never physically abandons her country but instead becomes an outsider to it by defying federal law as a participant in the Sanctuary Movement. She, like the author herself, is vulnerable to official charges of conspiracy against the US government for providing safe haven to undocumented Central American families fleeing rights abuses.

In representing such protagonists, justice plots explore a conflict that is built into the universalist ambition of human rights itself. How do you act for justice in a specific place when your right to claim authority in that place is precisely what's in question? How do you act out of care for others when your well-intentioned intervention involves not only altruism but also the projection of your own anxi-

THE US NOVEL OF HUMAN RIGHTS

eties, conflicts, and needs onto the other? Sarah Stone's *The True Sources of the Nile* and Douglas Unger's *Voices from Silence* are only two of the many available examples—some of them more, some of them less self-conscious—featuring human rights activists with over-determined motives who seek to claim as home the countries they also see themselves as serving. The recurring fictional device of the displaced protagonist in the justice plot—the one who is both at home and away, who has authority and doesn't, whose motives are both pure and suspect—offers a way of thinking about the strategies of human rights and humanitarian organizations working in emergency zones around the world. As Rony Brauman of Doctors Without Borders explains of fieldwork practices: "There must be a mediator—a personality or a volunteer from a humanitarian organization—to 'authenticate' the victim, channel the emotion generated and provide both distance and a link between the spectator and the victim."[3] Like the investigating protagonist of the justice plot, such mediating figures are always morally compromised.

Justice plots are explorations of legitimacy crises at the level of individual and system. Violations take place in settings where domestic populations or institutions—in part or as a whole—are perceived to be in crisis, illegitimate, or directly implicated in the crime itself. But justice plots are not only about the legitimacy crisis of the government under investigation as the content of the novel. They are also about the legitimacy crisis of the human rights regime that positions itself as the expert, external investigator, and, on top of that, the legitimacy crisis of the novel itself as a form.

Rights novelists face particular ethical challenges, for instance, due to the genre's reliance on spectacular bodies. There is often no clear line between the necessary and the exploitative, between witnessing and voyeurism. The range of strategies authors use to represent physical and psychological trauma is, therefore, wide almost to the point of polar opposition. Omar Rivabella's *Requiem for a Woman's Soul* relentlessly exposes the abused body of one torture victim. By contrast, Lawrence Thornton's *Tales from the Blue Archives* is about disappeared bodies that become the objects of obsessive, grieving imagination. In some works, the aesthetics of the body are integrated into the aesthetics of narrative closure, with an equally polar range.

Héctor Tobar's *The Tattooed Soldier* ruminates over gruesome images of a slaughtered family in order to emotionally amplify the conclusion, in which the surviving family member climactically murders the responsible Guatemalan death squad commando. Michael Ondaatje's *Anil's Ghost*, in stark relief, focuses on a forensic anthropologist's clinical analysis of inconclusive skeletal remains and concludes with the frustrating retreat of her fact-finding commission, in the stalling of revelation and closure. At the meta-narrative level, some novelists meet the challenge of what to do with the violently exposed body by thematizing the act of guilty watching. Stona Fitch's *Senseless* is about what happens when torture is televised for mass consumption. And Englander's *Ministry of Special Cases* tells the story of a young man's disappearance by making torture exclusively visible in the naked body of an unnamed, plot-irrelevant young woman, almost as if to directly ask, What right do we have to expose her like this?

Julia Alvarez makes anxiety over the "rights" of the rights novel explicit in her wrenching novel *In the Time of the Butterflies* (1994), which tells the story of General Trujillo's brutal dictatorship in the Dominican Republic and his infamous murder of the dissident Mirabal sisters. Only a handful of months after the murder, Alvarez— then only ten years old—was herself forced to flee the Dominican Republic because of her father's involvement in a failed plot to oust Trujillo. Conceived as a respectful commemoration of the murdered women, *In the Time of the Butterflies* nonetheless frames itself as an accusation against its own writing. It opens by describing the clumsy, intrusive efforts of a foreign writer who wants to interview the single surviving Mirabal sister, Dedé, on the anniversary of the murders. A stand-in for Alvarez's own worry over well-intentioned exploitation, the writer is a kind but nonetheless hurtful intruder into the life of a traumatized survivor who seeks, in her old age, only to be left alone, to cultivate an unpenetrated privacy that Trujillo never permitted. As Junot Díaz comments pointedly in his own Trujillo novel, *The Brief Wondrous Life of Oscar Wao* (which explicitly references Alvarez): "Rushdie claims that tyrants and scribblers are natural antagonists, but I think that's too simple; it lets writers off pretty easy. Dictators, in my opinion, just know competition when they see it. Same with writers. *Like, after all, recognizes like.*"[4]

Alvarez and Díaz are concerned about the arrogance of claiming a right to speak on behalf of others and about the aesthetic instrumentalization of trauma. "My God," Dedé declares, "how people romanticized other people's terror!"[5] More deeply, they and other rights writers are concerned about a fundamental conflict between the novel as a form and the aims of justice: namely, the problem of the one and the many. In the novel of human rights, the crime that is investigated represents systemic rather than exceptional abuse. It is decidedly not about one case or one person—but it is, ultimately, a single crime. In this way, rights violations present a challenge to the novel's ability to adequately describe the world, insofar as the novel as a form—that is, the realist novel, in the broadest sense of the word, ever since Defoe and Richardson—has tended toward individual identification, individualizing narrative, and individual problems. In other words, because the novel of human rights is dominated by individual crimes it is also dominated by individualizing conceptions of rights. It focuses upon first-generation civil and political rights by contrast to second-generation economic and social rights.[6] Civil and political rights, which include physical integrity rights along with freedom of speech and religion, emphasize protecting the individual from state interference. Economic and social rights, which include rights to employment, housing, and health care, emphasize the obligations of the state to its collective citizens.

Before moving forward with how this split plays out in rights novels, let me provide some background. At the World Conference on Human Rights in Vienna in 1993, representatives from 171 states reaffirmed two of the most important principles of human rights: universality and indivisibility. Universality means that human rights belong to all people everywhere and are not, for instance, contingent upon citizenship. Indivisibility means that human rights are conceptually intertwined and even interdependent. It is not permissible to sacrifice one category of rights—for instance, the rights of women—in order to pursue others. This idea of the indivisibility of rights is manifest in the primary expression of international human rights, the 1948 Universal Declaration of Human Rights (UDHR), which elaborates first-generation and second-generation human rights as an organic whole.

But the UDHR was a political document born in the post–World War II ideological competition between the United States and the Soviet Union. The Vienna conference's reaffirmation of the principle of indivisibility was at least in part a corrective response to the Cold War competition over which rights counted most: political and civil rights or economic and social rights. Antagonism over indivisibility in the composition of the UDHR—drafter René Cassin characterized it as the most emotional dispute in the negotiation process[7]— eventually culminated in the splitting of the UDHR into two separate and, in key ways, competing documents: the International Covenant on Civil and Political Rights and the International Covenant on Economic, Social, and Cultural Rights (both 1996). In the ideological contest that ensued over the next several decades, one thing would become clear. In the US popular culture of human rights, economic and social rights lose.

The defining image of human rights in US political imagination is Amnesty International's "prisoner of conscience." Founder Peter Benenson coined this phrase in his 1961 Appeal for Amnesty:

> Open your newspaper any day of the week and you will find a report from somewhere in the world of someone being imprisoned, tortured or executed because his opinions or religion are unacceptable to his government. There are several million such people in prison—by no means all of them behind the Iron and Bamboo Curtains—and their numbers are growing. The newspaper reader feels a sickening sense of impotence. Yet if these feelings of disgust all over the world could be united into common action, something effective could be done.[8]

Importantly, it's not only that this individual prisoner of conscience summarizes human rights for the United States. It's also that the kind of agency Amnesty International offered to its imagined newspaper reader was individualizing action: letter-writing campaigns from individuals in support of individuals imprisoned in other people's countries. The political prisoner and the Amnesty International member function as a political diptych: on the one hand, the person detained for free speech; on the other hand, the person exercising the right to free speech.

Two things, I should emphasize, are simultaneously true here. The rights of political dissidents are vitally important, and the work of Amnesty International and like organizations is vitally important. And, at the same time, the image of the political dissident has been a critical weapon in the United States' global political-image wars, which have aimed to destroy the idea that rights are indivisible and to repel economic and social rights as intrusive, foreign interventions.[9] However capacious Amnesty International's mission is now, with years of across-the-board human rights work, its origin story remains a powerful influence in the US popular culture of human rights.

This global political tension between competing conceptions of rights is also a formal narrative tension in US literature. For especially illuminating case studies, I will focus on John Edgar Wideman's *Philadelphia Fire* (1990), Karen Tei Yamashita's *I Hotel* (2010), and Francisco Goldman's *The Long Night of White Chickens* (1992). Wideman's and Goldman's novels model key features of the justice plot (Yamashita's adds a layer of complexity I will describe in more detail below). In *Philadelphia Fire*, systematic human rights violations against African Americans are narratively represented through the trauma of a single child. Simba is the sole survivor of the state police firebombing of the Philadelphia row house where members of the African American back-to-nature group MOVE lived, burning down sixty houses in the neighborhood and killing eleven people. The narrator, Cudjoe—who feels both connected to and anxiously alienated from the old neighborhood he abandoned—returns to try to find Simba, get the story, and achieve justice and truth through narrative. Cudjoe as returnee-protagonist, like Alvarez above, remains deeply concerned over the ethical complexities of writing on behalf of others. "You want Simmie's story so you can sell it," a former member of MOVE accuses.[10] Cudjoe is here a stand-in for Wideman himself, who asks in his memoir about the imprisonment of his brother, *Brothers and Keepers*: "Wasn't writing about people a way of exploiting them?"[11]

Philadelphia Fire is about what counts as a human right in US political discourse. It is also about the way the novel's pressure toward individualization *reaffirms* what counts. The book opens by generating desire for individualized narrative closure—Will Cudjoe find Simba?—but in the end refuses to provide it. The search for the child is hopeless. He is irretrievably lost into the city, and then lost from the narrative itself, replaced—in a startling moment when Wideman inserts himself as a character into the text—by another lost child, Wideman's own imprisoned son Jake. Jake is a wrenchingly personal stand-in not only for Simba but also for Cudjoe's own abandoned children. He represents, indeed, all the lost children of Philadelphia, who are apocalyptically emblematized in the adolescent gang, Kaliban's Kiddie Korps. The gang, which is allegedly conspiring to kill all adults in the city, links the plight of the novel's individual lost children to atrocities of near unnarratable scope, from US white supremacist terrorism to the long history of western European imperialism. Wideman connects them to the KKK, Shakespeare's Caliban, and the *"Kids Krusade"* (88)—the latter a reference to the thirteenth-century march of children across Europe to retake the Holy Land that ended with masses of children gone missing or sold into slavery.[12]

Just as the lost child who is the book's ostensible subject disappears, the narrator himself disappears. By the end of the novel, Wideman abandons the subplot of Cudjoe's effort to achieve self-understanding by reconciling himself to the love, hate, and guilt that binds him to his hometown. At one point, Cudjoe starts a "harebrained project" (146) to stage *The Tempest* in his inner-city neighborhood school—but after much preparation and work, the play is never staged. Wideman has remarked, tellingly, that the episode is based upon an experience from his own past, in which he remembers the deep "disappointment" of students who were abandoned by a teacher who—like a stereotype of the humanitarian interventionist—came and went and "didn't see it through."[13] But as Madhu Dubey also suggests, Cudjoe's project fails in the narrative because it is a self-serving fantasy of the artist's ability to play, as an individual, a "redemptive role in society."[14] Indeed, in *Philadelphia Fire*, Wideman rejects not only the authority but also the voice of the individual artist. Cudjoe as a guide is replaced by a series of narrators, including a homeless man named JB, Wideman himself, and others, who together produce a panoramic catalog of structural racism and economic and social rights violations in Philadelphia. Jan Clausen characterizes this series of disorienting perspectival shifts as an aesthetic flaw. *Philadelphia Fire*, she writes, "fails to fulfill the demands of a hero-centered narrative."[15] But as Susan Pearsall characterizes it, "the novel clearly calls for a turn from narcissistic, artistic-centered modernism to a form of community-constructed 'realism.'"[16]

Wideman's turn toward deindividualized narrative is an experiment with the novel's capacity to represent competing hierarchies of human dignity and need. *Philadelphia Fire* starts with the justice plot's typical pattern: the first-generation human rights violations of political persecution and police murder, summarized in a single disappeared body. But it then shifts from its individualizing opening toward a communitarian vision of the city and toward a plot-resistant depiction of economic and social rights violations. *Philadelphia Fire* simultaneously generates and disavows particularizing desire because to focus on the individual is both necessary for understanding systems of injustice and also a way of failing to understand them, a way of turning systems and larger context into mere background. For Wideman, the endangered individual who is the gathering point of our empathy can also make us forget that the rights of free individuals are not the only rights that matter. *Philadelphia Fire*'s careful attention to the problem of the one and the many characterizes Wideman's broader human rights work. Focusing on the one, Wideman asserts that his brother Robert, sentenced to life in prison for second-degree murder, is a "political prisoner." Focusing on the many, he insists that the story of the individual political prisoner must be part of a wider call for a "mass movement for human rights," beginning with the US prison system as a site for understanding the indivisibility of social and economic rights.[17]

Like *Philadelphia Fire*, Francisco Goldman's *The Long Night of White Chickens* examines the links between narrative practice and human rights in US culture. *The Long Night of White Chickens* is the story of the murder of a humanitarian worker. The narrator, Roger, is a young man living in the United States who returns to his childhood home in Guatemala to investigate the unsolved murder of Flor de Mayo. Flor was a Guatemalan orphan who came to live with his family as a maid, but quickly became something like a daughter and sister. In her adoptive community of Namoset, Massachusetts, Flor represents the prototypical refugee narrative. She is the Mayflower, an outcast who comes to America to become a success. To everybody's shock, however, the United States is not the end point of this particular refugee story. Flor returns to Guatemala after graduating from Wellesley to run a private orphanage and malnutrition clinic.

Much like *Philadelphia Fire*, *The Long Night of White Chickens* models basic features of the justice plot. The catastrophic civil war is represented by way of a single crime that will be solved when a murderer is named, satisfying the narrative desire it generates. And the investigating returnee, Roger, feels both a sense of belonging to and alienation from Guatemala. Indeed, much of the book is about Roger's struggle to understand his own identity and to reconcile himself to Guatemala, just as Cudjoe tries to reconcile himself to Philadelphia.

There are multiple theories for Flor's murder. Guatemala's devastating internal conflict has led to a massive displacement of populations, putting Flor's work with war orphans at the dangerous intersection of humanitarian need, criminal networks, government corruption, and potential guerrilla retribution. At one point shortly before her murder, for instance, a government official demands that she pay an excessive bribe to acquire an exit visa for an orphan who needs lifesaving surgery abroad as part of his adoption process. When the official threatens to arrest Flor on trumped-up charges of baby trafficking if she refuses to pay, Flor appeals for help from the Swiss Embassy and goes into hiding. Running alongside this plot of Flor's life and death is the present-day framing plot of the investigation Roger and the journalist Luis Moya conduct into her murder. This part of the story climaxes when the two men are confronted by a government death squad, which is targeting Moya for an article he wrote exposing government corruption. In short, with both the main plot and this subplot, Goldman is giving US readers what most justice plots give US readers: a story of first-generation human rights in which the characters of interest are all, essentially, variations on the prisoner of conscience.

Goldman sets up this narrative pattern only to undo it. Like *Philadelphia Fire*, *The Long Night of White Chickens* refuses to solve its own mystery. We never find out who killed Flor. Indeed, as I will argue later, this desire to "find out" is finally characterized as morally suspect. Refusing to provide individualizing answers to complex social problems, Goldman questions the exclusionary dominance of civil and political rights in US political discourse. At one point, for instance, Roger explicitly mocks the "certainties" he held as a visiting American, when he could understand Flor's life and death only as a human rights fable of first-generation violations: the individual savior of individual victims of physical integrity and freedom violations. Reflecting upon the case of one orphan, whose community has been decimated because of its association with guerrilla forces, Roger highlights how the vivid narratability of first-generation rights can occlude second-generation rights: "I thought Flor's orphanage must be full of little girls like that one, forgetting about all the children orphaned by the more mundane calamities of poverty and urban life. The Orphanage of the Revolution. Crazy. But I fantasized it. Nuns rescuing children who were in some kind of danger, because they were the offspring or siblings of guerrillas or union leaders or university students murdered or gone underground."[18]

Roger's final hypothesis about Flor's murder synopsizes the competing moral and narrative pressures of the individual / social binary. Flor was involved in a love affair with a political figure that went terribly wrong. In her distraction after the breakup, she arranged for a young girl to be sent to France for adoption. Years later, it becomes clear that the girl had a surviving older brother who was left behind because Flor (purposefully and illegally? negligently in her depression over the breakup?) conducted the adoption as if he did not exist. Roger considers the possibility that Flor was murdered to clean up the politician's love affair, but then comes to believe that the orphaned brother came back to murder Flor in revenge. Here, the scope of social concern is expanding at the same time that narrative focus is contracting. In other words, when Roger focuses on the separated children he is focusing on context. Flor's murder is the result of social breakdown so chaotic and severe that siblings can be orphaned and then separated as a matter of course, without any political or legal accounting (some accounts of the conflict in Guatemala in the 1980s estimate 38,000 orphans and 90,000 children losing one parent).[19] When Roger focuses on the turbulent romance, by contrast, he is focusing on the individual. The romance plot is effectively depoliticizing, turning our attention away from patterns of public life toward the satisfactions of peeping into the private.

In an essay for the *Washington Post*, Goldman discusses the formal pressures of the novel as they relate to the individual/social binary. He explains that early in his career he aimed to make a hybrid of two perceived traditions: the individual-driven North American novel and the "total" Latin American novel in which "entire societies speak" by way of very particular voices and places.[20] In *The Long Night of White Chickens*, hybridization means that Goldman wants us both to focus on the deep histories of his primary characters and to resist the insistent pull of the individual. He continually shifts our attention back and forth between the face-to-face and the encyclopedic, between personalizing drama and catalogs of life. His sweeping social vistas highlight the structural economic inequalities within and across national borders that set the conditions for war and political instability; and these, in turn, are revealed to generate systematic violations of civil and political rights. For Goldman, here and in his other work, it is impossible to tease apart rights that matter from rights that don't.

Notably, the narrative concerns of writers like Goldman and Wideman are also narrative concerns in human rights work. Consider debates over the concept of "the public" in human rights. At the most basic level, human rights have always been understood this way: violations that are private are crimes; violations that are public are human rights violations. If a private citizen uses force to imprison you and hide your location, that is a crime—it's called kidnapping. If state authorities use force to imprison you and hide your location, that is a human rights violation—it's called disappearing people. At the 1993 Vienna conference, NGOs managed to make the case that the framing idea of "the public" is a gendered category that relegates to the sidelines systematic human rights violations against women, in particular domestic violence. To make that case is a victory by any standard. But as Laura Flanders explained in *The Nation*, that victory was only achieved because advocates cannily used intense, individualizing narration of physical violations against women. In other words, Flanders lamented, the kinds of violations that could rise to visibility in human rights discourse had to be violations that are easily narrated as individual stories of direct coercion and violence, by contrast to less vividly narratable issues such as "labor rights, illiteracy, self-determination or poverty."[21]

Goldman, too, worries about the way individual rights narratives can sideline "the mundane calamities of poverty and urban life." But in *The Long Night of White Chickens*, this worry is matched by a competing anxiety over deindividualization. Here, the pressing concern is not the expansion of the individual at the expense of the social, but rather the expansion of the social at the expense of the individual. It's not about how a myopic focus on individual rights blinds us to social violations, but rather how a too-distant focus on social problems blinds us to individual suffering. In *The Long Night of White Chickens*, Goldman's concern over the individual / social hierarchy within rights discourse is a frame for a deeper concern over the individual / social hierarchy within personality itself. To explain that claim, let me step back a bit.

As *The Long Night of White Chickens* progresses, Flor's murder becomes increasingly less central to the narrative. Or rather, it continues to guide the actions of the narrator, but the secret Roger discovers, the secret that ultimately defines the novel and provides its tragic climax, is not about what the unknown murderer did to Flor. It is about what Roger and her adoptive family did to her. And to explain that claim, let me step back just a bit more.

Roger spends a good deal of the book lingering over memories of Flor, but two scenes stand out. The first is Roger's characterization of the typical bar nights in Boston when local young men try to get Flor's phone number. The monotonously predictable young men see her as an exotic conquest, attractive because she represents alluringly vulnerable "third-world" poverty. To Roger's annoyance and mystification, Flor always humors them. She tells the same stories about her adaptation to US life over and over again, playing the role they desire of her while also, quite clearly, holding them in contempt and waiting for the moment when she can refuse them.

The next memory is a brief moment in front of FAO Schwarz in New York City. Roger's father Ira has been hospitalized for

gallbladder surgery; the two are walking through the city seeking
distraction. At the toy store, Flor asks Roger what he wants for
Christmas. He replies that he wants hockey skates. When Roger
returns the question, Flor says, "All I want for Christmas is for Ira
to get better" (442). Roger is shamed by his comparative selfishness,
but bothered more by what he calls a mysterious "ping" in Flor's
voice, an odd, hollow noise that troubles him for reasons he cannot
understand at the time. Indeed, it isn't until the climax of the murder
investigation years later that Roger finally understands why that
single moment, why that "ping," has continued to haunt him.

Roger, like the reader, is prepared for that final epiphany by something he comes to realize during the death squad subplot. When
the masked gunmen appear on the streets, Roger heroically endan-
gers himself to save the journalist. He pulls Moya into cover and,
with the instincts of a protagonist from a spy novel, drags him out
of range behind the screen of a moving bus. Or that, at least, is the
story Roger constructs for himself after the assault. The protagonist, who is also the narrator, wants, indeed, needs to believe in himself as a heroic agent defending the target of rights violations. But in
the end Roger's story is revealed to be an exaggerated, narcissistic,
self-affirming misperception. The US Embassy informs Roger that
it was not a death squad, just a "heavy tail." The masked men were
directed to frighten rather than shoot the journalist. Roger realizes
that he saves people only in his imagination. Packaging the incident
later like a Walter Mitty comedy, he mockingly depicts himself
telling his lover Zamara about his ingenious, instinctive heroism in
order to earn her admiration.

Roger's preparatory epiphany here is about the things we want to
believe about ourselves, and about how this inspires the stories we
tell. It is also about the way we use the tragedies of others to come
to fuller understandings of ourselves. Because in the end, what is
most important about Moya's perceived near-death experience is that
it helps Roger to see that he is not the coward who, as a child, abandoned Moya when he was attacked by a dog. Rather, he is, and always was, a hero. In other words, *The Long Night of White Chickens* is
not only concerned about the pressures of the novel as a form. It is
concerned about the narcissism of authorship itself, and the narcis-

sism of the reader as a stand-in for those whose fantasies of moral self-affirmation include the work of rescue in any of its dramatic, individualizing forms—whether it is investigating an unsolved murder, saving a persecuted journalist, taking in a Guatemalan orphan and making it possible for her to go to college, finding a boy lost after a fire, staging *The Tempest* in the inner city, or even just reading with generous and humane attention fictional accounts of people doing such things.

By the end of the novel, Roger finally understands the reason for the troubling "ping" in Flor's voice. He finally understands that Flor was never in her life allowed to be more than the orphan who would embody his family's and Namoset's vision of their own generosity; that when Flor wished for Ira's recovery she was performing the role assigned to her upon her arrival in the United States; that she was in that moment little more than what she was for the young Boston men who tried to pick her up in bars: a performance of what they needed to affirm their worldview. What Roger realizes here is that Flor, even in their most intimate moments, had intentionally performed the gratitude appropriate to a rescued orphan. Flor was inventing herself for him, just as she invented herself to match the exoticizing desires of her Wellesley roommates when she fabricated a scandalously glamorous childhood love affair with Roger; and just as she invented herself to match the desires of Roger's disintegrating, loveless family, which needed the unrelenting charm and grace of a perceived innocent to hold them together in the illusion of harmony. Roger had loved Flor more than anyone else in his life, and even so he had never known her. Flor had functioned as an emblem of humanitarian tragedy that the community around her could use to come to a satisfying understanding of itself. Indeed, she remained so in her death. Roger's investigation into her murder was always, after all, a form of self-investigation, a struggle to come to terms with the fractures of his own identity.

Roger had *used* Flor. Goldman underscores this point in the Zamara story line. A *barra* show girl and an explicit double for Flor, Zamara is the woman Flor might have become had Ira not rescued her. Roger uses Zamara so he too can imagine himself as a savior like his father—until he loses interest and, with nonchalant emotional brutality, wordlessly abandons her. The question that had puzzled Roger, his family, and Namoset throughout the novel—Why did Flor throw away the American dream, the dream they gave to her, by returning to Guatemala to live once again in an orphanage?—returns here at novel's end as more important than the question of who murdered her. Why did Flor leave? She didn't leave. She escaped.

Goldman worries about the dominance of civil and political rights and the disfiguring prominence of the individual. But as the narrative entrapment of Flor reveals, he's equally concerned about the disfiguring prominence of the social, the way individuals can get swallowed up in social and political roles. Goldman's dilemma here points to a deeper irreconcilability than the first-generation / second-generation divide that I have been using to frame novels thus far. At its most inclusively abstract, Goldman's and also Wideman's individual / social binary can be identified as a tension within a variety of political and cultural discursive registers. It is the tension between the universal and the particular, between top-down fixed authority and bottom-up multiple authorities, between the theoretical and the lived, even between self and other.

In *The Endtimes of Human Rights*, Stephen Hopgood argues that these tensions reveal fatal contradictions in the human rights movement. He insists that the human rights regime is headed for historical obscurity because it cannot balance its universalizing, top-down tendencies with the needs of the local and particular.[22] Hopgood's is one of the most fierce articulations of concerns that have dogged human rights work since the American Anthropological Association's 1947 "Statement on Human Rights." Drafted in anticipation of the UDHR, the "Statement on Human Rights" frames the tension between the individual and the community as a starting point for understanding cultural relativism.[23] While the novel of human rights often draws upon such critiques, it also renders the binaries that subtend them illegible. In the novel's complexly layered relations, every unit of social analysis admits of further subdivision. Every local is universalizing, composing and composed of claims reaching beyond; and every universal is local, built out of competing and collaborating local becomings. Indeed, as many rights advocates have argued, it is a performative contradiction for critics to assert that human rights is conceptually unsustainable because it founders on the problem of the universal and the particular. That is, the accusation that human rights is undone by its reification of imperial binaries between center and periphery is an accusation that itself relies upon binarizing conceptions of politics and culture. In my view, it is a mistake to say that human rights work fails because it cannot resolve the problem of the universal and the particular. Human rights work is, in some ways, nothing more than an insistence upon occupying that tension, an insistence upon articulating in specific contexts the ever-present conflicts around varying ideas of community.

Karen Tei Yamashita's *I Hotel* is aesthetically organized around this intrinsically conflictual relationship between different conceptions of rights and the ever-shifting boundaries of community. A finalist for the National Book Award, *I Hotel* is a series of ten linked novellas that center on the conflicts and confluences of Asian American intellectuals, artists, and activists in the Bay Area from 1968 to 1977. Resisting singularization with even more radical narrative experimentation than *Philadelphia Fire* and even greater sprawl than *The Long Night of White Chickens*, the novel has no single plot to summarize and no single character or even set of primary characters to track. It mixes a kaleidoscopic range of forms, including poetry, newsletters, short stories, illustrations, playwriting, and scriptwriting. In the *Chicago Tribune*, Alan Cheuse describes it as a "grand failure," noting that he wishes "Yamashita had stuck with a more traditional form in telling this important story, something more akin to the great novel *East of Eden*, the first book, as those who know the novel will recall, in which a Chinese character appears on American soil in all of his complexities and human potential. Or perhaps a *Portrait of the Chinese Artist as a Young Man*, with a bit more lyric to enhance the prose and the political arguments."[24] While the novel's formal pyrotechnics admittedly make it no easy read, I—like most, I imagine—disagree with Cheuse. I think that *I Hotel* is necessarily conceived as the narrative equivalent of its own ideological center, a story whose pleasures resemble the jazz music that it returns to again and again.

Invoking Marxist critiques of Western rights discourse, *I Hotel* takes as its ideological starting point the first-generation / second-generation rights split that concerns Wideman and Goldman. But Yamashita quickly reaches past this binary to explore the evolution and conflicts of third-generation human rights. The generations of rights—a heuristic organizer first proposed by the legal scholar Karel Vasak—are modeled on the motto of France, which is drawn from the French Revolution: "Liberté, égalité, fraternité." While the first two terms are relatively clear concepts in human rights, the last term has moved more slowly to conceptual and legal solidity.[25] A marker for the third generation of rights, fraternité encompasses a broad range of ideas on human flourishing, from peace and sustainable development to a healthy environment. As a historical matter, however, fraternité begins with a single and powerful directive. As Yamashita puts it at the opening of her novel: "This is about self-determination, you dig?"[26]

In the standard historical narrative, the chronologically first generation of human rights is born in the eighteenth century with the Enlightenment. It emphasizes civil liberties, focusing primarily on political participation and the protection of individuals from excessive state power. The second generation of human rights, emerging with socialism and the rise of organized labor, encompasses social and economic equality. Concentrating on the rights individuals have to all those things necessary to the full realization of personhood, including health and employment, second-generation rights emphasize not what the state should refrain from doing *to* its citizens but rather what it must do *for* them. Third-generation rights, often described as collective rights, emerge after, with what is arguably the most dramatic wave of political liberation in global history: the post–World War II decolonization of Asia and Africa.

For many, third-generation rights are a historical culmination, providing a final counterbalance to both individualist and statist conceptions of human flourishing. They emphasize that community and trans-state solidarity are aspects of individual well-being and are, moreover, critical as political and philosophical worldviews if we are to have any hope of addressing the most pressing problems of global interdependence. Decolonization, understood a particular way, becomes the first step on the conceptual path to collective rights and responsibilities that are required for species preservation. As the UN's 1972 Stockholm Declaration characterizes it:

> A point has been reached in history when we must shape our actions throughout the world with a more prudent care for their environmental consequences. Through ignorance or indifference we can do massive and irreversible harm to the earthly environment on which our life and well being depend. Conversely, through fuller knowledge and wiser action, we can achieve for ourselves and our posterity a better life in an environment more in keeping with human needs and hopes . . . To achieve this environmental goal will demand the acceptance of responsibility by citizens and communities and by enterprises and institutions at every level, all sharing equitably in common efforts.[27]

Yamashita's concern with collective duties for collective well-being focuses on the way decolonization and third-generation rights overcome the Roosevelt-Du Bois divide of domestic and international (described in the Introduction). As Yamashita said in an interview with the National Book Foundation about her research for *I Hotel*, the "Asian American or yellow power movement has perhaps been characterized as a circumscribed movement for ethnic identity, but it became evident to me that international and global connections and histories had tremendous influence and play. The birth of the Asian American movement was always transnational."[28] Throughout *I Hotel*, Yamashita tracks the way decolonization, as articulated in the language of universal human rights, provided political and rhetorical resources to civil rights activists in the United States.

At the physical and, in some ways, ideological center of *I Hotel*, Yamashita features a section entitled "Malcolm X at Bandung." The section stitches together a story fragment about the romantic tension between two Asian American civil rights activists with human rights communiqués from the 1955 Bandung Conference. The historian Roland Burke describes Bandung as a "landmark in the emergence of the non-aligned movement and the birth of the Third

World" that exercised a "revolutionary influence" on emerging UN-based human rights debates.[29] At Bandung, African and Asian nations articulated a strong commitment to the universality of human rights, as expressed in the UDHR. But they did so, importantly, by first emphasizing "full support of the principle of self-determination of peoples and nations," declaring that self-determination was "a pre-requisite of the full enjoyment of all fundamental human rights."[30] Reinforcing a 1952 UN General Assembly resolution that emerged against racist pushback from European delegations, Bandung helped codify the idea that colonialism was a grave human rights violation.[31] Bandung, interpreted thus as a synthesis of individual rights and sovereignty, of liberté and fraternité, offers a mutual promotion. That is, antiracist solidarity movements fortify themselves by drawing upon the political and rhetorical power of universal human rights. In doing so, they grant to universal human rights the legitimacy that comes from proving its relevance to the needs of populations assaulted by globally Western and nationally white power structures. In this frame, human rights displays power and coherence not only across continents but also across its generations.[32]

While "Malcolm X at Bandung" is a story of the aspirations of human rights, *I Hotel* as a whole, like *Philadelphia Fire* and *The Long Night of White Chickens*, is a story of the movement's internal tensions and historical contradictions. Third-generation rights are perceived by many to be the natural next stage of rights. By many others, however, they are viewed as a contradiction of human rights foundations. Human rights, the latter group argues, are as a simple matter of definition rights that are held by individuals. They are claims that individuals make *against* the power of states and other large social groups. The concept of collective rights is, then, a potentially incoherent conceptual shift. Indeed, some even see it as a very real danger, offering moral justification to those who would deny individual rights in the name of a purported social good. Jacob Mchangama and Guglielmo Verdirame go so far as to argue that the main proponents of third-generation rights are authoritarian states, who use them to "knock liberal states off the moral high ground and shore up their own political legitimacy." Citing a handful of examples, they note that in 2013 widely perceived abusers North Korea and Sudan encouraged Cuba to "work through the UN mechanism in progressive development of the third generation of human rights, particularly the value of international solidarity."[33]

Wideman and Goldman explore the philosophical tensions between liberty and equality. Yamashita completes the human rights triptych by staging the conflict between liberty and fraternity. In *I Hotel*, they are not incompatible—the novel celebrates the passions and ideals of solidarity movements that embrace both concepts—but neither are they seamless.[34] "Our transformation from individuals into collectives was precisely the thing that gave us power," Yamashita summarizes at the close of the novel, "but power has many sides to it" (599).

The individual-group contradictions explored throughout *I Hotel* are perhaps most overtly staged in the narratives around Chairman Mao. The novel details adulatory study of Mao's thought throughout, including important declarations from Mao calling for solidarity between people of color all over the world in support of the US civil rights movement. But the novel also includes one professor's acknowledgment that he must hide from undergraduates studying Mao's revolution the unavoidable contradictions between collective and individual—in this case specifically, between the "revolution" and the "poet intellectual." "Poetry for the Marxist-Leninist must be written for the proletariat. Everything that Chen loved about art and literature had to be destroyed or changed" (26). Later, an aging Chinese writer looks back with regret upon his life: "Yes, the pen can be a revolutionary force and a weapon, but we did not entirely understand what that means. The pen is also used to ensure conformity and political order" (74). Yamashita depicts a similar contradiction when Chinese American journalists traveling to the People's Republic experience for the first time the exhilaration of international belonging and solidarity. While on their way to Tiananmen Square, they interview a young man who explains with doctrinal acquiescence and a poignant conditional that he is content to have been consigned to work on a train rather than go to college, as he had originally hoped, because "it's my country's wish." "If my work benefits the country, then I do it wholeheartedly" (67).

I Hotel does not fit neatly into the justice plot framework I have thus far used for understanding the novel of human rights, just as it does not fit neatly into the traditional form of the novel itself. For that reason, it is a useful text to transition away from justice plots to the other dominant pattern in the novel of human rights: the escape plot. The escape plot is defined by a different set of creative tensions than the justice plot, foremost among them the problem of representing the United States as the end point of refugee narratives.[35]

In his critique of parochialism in contemporary US novels, Bruce Robbins argues that the theme of immigration as redemption goes back at least one hundred years in US novels. This celebratory "coming to America" narrative is visible even now, he says, in the work of novelists as ethically self-conscious as Junot Díaz and Dave Eggers. Discussing *What Is the What* and *The Brief Wondrous Life of Oscar Wao*, Robbins writes: "The same underlying schema, however inflected with irony, remains visible . . . Step one: atrocity in a foreign country. Step two: escape to the US."[36] I disagree with Robbins's characterization of Diaz and Eggers, and would for a counter-example point to *I Hotel*, which begins where "coming to America" myths end. With these key examples aside, however, Robbins's criticism feels generally apt for a large swath of US writing.

For a clarifying example of the narrative pattern Robbins identifies, along with its attendant ethical risks, it is hard to do better than the *New York Times* best seller by Blaine Harden, *Escape from Camp 14* (2012). *Escape from Camp 14* is the account of the life of Shin Dong-hyuk, the world's only surviving escapee from one of North Korea's total-control slave labor camps. While a work of nonfiction, the book nonetheless reveals basic, shaping narrative devices helpful for understanding novels. Before proceeding, let me emphasize clearly: disputes about the book's reliability notwithstanding, North Korean slave labor camps are a fact in the world that defy comprehension in their brutality. They are genocide in slow motion, and future generations will look back on our inaction around those camps with the same astonished outrage that we direct at past examples of gross, negligent global inaction. Books like *Escape from Camp 14* are therefore important works of witness. To criticize them for relying on simplifying formulas designed to generate broad interest is to miss the point almost entirely.

Escape from Camp 14 is a difficult book to read, however, not only because of the atrocities it recounts, but also because it uncomfortably coerces the reader into a vision of the world that consolidates reductive and self-serving US-centric "city upon a hill" narrations of global order. It is difficult to read because it appears to serve US political agendas as much as it serves victims of North Korean totalitarianism. Notably, human rights violations within North Korea seem to matter in the United States only when North Korea is felt to be a threat to the United States. The regime's atrocities then become opportunities to reaffirm that, for those suffering abroad, the United States is the inevitable redemptive end point. As I see *Escape from Camp 14*, for instance, Shin's escape to South Korea is depicted as only a partial step toward full human dignity, and that it will require the test of freedom in the United States for him to discover himself. Moreover, when Shin fails to adapt here it is not because the United States did not suffice, but because of what had been broken in Shin.[37]

Shifting back to fiction for a contrast study, Viet Thanh Nguyen's Pulitzer Prize–winning novel *The Sympathizer* turns such coming-to-America tropes upside down. An English professor and literary critic, Nguyen has written trenchantly about the ideological function of US exceptionalism in refugee narratives.[38] In *The Sympathizer*, Nguyen gives readers a protagonist who escapes to America not once but twice. In his first escape, the protagonist flees the war in Vietnam to come to America as a Communist spy. He is tasked with tracking the South Vietnamese military leadership-in-exile, which is impoverished and depressed, disillusioned by the US lie of prosperity and freedom. Among his more notable experiences is his work for an infuriating Hollywood director who is shooting a shallow, sappy, United States-as-tragic-hero film about the Vietnam War that, incidentally, exploits the labor of impoverished Vietnam War refugees. At one point the protagonist loses his patience with the director for centering the movie on the brutal rape of a young

Vietnamese woman (another troubling literary device Nguyen critiques that I will discuss in Chapter 3). When the director calls him a sellout and a loser, the protagonist responds: "I'm a loser for believing in all the promises your America made to people like me. You came and said we were friends, but what we didn't know was that you could never trust us, much less respect us. Only losers like us couldn't have seen what's so obvious now, how you wouldn't want anyone for your friend who actually wanted to be your friend. Deep down you suspect only fools and traitors would believe your promises."[39]

The protagonist's second escape to the United States comes after horrifying torture during "reeducation" in Vietnam. But even here, after the very worst of atrocities abroad, the protagonist comes to America not with hope but rather with the existential conviction that nothing awaits him, that US democracy is as ideologically bankrupt as the communism he finally fled. Ho Chi Minh's revolution had revealed only that Vietnam was much like the United States. Both could "abuse grand ideals" and transform "the vanguard of political change" into "the rearguard hoarding power" (376).

Francisco Goldman's *The Ordinary Seaman* is another escape-plot novel that organizes itself around the narrative problem of the United States as refugee end point. Here's the story in brief. Two unscrupulous US investors purchase a derelict ship, hoping to use undocumented workers to repair it while it is docked at a US port so they can sell it for an outlandish profit. For the protagonist, Esteban, having the opportunity to work in the ship represents escape from a life of constrained opportunities in Nicaragua, where he has suffered trauma fighting the Contras. But the ship (somewhat heavy-handedly named the *URUS*) is a trap. The *URUS* has been registered under a "flag of convenience," making it an extension of Panamanian sovereignty—which means that the workers aboard cannot leave it because, once on US soil, they risk deportation. The shipowners use the workers as "slave labor" in brutal and unsafe working conditions because there is no governing authority to stop them from doing so.[40] Esteban's escape from the war against the Contras is therefore incomplete until he sneaks off the ship, risking assault, homelessness, and deportation to start life as an undocumented worker in the United States.

As in *The Long Night of White Chickens*, Goldman is highlighting the conceptually incoherent split in US political culture between political and civil rights and economic and social rights. Esteban cannot claim asylum because he is an economic migrant, not a political refugee, and economic migrants do not have rights of access. But the reason Esteban arrives in the United States as an economic migrant is because of the United States' politically sponsored war against the Sandinistas and the violation of his civil and political rights as an undocumented worker. Representing the *URUS* as a vessel of freedom that becomes a prison, Goldman invokes Melville's *Tryal* and *Pequod* and even Huck Finn's raft.[41] With these novels as backdrops, Goldman rewrites the contemporary popular culture's refugee plot. Freedom in the United States can never be an end point for Esteban because freedom in the United States is a citizenship right rather than a human right. Esteban will remain, but he will remain in a state of permanent escaping. As Arendt argued after World War II of rights and refugees: "The conception of human rights, based upon the assumed existence of a human being as such, broke down at the very moment when those who professed to believe in it were for the first time confronted with people who had indeed lost all other qualities and specific relationships—except that they were still human. The world found nothing sacred in the abstract nakedness of being human."[42]

As I have been arguing throughout this chapter, formal pressures generate ethical concerns, and ethical concerns generate formal pressures. Here, concerns over political teleology press plot structure and characterization toward the picaresque. In this way *The Ordinary Seaman* is a useful example for identifying a pattern typical to escape plots, including texts like *What Is the What*, Ha Jin's *War Trash*, Edwidge Danticat's *The Farming of Bones*, and Adam Johnson's *The Orphan Master's Son*. Instead of a tightly plotted narrative that builds upon itself with "necessary and probable sequence," the escape plot tends toward episodic narratives governed by the structure of "and": and then this happened, and this happened, and this happened. The protagonist of the human rights escape plot, as in the picaresque novel, is often a first-person narrator who comes from a socially marginal position. The protagonist moves laterally from

disaster to disaster through a world of moral chaos, rather than
vertically through the organizing, socializing structures of the bildungsroman. If the primary worry of the justice plot is individualization, the primary worry of the escape plot is inevitability. To
satisfy readers, plots must entail their endings, but entailment in
the novel of human rights is a risk. Authors like Goldman do not
want to endorse a form that represents US resettlement as an
adequate answer to atrocities traceable to the United States. They
do not want the logic of emplotment to make such political patterns
seem inevitable. And finally, they do not want their endings to transform the suffering of their protagonists into worthwhile "experience," that is, into the necessary challenges that produce them in all
of their complicated and tragic fullness.

I want to close by talking more about that last point, because it has
generated heated dispute among authors and critics. It could be argued that I have throughout this chapter implicitly validated an
aesthetic hierarchy that prioritizes texts that resist conventional
narrative patterns, expectations, and desires. Indeed, my analysis of
novels seems to map quite neatly onto the models of human rights
described in the Introduction. "Human rights teleology" reinforces
and is reinforced by the US-centripetalism of Blaine Harden–like
novels (some of which I will discuss in Chapter 3) that offer satisfying, conventional narrative closure by way of redemptive human
rights work. By contrast, "human rights pragmatism" and "skepticism" reinforce and are reinforced by novels like Goldman's and
Wideman's, which refuse the easy plot closure of human rights do-
goodism, relying instead on satisfaction-denying narrative devices
that generate sustained critical engagement. If this were my evalua-
tive framework, then clearly the latter novels would be the winners.
But as I hope to make clear now, this kind of argument would be a
reductive modeling of the genre and the texts, which offer possibility, multitude, and contradiction rather than ideological clarity. I
believe any attempt to do justice to an emerging genre must acknowledge that to work within convention or toward reader expec-
tation is to be neither aesthetically nor politically lesser. To briefly

frame this closing point, I will focus on Isabel Allende's *Maya's Notebook*.

Allende, who fled Chile under threat of death in 1973 because she was related to the deposed Socialist president Salvador Allende, is a complicated case study in rights writing. On the one hand, *The House of Spirits* (1985) is arguably one of the seminal hemispheric texts of rights writing. A landmark novel that fictionalizes Chile's history of counterrevolution and atrocity in a powerful, multigenerational family saga, it was described in the *New York Times Book Review* as a unique achievement of "personal witness and possible allegory of the past, present and future of Latin America."[43] On the other hand, Allende has been repeatedly taken to task for the perceived moral failures of her writing. Allende has characterized herself as a writer who feels a special "responsibility" in her fiction to "speak for others who are kept in silence," to communicate the truth of atrocity to the world.[44] Nonetheless, she is repeatedly criticized on precisely this issue of responsibility, primarily because she appears to rely on fixed narrative conventions that achieve popularity through moral compromise. Allende has replied by arguing that the violence totalitarian regimes have committed against writers makes reaching "a large number of readers . . . a great responsibility."[45] Elsewhere, Allende has characterized the criticisms against her as an elitist disapproval of popularity in and of itself. As she said once in an interview:

> The fact [that] people think that when you sell a lot of books you are not a serious writer is a great insult to the readership. I get a little angry when people try to say such a thing. There was a review of my last book in one American paper by a professor of Latin American studies and he attacked me personally for the sole reason that I sold a lot of books. That is unforgivable.[46]

While there may be something to Allende's claims about suspicion of broad popular appeal, criticisms against her work tend to be rather more focused than that. Here is a representative question posed to Allende in an interview published in the *Kenyon Review*:

How would you respond to critics who allege that Isabel Allende is writing popular romance, or even kitsch, which is escapist and ultimately conservative because it doesn't fundamentally challenge readers? Some readers have charged that you write literary soap operas. How do you respond to criticism that your work is implicitly conservative because it merely confirms readers' extant worldviews?[47]

The interviewer also asked Allende to respond to the charge that she writes books about human rights violations in which villains generally receive their due punishment, thereby presenting to readers a world of easy justice that does not require their continued outrage. In her immediate response to these questions, Allende defended herself by denying that the charges were true of her fiction. That is, her first response was to *not* challenge the premise of the questions: namely, whether as a writer who focuses on human rights, she should be judged by the degree to which she challenges worldviews and avoids narrative closure.

Maya's Notebook, on a first read, would seem to be the worst novel to choose from her corpus to alleviate the concerns of the *Kenyon Review*. It is the story of a US teen runaway, Maya, whose path to social reintegration mirrors the recovery of her caretaker, Manuel, detained and tortured years before in Chile. As part of her recuperation from abuse and addiction, Maya investigates Manuel's mysterious past, learning about the hidden details of his torture and uncovering the secret that he is in fact her grandfather. These coupled revelations are, at novel's close, tied into a romantic breakthrough for Manuel and a romantic recovery for Maya. As Allende's critics might charge, the revival of both exiles is celebrated as an extension of each of their romance plots, and Manuel's torture plot is reduced to a device for amplifying narrative closure in Maya's heterosexual coming-of-age story. Moreover, the protagonists are able to reconcile themselves to their pasts because their suffering has made them into who they are today, and we readers are meant to find this end point deeply satisfying. Their suffering is not senseless trauma but rather valuable, personality-enhancing tragedy.

It is possible, however, to see *Maya's Notebook* differently, to see how Allende has attempted to embody a different kind of responsibility. The first thing to underscore is that Allende, like Goldman, reverses the vector of rescue in novels that feature political violence in Latin America. In her story, the protagonist must leave the United States to escape persecution. This critique of US exceptionalism by way of narrative structure echoes Allende's own personal life. Discussing her immigration to the United States, Allende explains: "I didn't come for the American Dream. I had no interest in being in the United States . . . The American CIA had intervened in my country, toppled a democratic government, installed a military dictatorship, and I thought they were my personal enemy."[48] The second thing to underscore is that "human rights violation as vehicle for self-discovery" is a trope pervasive throughout the genre. For instance, the orphaned protagonist of Arlene Chai's *Eating Fire and Drinking Water*, like the protagonists of *The Long Night of White Chickens* and other novels, conducts an investigation into human rights violations as a way of examining her own identity, in this case by discovering her own biological parents.

It could be argued that Allende reductively uses Manuel's torture as a subplot to enhance the existential depth of Maya's romantic self-discovery. But it could also be argued that Allende does so as an ethically engaged response to the challenge Goldman presented with the character Flor. That is, Allende is insisting that refugees and torture survivors in human rights novels need not only or even primarily be understood as refugees and torture survivors. She is trying to show that subordinating a trauma plot to a romance plot can sometimes function as character expansion rather than constriction. Allende recalls the way reviewers criticized her novel *Of Love and Shadows* because of its "sentimental" approach to atrocities that took place in Chile in 1973. "If the main characters . . . had died in a torture chamber, or at least if the violent experiences they endured had drowned them in despair and destroyed forever their capacity to love and to dream, these critics might have been more tolerant." But such a stance, she argues, promotes a needlessly impoverished view of the capacities of both art and the human. Political responsibility in her novels is revealed precisely because a character "who has been raped, tortured and mutilated, is able to reconcile herself with life . . . [to] make love in spite of terror."⁴⁹ For Allende, it is not a moral betrayal to narrate atrocity as a component of a person's story rather than its entirety.

Novelists like Helon Habila and Dave Eggers have taken similar approaches. In *Measuring Time*, Habila subordinates accounts of the Biafran War and child soldiers in the First Liberian Civil War to the romantic coming-of-age narrative of a young African writer. This narrative hierarchy is deliberate, as Habila reveals in a meta-textual moment when the young writer receives a rejection letter from a London magazine: "We regret that the subject does not suit our particular demand at the moment. However, if you have other pieces that address such issues as the AIDS scourge, or genital circumcision, or other typical African experiences in a challenging and progressive way, we'd like to take a look at them."⁵⁰

Emphasizing a similar concern, Eggers once explained to me the importance of threading humor and romance through his biographical novel about the Sudanese refugee Valentino Achak Deng, *What Is the What*:

> Early on [the manuscript] was just sort of jumping from headline to headline and calamity to calamity. I think that's a narrator's temptation, and that certainly was Valentino's way of telling his story. He thought I was only interested in the most grievous atrocities, and so whole years would be skipped because "nothing of note" had happened that year in terms of the terrible things he had seen. [But I needed to] balance all the horrific parts with some measure of relief and calm and the other aspects of life, laughter and romance, all these things that make a full human life. If I didn't do that I would be ignoring his whole humanity, saying all he is is a product of statistics, all he is is somebody who's seen atrocity—there's no other aspect of his life that's of value. That's what I would be saying, and that's sometimes what we do say.⁵¹

Whether or not such a recuperative reading is plausible or appealing in Allende's case, however, it is *not* the argument I wish to make as I close this chapter. Such an argument suggests, once again, that novels must have ironic relationships with reader expectations to merit critical attention. I am interested in moral and aesthetic criticisms of Allende not because I accept or reject their premises—that is a question for a different study—but rather because they are salient, public expressions of the internal formal tensions I've been discussing throughout this chapter.

Atrocity as material for representation exerts aesthetic pressure on writers and on the novel as a form. It raises unique questions about the ethical responsibilities of authorship. The genre I am identifying is, in this sense, the product of an array of common structural questions. How do stories about steady, unremitting suffering adjust the novel's more typical rhythm of alternating tension and relief? (Often a loose accumulation of settings stands in for the development and resolution of narrative desires.) How do authors make acute, recurrent suffering matter freshly? (Novels about torture are often short, or rely on braided plots and tone-resetting flashbacks to minimize the cumulative deadening effect of brutality.) How do stories written in the voice of the survivor or perpetrator generate character identification in the face of unbridgeable moral gulfs? (Authors counteract both distancing sacralization and revulsion in a range of ways, including irony and fish-out-of-water humor.) As the novel of human rights develops, and the academic subfield of literature and human rights evolves, more patterns and questions will emerge. Part of what will make future work in this area so rewarding is that, in analytic projects where the intersecting texts and political movements are still in formation, to historicize is also to forecast.

CHAPTER 2

The Central Features of the Novel of Human Rights

Article 12
No one shall be subjected to arbitrary interference with his privacy, family, home or correspondence, nor to attacks upon his honour and reputation. Everyone has the right to the protection of the law against such interference or attacks.

Article 13
(1) Everyone has the right to freedom of movement and residence within the borders of each state.
(2) Everyone has the right to leave any country, including his own, and to return to his country.

Articles 12 and 13 of the Universal Declaration of Human Rights (1948) are about the home. The right to privacy is the umbrella concept for all of the rights enumerated in Article 12, and privacy is epitomized in the idea of a home that is "inviolable"—a word that appeared frequently in the world constitutions that John Humphrey collected as background documents for drafting the UDHR.[1] Much of the debate around Article 13 focused on free movement across state borders, but free movement within the state was also a central topic. In particular, the freedom to choose a residence was a dominating concern, given both the specter of Nazi ghettoization and the appearance of a right to choice of domicile in half the constitutions Humphrey collated.[2] While Article 13's key sites of protection—home and travel, residing and departing—at first seem to define opposed poles of bodily experience, they have been linked in political philosophy as far back as John Locke's *Second Treatise of Government*. Locke explains how we come to our duties of citizenship through the concept of "tacit consent" to state authority, which he illustrates with the parallel examples of choosing a residence and traveling freely on the highway.[3]

Articles 12 and 13 are linked not only by the superordinate concept of home, but also by the narrative pivot of Article 12. At this point, the UDHR swerves away from the focus of the previous six articles (rights realized through a public judicial system) to a pair of articles that illuminate the front edge of our private vulnerabilities in day-to-day, lived experience: our homes, our letters, our reputations, our children and loved ones. As discussed in Chapter 1, rights are deemed indivisible as a legal matter. But as a matter of literature, the rights of Articles 12 and 13 take precedence. They are the rights, so to speak, not of legal personhood, but of *character*: privacy, mobility, and family. Across the novel of human rights, these sites of protection are unifying topics of concern. Indeed, they form the three primary themes of the genre as a whole: endangered privacy, restricted movement, and damaged families.

This chapter is broken into three sections, one for each of the topics listed above. I use an interpretive practice here that is quite different from Chapter 1, which premised assertions upon emblematic close readings. In what follows, I flip the lens of analysis, working in the spirit of what Franco Moretti has termed "distant reading." For Moretti, to practice distant reading is to meta-read rather than read texts, focusing on units that are "much larger than the text," including "genres and systems."[4] Todd Presner, applying the concept to searches in vast digital archives rather than to Moretti's studies of studies, explains that distant reading is exciting precisely because it eschews literary-critical close reading, in which a small handful of (sometimes unrepresentative) literary texts are hermeneutically mined, in favor of keywords and other pattern searches through "big data" quantitative analysis. This computational mode, Presner advocates, will allow new research questions to emerge by enabling searches for correlations across "thousands, if not millions" of texts.[5] At the moment, I am still working from a human scale—finger-and-toe counting, with no digital archiving yet for me. But I will seek to approximate distant reading by scanning for information across larger swaths of texts. Hopefully, this will feel more like a nimble scamper through a field of reading options and less like an archival slog.

Privacy

In the literature of war and state-sponsored violence, privacy is endangered. The aim of war is the elimination of private space. Rey Chow takes the bombing of Hiroshima and Nagasaki as the catastrophic end point of modern war's drive to "maximal visibility and illumination," to the idea of the world as target.[6] In many ways, however, it is better to understand nuclear war's totalization of the planet's surface not as an assault on vast regions but rather as an assault on individual homes, one by one by the thousands. The nuclear age is less a technological transformation than a technological fulfillment of total war's basic aim: namely, the elimination of off-limit space. As Carlos from Lawrence Thornton's *Imagining Argentina* says about the military junta's invasion of privacy in his nation:

> Just think about the helicopters, the cameras, the tape recorders, the tapped telephones. They can penetrate every street, house, apartment, even this garden is not immune to their eyes and ears. They have penetrated the cafés and restaurants and melon shops, they have men like Gustavo on board ships in the harbor, and men like Gustavo have learned how to loiter in the dark corners of pool halls, dance halls. They want to make the city transparent, a city of glass. They can see everything they want to.[7]

The novels I will discuss in this section model the relationship between human rights and violated privacy through three tropes, each conceptually linked by the way they mark the boundaries of our intimate identities: homes, secrets, and names. Each trope is, if in different ways, a site of negative and positive vulnerability. That is, they are physical or psychic sites that establish the boundaries of our identities, creating safe spaces that are also targets. Or better yet, they are *practices* that lay bare our private selves in ways that simultaneously enable our deepest intimacies and also subject us to the greatest risk. As this section progresses I will question, just as the novels themselves do, the ideological implications subtending this model of the private self—the self that comes into being through its separation from others. But for now, such aesthetically modeled individualism is a reasonable starting place for thinking about one of the most common models of what human rights are: namely, that rights are ways of protecting individuals (as opposed to the idea, for instance, that they are ways of enshrining mutual obligations).

Homes

In her statement of the "perplexities of the Rights of Man," Hannah Arendt famously linked homelessness and rightlessness. Perhaps unsurprisingly, this link is a central focus in the novel of human rights. Arguably, the novel's summary image of the state's capacity for violence is the home invasion. The trope is pervasive rather than symptomatic. Whether it is US-based novels about the Dirty War in Argentina, the internment of Japanese American families during World War II, Russian war crimes in Chechnya, global war on terrorism (GWOT) surveillance, atrocities committed by the Tonton Macoute in Haiti, or police brutality and murder in Philadelphia, the violated home is trauma's symbolic gathering point.

Dave Eggers's *What Is the What* is an emblematic case. The novel tells the story of Valentino Achak Deng, one of the more than 20,000 "Lost Boys" displaced or orphaned during the civil war in southern Sudan (1983–2005). A relentless account of suffering that spans decades and continents, the novel begins with a single home invasion: the gunpoint robbery of Valentino in his US apartment. A deliberate

echo of the destruction of Valentino's childhood home in Sudan, this
opening assault becomes the novel's through line, suturing together
all of his memories of the war. By interweaving past and present in
this way, Eggers shows how war's trauma insinuates itself into the
psychic life of aftermath, how war's elimination of private space is
best understood when seen as an elimination of all nonwar space and
time, the creation of a condition for which there is no outside.

Dinaw Mengestu's *The Beautiful Things That Heaven Bears* is
the story of a refugee from the Communist revolution in Ethiopia.
Here, too, the violated home is the primary structuring narrative
device. Stephanos abandons Ethiopia after the police invade his
home, beating his father nearly to death before disappearing him.
Stephanos then abandons his home in the United States after a desperately troubled homeless man burns down the renovated home of
his would-be lover Judith, hoping to claim the abandoned home as
his own afterward. And Judith's home is itself experienced as a meta–
home invasion by the long-term residents of the gentrifying neighborhood who now face a wave of evictions. "It's not right," a neighbor
declares. "These people coming in like that and forcing us out."[8]

These explicit home dispossessions are echoed throughout the text
in key moments. Stephanos feels uncomfortable whenever he and
Judith enter each other's homes, for instance, because they are crossing
rigid lines of race and class; they are, so to speak, entering the wrong
homes. Similarly, during an intimate holiday moment in Judith's
home, Stephanos begins to dream that he, Judith, and her daughter,
Naomi, might become a family—until Naomi opens a Christmas
gift from her absent father: an expensive dollhouse. And in the final
unhousing, Stephanos and Naomi transform his grocery store into
a symbolic home for themselves, ignoring customers for hours on
end as he reads aloud to her in a poignant miming of family—until
the bank forecloses on his failing store.[9]

Mengestu reprises these themes in his second novel, *How to Read
the Air*. This novel tells the story of a young Ethiopian American
man, Jonas Woldemariam, who is struggling to come to terms with
the domestic violence perpetrated by his father, Yosef. Jonas works
at a refugee legal center where he helps asylum seekers refine their
raw testimony into legally effective narratives. Over time the par-

ticularities of each story become increasingly unimportant to Jonas: "I read through them quickly, but in each case I could've stopped after the first couple of paragraphs. The rest was familiar, and had already been spoken or written hundreds of times before in this office."[10] Jonas soon begins to openly fictionalize survivor stories, deleting whole swaths of people's lives—a practice that both reflects and reinforces his emotional numbness, his inability to connect authentically to others. As his marriage begins to break down, Jonas realizes he is building isolated emotional forts that recall the obsessive fort-making of his childhood.

> As a child I built dozens of forts in my bedroom . . . In later years I studied how-to books written for children. How to build an igloo, a tee-pee, a birdhouse, a tree house . . . For seven years I tried to construct as many versions of home as I could find. By the time I was twelve I had probably tried them all, but always with one distinct variation that was of my own making. I built each, regardless of how poorly it may have been constructed, as far as possible out of anyone's general line of vision. I put the birdhouse in the closet and kept a small circle of rocks near the head of my bed. There were no back- or front-yard forts for me. I didn't build protective cocoons to fight from or to defend. I built mine to hide in because I always knew an attack would come, and that even at their best, the most my forts could do was soften the blows when they came. (119–120)

As the novel proceeds, the story of his mother's dramatic attempt to escape her husband is intertwined with the story of his father's escape from Ethiopia. It soon becomes clear that the forts of Jonas's childhood are intergenerational reverberations of Yosef's original trauma. A refugee from the Communist purges, Yosef is haunted by memories of escapes across borders and "abandoned thatched-roof huts all over the countryside in Ethiopia and again in Sudan" (160). In the enraged paranoia that precedes his assaults on his wife, Yosef repeatedly accuses her of undermining him because she wishes "to see us with no home, so I can go begging like a dog for a new place to live" (264). Yosef's fear of losing his home has its ghastly origins

in traumatic entombments from his past. As a prisoner in a cell just
outside of Addis, he stands for 133 days packed tightly against dozens
of men and boys, sleeping upright and taking turns sitting on the
feces- and urine-covered floor. Later, he is boxed up in a storage crate
as a stowaway on a ship bound for Europe. For Yosef, the conversion
of the sheltering room into the entombing box is the source of nightmares that recur for the remainder of his life: nightmares about
boxes, "boxes large enough to hold a man" (39).

Discussing the psychic damage that attends the conversion of domestic safe spaces into sites of terror, the rights scholar Elaine Scarry
explains:

> In normal contexts, the room, the simplest form of shelter, ex-
> presses the most benign potential of human life . . . In torture,
> the world is reduced to a single room or set of rooms. Called
> "guest rooms" in Greece and "safe houses" in the Philippines,
> the torture rooms are often given names that acknowledge and
> call attention to the generous, civilizing impulse normally
> present in the human shelter. They call attention to this impulse
> only as a prelude to announcing its annihilation. The torture
> room is not just the setting in which the torture occurs . . . It is
> itself literally converted into another weapon, into an agent of
> pain. All aspects of the basic structure—walls, ceiling, windows,
> doors—undergo this conversion . . . The domestic act of pro-
> tecting becomes an act of hurting and in hurting, the object
> becomes what it is not, an expression of individual contraction,
> of the retreat into the most self-absorbed and self-experiencing
> of human feelings, when it is the very essence of these objects
> to express the most expansive potential of the human being, his
> ability to project himself out of his private, isolating needs into
> a concrete, objectified, and therefore shareable world.[11]

During his displacement, in other words, Yosef does not simply lose
his home; he loses his concept of home. It is the novel's contention
that this kind of trauma cannot be escaped, even across generations.
When Yosef dies in the United States as an elderly man many years
later, he is effectively homeless, living in a YMCA. In the final para-

graph of the novel, Jonas reenacts his father's traumatic homeless-ness. He packs his bags and leaves the apartment he shared with his wife, in the last of their "best attempts to escape one another" (305), with no clear destination.

In *Plowing the Dark*, Richard Powers invokes Scarry's concept of the room as a primordial site of either making or unmaking. The novel is organized around events occurring in two different rooms. The first is a torture chamber where a hostage's world is unmade. The second is an experimental virtual reality chamber where human creativity, now unshackled from the limits of the body, can create world after world. Deliberately and elegantly echoing Scarry's rhe-toric, Powers's work is uniquely grounded in academic scholarship. This makes it an excellent text for seminars on literature and human rights. However, novels like Mengestu's, which emerge from a con-ception of an individual character rather than a theoretical construct, are more representative of the genre. And these character-driven novels tend to focus less on the bare structure of the identity-stripped room and more on the character-saturated space of the home.

In the novel of human rights, homes are more than content-entailed settings and repositories for narrative action. They are resonant images of the right to safety, idealized conceptions of phys-ically bounded private identity, and metaphors for belonging within a range of aggregate identities, from family, to neighborhood, to nation-state. Violated homes are, therefore, the recurring drivers of plot and central thematic gathering points throughout the genre.

Nathan Englander's *The Ministry of Special Cases* is a fictional account of the Dirty War in Argentina. It tells the story of Kaddish and Lillian Poznan, whose son Pato is disappeared. As Jews in Buenos Aires during the rule of the junta they are vulnerable—uniquely so, because they cannot turn even to the scant protection offered by their already-targeted Jewish community (Kaddish has been ostracized for his brazen refusal over the years to erase the memory of his mother, a young woman who was trafficked into prostitution and became a historical symbol of community dis-grace). An unsettling mix of the comic and horrific, *The Ministry of Special Cases* is a study of helplessness in the face of state force. The novel's most significant image of despotism—the image that sharply

marks the beginning and end of the plot's tragic arc—is the "industrial and oversized steel" door that Kaddish's wife purchases at dear
expense to protect her son Pato.[12] As students are disappeared around
her during the terror, Lillian takes comfort in her impenetrable
door. It physicalizes her desperate belief in individual agency, in
the capacity of a mother to protect her child. But in the end, when
the security forces come for Pato, Kaddish mistakes their knock for
his wife's and simply holds the door open for them as they take his
son. He becomes at that point an emblem of paternal failure and
always-already submission to the state.

> "You opened what should stay closed, what I told you to keep
> closed . . . Lost your mind," Lillian said. "Lost our son."
> "Yes," Kaddish said. "And I held it for them." Here his voice
> broke hard. "I held open the door." (123)

The Ministry of Special Cases is not only thematically but also structurally organized around the door, which ultimately separates each
member of the family from the others. Part 1 closes when the security forces knock on the door, just as Kaddish has unforgivably cursed
his son in an out-of-control argument. The third and final part opens
with Lillian explicitly blaming Kaddish for their son's disappearance:
"You brought a curse on our house and then you opened the door"
(231). And on the novel's final page, Lillian closes the door—the door
that had been left "always-open" in the vain hope that Pato might
return (278)—locking Kaddish out of her life for good.

Anthony Marra's *A Constellation of Vital Phenomena* is a justice plot
about one woman's search for her trafficked sister amid the atrocities of the Chechen wars. It is a story about homelessness and
home invasions. The novel's first page depicts eight-year-old Havaa
watching as Russian soldiers burn down her house and abduct her
father. When the novel shifts its narrative perspective for the first
time to Sonja halfway through the first chapter, it describes two more
displacements. Sonja's sister Natasha has disappeared from their
shared flat for the last time to become a homeless refugee. With no
family to hold her, Sonja abandons their home as well to live in the
public hospital where she works. (Later, Havaa also moves into a hos-

pital room, but never unpacks her suitcase lest she need to flee suddenly.) Chapter 2 begins with Sonja abandoning her home in London to return to Chechnya to find her sister, and part 2 opens with the arrival of the first war refugees at Havaa's home, which soon comes to be known as a hostel for the war homeless. The plot reaches its climax when soldiers wake the neighborhood by knocking loudly on the door of the home of Havaa's protector, Akhmed. At this point in the novel, the sound of knocking on doors can only be experienced as a jolt. For those inside, it could mean the dreamt-for return of a lost refugee or "a rifle butt to the forehead" from security forces.[13] For Akhmed, now, it announces abduction and death. The novel closes with a flash-forward through time to Havaa's death:

> She would die at the age of one hundred and three, in the geriatrics ward of the Hospital No. 6, in a room that had been the director's office, then Sonja's bedroom, and finally a regular hospital room, a room Havaa would remember as many thousands of refugees remembered her own childhood bedroom, a room that had been there when it was needed. (375)

Ann Patchett's *Bel Canto* is organized around a space that, like Havaa's room and Sonja's hospital, becomes a home for displaced persons. The story takes place entirely within the residence of the vice president of an unidentified South American nation. During a party for international power brokers, terrorists invade and seize the estate, taking dozens of hostages. Families are broken up as all but one of the women—the internationally renowned soprano Roxane Coss—are separated from their partners and released. The invasion is violent and terrifying; everybody believes the terrorists are from a revolutionary group known for indiscriminate murder. But soon the ICRC delegate negotiating with the terrorists discovers that they are from another, less radical group, La Familia de Martin Suarez. Named for a ten-year-old boy murdered by government forces, the rebel group is led by a man desperate to have his brother released from prison before he dies, and is composed of young villagers who had watched as family members were seized from their homes and disappeared by security forces.

Initially, hostages are consumed by thoughts of the homes they left behind and the families they might never see again. But as the standoff extends into months, terrorists and hostages begin to establish friendships and romances. The vice president even plans to adopt one of the young terrorists. Early in the novel, the vice president reflects that he lives in a residence rather than a home—nothing there is truly his. With the terrorists, however, he and the other hostages begin to experience his residence as a new communal home, a place they might stay indefinitely and even happily. Hostages and terrorists alike abandon thoughts of escape. "They were in love with the place. They wouldn't leave if you tore the wall down. If you poked them in the back with your gun and told them to get going they would still run to you."[14] Carmen, one of the terrorists, prays: "She prayed while standing near the priest in hopes it would give her request extra credibility. What she prayed for was nothing. She prayed that God would look on them and see the beauty of their existence and leave them alone" (156).

The novel indexes this transformation of residence into home, and homeless displacement into belonging, through a shift in the representation of privacy. At the start of the occupation, hostages complain that they must live with no privacy, as all share common spaces. Gen, the translator, emblematizes the obscene visibility of their situation. Because all information, from political negotiations to romantic messages, must pass through him, there can be no secrets. And because everyone needs to communicate so desperately, he can never be left to himself. Soon, however, Gen falls in love with the terrorist Carmen, and together they begin to enjoy a privacy unprecedented in their lives. So does Mr. Hosokawa, who begins a love affair with Roxane. "The private life. Mr. Hosokawa had a private life now. He had always thought of himself as a private man, but now he saw that there was nothing in his life before that had been private" (291). And it is precisely at this point—when the communal space has been established as the protector of privacy—that a second home invasion begins. Government forces mount what they see as a rescue. But they are received by the hostages as violent strangers. The hostages watch in terror as their home is destroyed and all the terrorists are killed.

Paolo Bacigalupi's sci-fi biopunk *The Windup Girl* is fundamentally a refugee novel. It depicts a post-petroleum world of famine and climate-change flooding that is re-globalizing in the wake of self-inflicted economic and ecological collapse. Science fiction is often overlooked in literary criticism focusing on human rights. I think this is a lost opportunity. Science fiction, our primary literary site of utopian and dystopian imagination, takes up the deepest questions of human rights. From Isaac Asimov and *Blade Runner* to Octavia Butler and *Ex Machina*, the genre asks: What constitutes a just or unjust social order? What costs to human flourishing will we ultimately face if we continue to tolerate the injustices that define our current social order? And what is the nature of "the human" such that it merits rights and protection?

The Windup Girl examines each of these questions through two parallel refugee plots: the story of Hock Seng, the "yellow card" Chinese businessman, and the windup girl Emiko, one of the "New People" bioengineered and crèche-grown to serve. The backstory for both is homelessness. Once a business magnate, Hock Seng is starting over in Bangkok after fleeing ethnic cleansing in Malaysia. Traumatized, discriminated against, and surviving on a thin shelf of possibility while his fellow refugees starve in the streets, Hock Seng is perpetually "looking for a future."[15] At the novel's catastrophic climax, his home is burned down and he must flee violent civil insurrection once again. Meanwhile, Emiko comes to Thailand as the companion and secretary of her former owner, who abandons her there so that he can upgrade to a new model. Emiko's life in Bangkok is a brutal allegory for contemporary sex trafficking and racism. She is unable to return to Kyoto—"the only home you knew," she tells herself (35)—because of the "debts" she soon runs up to the vicious pimp who enslaves her. Emiko's escape plot begins with the dream of escape to a free North, where "her kind" (39) build their own, safe villages. It ends with Emiko free, finally, in an apartment that is her own because the city has been wiped clean of its human inhabitants.

Like any genre in formation, the novel of human rights is being pieced together with relative degrees of consciousness by authors borrowing from one another and from preexisting forms. In this way, it invites cross-genre work. The genre includes not only the otherworldly speculative fiction of Bacigalupi, but also the testimonial realism of authors like Dave Eggers, who based his biographical novels *What Is the What* and *Zeitoun* on in-depth interviews and testimony. *Zeitoun* tells the story of the survivors of Hurricane Katrina. Best understood as Eggers's premier novel of place, *Zeitoun* documents the hurricane as both a historic natural disaster and a human rights catastrophe. Discussing the book in *Mother Jones*, Eggers elaborates:

> Zeitoun was among thousands of people who were doing "Katrina time" after the storm. There was a complete suspension of all legal processes and there were no hearings, no courts for months and months and not enough folks in the judicial system really seemed all that concerned about it. Some human-rights activists and some attorneys, but otherwise it seemed to be the cost of doing business. It really could have only happened at that time; 2005 was just the exact meeting place of the Bush-era philosophy towards law enforcement and incarceration, their philosophy toward habeas corpus and their neglect and indifference to the plight of New Orleanians.[16]

Eggers structures *Zeitoun* through juxtaposed settings of "housing." The through line of the first two-thirds of the book is the path of the eponymous protagonist's canoe, as he paddles freely through neighborhoods of destroyed homes to offer assistance to the stranded. The last third of the novel is the infuriating account of his detainment seven days after the storm in "Camp Greyhound," a prison the government hastily constructed as thousands of residents languished on rooftops across the city. Accused by soldiers of being "al Qaeda" and "Taliban," Zeitoun is locked in a cage in an orange jumpsuit, "housed" in a facility whose similarities to Guantánamo "were too strong to ignore."[17] The book's last paragraphs offer revitalizing counter-images of homebuilding. In what turned out to be tragically misplaced optimism about both New Orleans and Zeitoun himself, Eggers concludes: "There is no faith like the faith of a builder of homes in coastal Louisiana . . . So let us get up early and stay late, and, brick by brick and block by block, let us get that work done" (325).

Julie Otsuka's *When the Emperor Was Divine* likewise designs its plot as a series of jarring shifts in setting. The novel begins when the unnamed mother reads a sign in the post office in Berkeley declaring that Japanese families must prepare to be relocated to internment camps. At the halfway point of the book, the unnamed son remembers the FBI storming into his house at midnight a few months before—shortly after Pearl Harbor—to take his father into custody. And the novel concludes three and a half years later, after the war is over, when the mother and children return to Berkeley. They find that their home has been serially occupied by unidentified strangers who leave behind broken bottles, pornography, graffiti, and water stains on the ceiling. This vandalism is a grotesque inversion of the book's opening, in which the mother packs all the dearest belongings that made their home into an intimate extension of their personalities: pictures on walls, books on shelves, stamp collections, and china. As the novel closes, the mother takes a job as a cleaner of other people's homes—no company wants to hire Japanese citizens. And the father, finally returned from custody, falls into a semipermanent quiescence. The horizon of his settings shrinks to his room, and he finds himself unable to walk out the front door of his house. In Joy Kogawa's *Obasan*, a novel about the internment of Japanese citizens living in Canada, the violation of homes is also a dominating concern. The novel's central question—"Will we go home again ever?"[18]— is literal but also symbolic, and reflects Kogawa's own experience as a childhood detainee.

Violations of homes recur as especially powerful images in the genre because, as Scarry has described it, our homes are physical extensions of our bodies. Walls, like skin, protect and enclose the individual. Windows and doors function as "crude versions of the senses," enabling "the self to move out into the world" (38) in controlled ways. Our rooms are material extensions not only of our personalities and interior desires but also of our most basic and private animal needs. Like organs of the body, rooms specialize in particular bodily functions: "the kitchen and eating, the bathroom and excreting, the bedroom and sleeping" (39).

Vyvyane Loh's *Breaking the Tongue* is the story of Japan's 1941–1942 invasion of Singapore, then an outpost of the British Empire. It opens by establishing an immediate parallel between the protagonist Claude's body and his childhood home. Both are explicitly characterized as containers for his consciousness, which begins to float away because of the disassociating effects of extreme torture. The interrogation plot—which Loh characterizes as war waged on "Claude the Body"[19]—parallels the plot of war on the city. Claude's torture, depicted as the relentless invasion of his body, secrets, and memory, doubles the indiscriminate shelling that forces Claude and his family to abandon their home. The novel becomes a plot of forced movement out of the private into increasingly public spaces: from home, to workers' residence, to private hotel, to public hospital.

Political violence visited upon people *inside* their own homes is a self-amplifying metaphor of violated privacy, of bodies turned inside out and then turned inside out again. As one critic summarizes of Edwidge Danticat's work: "Dictatorship, occupation, coups, gang violence, murder, and detention centers are just some of the ways the outside world enters the home, determining how families will divide and dissect their lives."[20] Héctor Tobar's *The Tattooed Soldier* is the story of a refugee who escapes Guatemala after a death squad storms into his house and murders his wife, who was a political dissident, and their baby. The novel opens as the protagonist is being evicted from his apartment in Los Angeles years later. Walking the streets with a plastic bag full of his few possessions, he relives traumatic memories of the day he became homeless in Guatemala, fleeing then with nothing but a cardboard box to hold all of his belongings. The soldiers had dragged his wife and son through the house, "painting the floors with their blood" and leaving their bodies on the front steps for the public to see.[21]

At the most extreme edge, the state's power to limitlessly invade is depicted in scenes of rapes performed in front of families in their homes. These crimes are central points of anguish in a range of rights novels. Danticat's *Krik?Krak!* opens with the story of Célianne, who is in her home when soldiers burst inside, force her brother to have sex with his mother at gunpoint, and then brutally gang-rape her in front of them. In Chris Abani's *Song for Night*, a child soldier is forced at gunpoint to rape a woman in her home as a way of finally and fully separating him from the rest of his moral world. Graciela Limón's

In Search of Bernabé opens with the revelation that Nestor's sisters were raped in front of him and his mother in their home. It closes with his brutal retribution against the perpetrators: he finds them, castrates them, and feeds them their testicles before they are shot in the head.

The most urgent emotional priority for many of the novels I have discussed is bodily integrity. Elizabeth Anker has written trenchantly about the problem of the body in human rights discourse. She argues that the focus on bodily integrity in human rights work has furthered, and been furthered by, a deep insecurity about our real-world bodies. This insecurity, she explains, pushes those who theorize rights to conceptualize the self through the figure of the idealized, sacred body. The result is a "fleshless, decorporealized" vision that exacerbates historical exclusions based on race, class, gender, and disability.[22] She argues further that corporeal pain need not be modeled as that which must be compartmentalized and mastered but can instead help us to conceptualize a subjectivity through wounding that does not rely on a liberal calculus of autonomy and self-determination. How much has the concern with establishing protection for vulnerable bodies led to an unwitting mythologization of an integrated, dignified body, and to a deepening of the center-periphery contrasts that so many have struggled against? Many of the novels I discuss in this chapter do not self-consciously engage that question. The novel of human rights seems most often to use the appalling power of physical integrity and privacy violations to generate reader outrage rather than to question hidden normative assumptions. There are important exceptions to this pattern, however. Two of the novels that I examine in the next chapter, Richard Powers's *Operation Wandering Soul* and Chang-rae Lee's *The Surrendered*, take up the problem of the norms that govern rights and bodies in complex and unique ways.

Secrets

In the novel of human rights, the concept of the secret is the narrative counterpoint to home invasion. It symbolizes the preservation of interior space. Madeleine Thien's *Do Not Say We Have Nothing*

dramatizes the harms of the Cultural Revolution with a brutal
scene of a family being displaced from its home—the first of many
such displacements in the novel. It then immediately contrasts their
privacy-erasing homelessness to their clandestine retrieval of a politically forbidden, piecemeal novel, the "Book of Records." Throughout
the novel, people will hide, preserve, and secretly pass on the manuscript to "courageous cliques, resistance fighters, spies and dreamers."[23]
In Chris Abani's *The Secret History of Las Vegas*, apartheid is defined
by the way homes either preserve or fail to preserve secrets. Describing white South Africans, he writes: "It was common knowledge that most led a double life. What was shown in public was a
repressed, conformist, and exaggerated morality. But the home life
was completely different, revealing everything from messiness to
deviant sexual behavior. A double life, however, was a privilege no
blacks had because while whites were safe from scrutiny behind
their front doors, blacks were always under scrutiny."[24] In Loh's
Breaking the Tongue, Claude endures unspeakable torture so that he
can preserve the secret of his relationship to Ling-li, a young Chinese nurse suspected of anti-Japanese espionage. In the end, he has
no information about her worth hiding. What is valuable about
their relationship is only the fact of its secrecy as such. Throughout
the genre, novel after novel is structured as a contest between exposure and camouflage, between accurate public identification and
codes, aliases, and hidden identities.

Susan Choi's examinations of the relationships among secrecy,
safety, and dignity are both exemplary and representative. Her novels
The Foreign Student and *A Person of Interest* are fundamentally narratives of privacy. The former is the story of Chang Ahn, a war refugee
from Korea who is relocated to Sewanee College in Tennessee. Chang
struggles to achieve "happy anonymity" as a student, desperate to
hide the traumatic secret that under torture he betrayed the priest
who helped him escape.[25] Eventually he becomes involved with a
woman, Katherine, who also lives with a traumatic past. As a child,
Katherine was sexually abused by a local professor. The two are at
first attracted to each other because they can spend hours together
in silence. As Katherine puts it to Chang, she likes that she can have
"privacy in front of [him]" (55). But soon, in a gentle, restorative

miming of Chang's interrogation, Katherine begins to desire his secret and to share hers with him. "Listen: give me whatever you're holding apart from me" (151). For Chang, however, it is too close; he resists her just as he resisted his interrogators. "It is a secret . . . I want that you keep it. Not give it to me . . . Sometimes somebody tells too much. Later on they want to die instead of telling it, but it's no any good then. They tell it" (172).

Ultimately, Chang's secret is about secrets, or his perceived inability to keep them—a charge that, in a continuation of the relentless parallels, is also leveled against Katherine by her mother, who wishes to keep her daughter's abuse a secret. As with so many of the novels discussed so far, the theme of endangered privacy is manifest most powerfully in images of violated homes. Chang tries to find a hiding place after the "desecration of the house" (102) by North Korean soldiers during the invasion of Seoul. He takes refuge in the crawlspace under the stairs, where he stays for three months, starving, feverish, and claustrophobic to the point of "going insane" (102). In an amplified parallel of constraint, Chang is tortured in a schoolhouse. A physical structure organized around the raising of children, the schoolhouse functions as the public equivalent of a home. With Chang's torture, it is transformed into a site of terror, becoming a chilling instance of what Scarry describes as torture's logic of civilizational undoing. Finally, in the novel's final paragraphs, the sites of physical belonging in Chang's life are synoptically linked both to this torture and to his relationship with Katherine. Watching him leave, she blends into his consciousness with a realization: "He had thought he would always have two things, the great space within him where his home had to live, and that diminishment, when his body had imploded" (323).[26]

Choi's later GWOT novel, *A Person of Interest*, returns to similar themes. It tells the story of Professor Lee, an aging math teacher who is a suspect in a case of domestic terrorism. Accustomed to decades of "invisible life," Lee becomes the hypervisible target of private vendettas, public racism, and intrusive government surveillance that culminates in the "rape" of his house.[27] Local television crews and FBI agents—who see Asians as inherently secretive, incapable of being polygraphed—storm in and seize as evidence his most private possessions, down to a treasured letter from his dead wife. Mean-while, Lee seeks throughout the novel to evade scrutiny, hiding his car, tearing his phone out of the wall, and hiding in unlit rooms to avoid detection by his neighbors.

In an illuminating contrast, Adam Johnson's *The Orphan Master's Son* is the story of a protagonist who lacks the capacity for secrets. In this picaresque novel, the protagonist, Jun Do, passes through a series of loosely connected adventures as a North Korean tunnel sol-dier, kidnapper, fishing boat spy, slave camp prisoner, foreign dele-gate, traitor, and national military hero. Simultaneously an everyman and a cipher, Jun Do is so thoroughly constituted by the scripts of the Dear Leader's totalitarian dictatorship that he is incapable of forming durable private attachments or even a stable, role-resistant identity. In this way he is an exaggerated extreme of all the citizens depicted in the novel. The regime insinuates itself even into the most intimate moments of family lives, systematically converting private self-expression into self-evacuating, public performances of loyalty.

This all changes, however, when Jun Do falls in love with the beautiful actress Sun Moon. Jun Do's capacity to achieve a secret by helping her defect at the climax—thus delivering her from the pred-atory desire of the Dear Leader—is figured simultaneously as personal fulfillment, interpersonal connection, political resistance, and final escape. Inexorably, however, Jun Do's treason leads to detention and to an extended series of torture sessions—sessions de-signed not so much to target particular secrets as to target the *ca-pacity* for secrets.

> In Prison 33, little by little, you relinquished everything, starting with your tomorrows and all that might be. Next went your past, and suddenly it was inconceivable that your head had ever touched a pillow, that you'd once used a spoon or a toilet, that your mouth had once known flavors and your eyes had beheld colors beyond gray and brown and the shade of black that blood took on. Before you relinquished yourself—Ga [Jun Do's alias] had felt it starting, like the numb of cold limbs—you let go of all the others, each person you'd once known. They became

ideas and then notions and then impressions, and then they were as ghostly as projections against a prison infirmary.[28]

As the novel demonstrates, the point of torture is to return dangerously opaque, private subjects to the unselfed condition that the absolutist state desires.

In Danticat's *The Farming of Bones*, secrecy and privacy are the survival conditions of the protagonist, Amabelle. She notes that as a servant she can remain invisible in public and private space.[29] This invisibility is figured as a positive through the lyrical sexuality of her private life with Sebastian, in which bodily interpenetration and the coerciveness of sensual pleasure are celebrated. These images of sensuous intimacy are inverted during the genocide, when Trujillo's regime seeks to turn its targets inside out in public, revealing their "hidden" identity by way of a different kind of corporeal coercion. Those who pronounce "perejil" (the word for parsley) with a perceived Haitian Creole accent are targeted for murder, which the genocidaires precede by forcing parsley inside of their bodies. Danticat's concern with this kind of coercive, out-grouping identification recurs in *Krik?Krak!* Here, a group of doomed Haitian refugees, who have surrendered all physical privacy on their exposed boat, fear their bodies will betray them to the Coast Guard as the sun burns them too dark to pass, in their minds, as Cubans. April Shemak characterizes this as an "obscene visibility" that is echoed in the rape of Célianne.[30]

Ha Jin has described "the private sphere and the public sphere" as the key themes of his work as a whole.[31] In *War Trash*, he explores these concepts by way of two binaries: visibility and invisibility, and public and private writing. *War Trash* is the fictionalized memoir of a Chinese soldier held in a US prisoner-of-war camp during the Korean War. The narrator, Yu Yuan, wants only to return to his family in China. He finds, however, that this desire puts him at the center of a lethal dispute between two factions of prisoners: the pro-Communists, who want to be repatriated to North Korea or China, and the pro-Nationalists, who want to be sent to South Korea or Taiwan. As the plot of Yu Yuan's long exile unfolds, he returns continually to images of writing as echoes of his primary purpose:

to bear witness to what happened to China's "war trash." Amidst
scenes of massacres and torture, a special cluster of humble details stubbornly demands attention. These details express the humane desire to expand public legibility: translating, teaching illit-
erate prisoners to write, teaching calligraphy to his camp doctor,
admiring good handwriting, recalling the theft of a pen and the astonishment of discovered or cherished pencils, stealing newspapers,
and craving books. The special value of public writing is embodied
most explicitly in the Geneva Conventions, which are translated
and posted throughout the prison camps, as required by Article 41
of the Third Convention. Yu Yuan and his colleagues memorize
them, hoping the pressure of the documents might help protect
their "human rights."[32]

At the same time, however, *War Trash* also reveals the desperate
need for private writing, for writing that cannot be translated. At the
metaphorical center of the novel is the moral opposition between two
kinds of "texts": the secret code the protagonist works on so that prisoners can safely communicate, and the obscenely visible tattoo
("FUCK COMMUNISM") that pro-Nationalists violently inscribe on his
body to make it impossible for him to return safely to China. *War
Trash* stages a competition between the translatable and untranslat-
able, between systems of prisoner control and prisoner resistance,
between surveillance and hiding. Indeed, Yu Yuan's own act of
witnessing—that is, the novel itself—is defined by the binary of
public and private. On the one hand, he is motivated by the dying
words of his former leader, who pleads for a public act of collective
representation. "Please write our story!" (349). On the other hand,
Yu Yuan insists that he can never speak for the "our," that he was
never "one of them" (350). *War Trash* is his private story, and he writes
it only for his American grandchildren.

Names

As *War Trash* demonstrates, the concept of the secret, like the other
topoi discussed in this chapter, functions differently depending upon
the moral vector of the novel. The two basic plots of the human rights
novel, the escape plot and the justice plot, embody contrary moral

desires that exert differentiating aesthetic pressures. These pressures help illuminate consolidating patterns across the genre. One of the key differences between these two plots—a difference that clarifies the function of secrets and privacy in the genre as a whole—is the contrasting function of names in each.

Let's start with the act of naming in escape plots. In the escape plot, the protagonist is named and renamed, sheds names, takes aliases, or avoids names. In this way the escape plot echoes both the original human rights text of US literature, *Narrative of the Life of Frederick Douglass,* and later works in African American literature like Ralph Ellison's *Invisible Man,* in which the protagonist remains unnamed and the names of other characters, as Mark Greif puts it, function as "the verbal equivalent of the mask that covers the face."[33]

Stona Fitch's Kafkaesque escape novel *Senseless* is a vivid contemporary example. It is a story of unnaming through torture, of names revealed to be masks. The protagonist, Eliot Gast, is a successful businessman who is kidnapped and tortured by terrorists. His masked torturers, referred to only by the aliases he gives them, repeat his full name every time they speak with him in a parodic reaffirmation of the identity they are seeking to unmake. They devise hideous tortures to remove each of his five senses, culminating in scooping out one of his eyes with a coffee spoon. As the novel advances, the protagonist's name is increasingly emptied of personal content. The self-evacuation begins with the depersonalized thinness of allegory. The author once told me that he chose the name Gast because it means guest in Flemish and because a *gasthuis* is a hospital. By midnovel, Gast's torture—which the terrorists have broadcast over the Internet—has converted his personal name into the pop-culture equivalent of allegory: celebrity, in which the self is transformed into the symbol. At the end, when Gast escapes, he is instantly recognized by the crowd that discovers him, but he cannot hear the name they are shouting at him because the torturers took away his hearing by jamming ice picks into his ears. Indeed, the protagonist no longer recognizes the name Gast as his own, or rather—as the past tense emphasizes—no longer recognizes himself as a subject capable of bearing a name. "I was surrounded by people,

their faces peering down at me, some curious, others frightened . . .
One of the businessmen took out a silver pen and wrote on the brilliant white cuff of his shirt. *Are you Eliot Gast?* I stared at the crowd
of faces, my audience, and nodded slowly. Yes, I was Eliot Gast."[34]
This closing paragraph is a deliberate and stark contrast to the first
days of Gast's detention, when he tries to effect a rescue by writing
notes to distribute—"*My name is Eliot Gast*" (20)—and to anchor
himself to reality by repeating to himself in a mirror, "I am Eliot
Gast" (20, 49).

The Ordinary Seaman is another escape plot fundamentally about
the instability of names. The protagonist, Esteban, cycles through the
nicknames Rambo, El Piricuaco, El Piri, and El Nieto, and one from
his irregular battalion in Nicaragua "which made him blush and grin
like crazy" (42). In the end, however, none stick, and his shipmates
decide he is un-nicknameable. "Esteban is slippery with nicknames"
(42). Esteban's structural opposites in the novel, the shipowners Mark
and Elias, are also slippery with names. They hide their identities
behind the construct of an unnamed, "phantom owner" (350). Mark
keeps "his personal credit cards out of all *URUS* transactions" (321)
so that when he steals his partner's money and flees to the Yucatán,
it is as if he has "vanished off the face of the earth" (371). And Elias,
who assumes the false title "captain," makes certain from the start
of their partnership that anybody investigating the *URUS* will be
unable to "find his name on a single piece of paper" (371). The ship's
own name, the *URUS*, is an alias. The original name was painted
over so that the owners could avoid paying overdue fees and taxes.
Even the pier where the ship is docked is described as having lost
its name long ago. One of the shipmates, Bernardo, explains this
fact to an elderly couple who have wandered out toward the ship.
Notably, they are looking for a doctor whose name they have forgotten and, despite Bernardo's desperate plea for help, they depart
without even "having asked him his name" (122).

In *The Foreign Student* the protagonist's Anglicized name, "Chuck,"
is effectively an alias, and he creates a fraudulent identity card when
fleeing Seoul. In *War Trash*, the protagonist takes on the alias Feng
Yan so that he cannot be targeted as an officer while in prison camp;
later he assumes the identity of another soldier, Chang Ming, in an

effort to protect him. In *When the Emperor Was Divine*, the members of the displaced family are never named. *The Sympathizer*'s protagonist is also nameless. In *Maya's Notebook*, the fleeing protagonist takes two aliases and one nickname, and studiously hides identity traces in all of her communications back home. And the protagonist of *What Is the What* takes on many names in his flight from war: he is Achak, Valentino, Dominic, and Gone Far. When a woman in the refugee camp calls him Sleeper, he comments: "I had so many names at Kakuma and this was the most poetic. I would allow Maria to call me anything she wished."[35]

Demetria Martínez's *Mother Tongue* is the story of a relationship between the protagonist, Mary, and a torture survivor who has escaped to the United States from El Salvador with the help of the Sanctuary Movement. He enters the country under the alias A. Romero, but in their first conversation Mary persuades him to pick a new alias, one that he can answer to in his sleep. He picks the "ordinary" name José Luis.[36] In that moment, Mary begins to fall in love with him. As she explains it, she was like many women in that time who "questioned their own names." She believed that this man, whose real name she would never know, embodied a "mystery" that had the power "to tear apart the dry rind" of her own "ordinary" name and all that it entailed (16).

Mary's great struggle in the novel is her attempt to determine, after José Luis has disappeared back in his home country, whether or not she ever truly knew him, whether she loved him as an individual or as a projection of her own fantasies and needs. Many readers have argued that their relationship begins, at least, as the latter. One critic writes that the novel destabilizes Mary's "fantasy of connectedness" by showing how her "experience as a Mexican American and José Luis's experiences as a Salvadoran have created fundamentally different subjects." Another emphasizes that Mary sees José Luis as "generically 'other,'" and El Salvador as "empty of people, full only of romantic ideas."[37] But critics also agree that by the end, the novel has revealed Mary's capacity to transcend such narcissistic reductions by accumulating diverse community experiences. In the novel's final moment of emotional closure, Mary—now twenty years older— finally finds her answer to the question of the authenticity of their relationship. She tracks down records of him and learns that his alias, José Luis—the name she gave to the son he unknowingly left her with—had been his true name after all.

Like the morally compromised, identity-shifting protagonists of Anchee Min's *Becoming Madame Mao* and Laleh Khadivi's *The Age of Orphans*, the protagonist of *The Orphan Master's Son* shifts effortlessly among disguises, identities, and names. As an orphan who lost his original name, Jun Do gives himself the name of a Korean War martyr and takes on the job of naming all the other orphans. Later, he sheds his name and assumes the identity of the war hero Commander Ga. "Names come and go," he says. "Names change. I don't even have one" (379). The torturer who ultimately kills him—and who yearns to have his own name acknowledged—believes that discovering Jun Do's "true name" will be his greatest accomplishment. But finally, in an act of perverse mercy, he decides to kill Jun Do before his colleagues can permanently set his identity by branding him before a large crowd in a soccer stadium with the label "Property of the Dear Leader Kim Jong Il" (399). Sent to the United States on a government mission earlier in the novel, Jun Do comes across a phone book in astonishment.

> Inside were thousands of names. It took him a while to understand that everyone in central Texas was listed here, with their full names and addresses. He couldn't believe that you could look up anyone and seek them out, that all you had to do to prove you weren't an orphan was to open a book and point to your parents. It was unfathomable that a permanent link existed to mothers and fathers and lost mates, that they were forever fixed in type. Donaldson, Jimenez, Smith—all it took was a book, a little book could save you a lifetime of uncertainty and guesswork. Suddenly he hated his small, backward homeland, a land of mysteries and ghosts and mistaken identities. (146)

On that same trip, Jun Do meets an English-speaking character who mistakes his name for "John Doe." "Isn't that the name that you give a missing person?" she asks (140).

The function of names is very different in the justice plot. Justice plot protagonists are investigators rather than escapees. They retain a single name and hold dearly to names. They are the relentless givers, seekers, or displayers of names that would otherwise be lost. *When the Ground Turns in Its Sleep* is about the revelation of true names and the ritualistic reading of the names of the lost. *Philadelphia Fire* begins with the search for a name: Who is the boy who survived the fire? It proceeds with Cudjoe anxiously trying to remember names from his past. It concludes with a memorial service in which citizens and mourners protest police brutality by reciting the names of the dead and holding posters with their names, "the ones gone who must not be forgotten" (197). *The Long Night of White Chickens* is centrally about identifying names (of a murderer, a secret lover, and a lost orphan boy), just as *A Person of Interest* centers on the protagonist's quest to identify the name of a terrorist. Elvira Orphée's *El Angel's Last Conquest* is a torture novel that viciously parodies the justice plot. Here, truth is not discovered through evidence but rather manufactured through pain. Significantly, torturers demonstrate their absolute power by arbitrarily renaming their victims.

In *The Ministry of Special Cases*, names are, for the families of the disappeared, "all we have left" (231). Describing a list of names the United Jewish Congregations keeps of those disappeared from its community, the Rabbi explains: "We have it right out in the open, for anyone to see. It's a protest. It's a list that contradicts and calls the government to task—of this I'm proud. Our staff does the research, working in tandem but independently. We use the government's very resources to challenge its claims with our own official roll . . . We can renegotiate names, and it's a fight to get each one" (244). Lillian pleads to have her son's name added to the list, but there is only one place Pato's name will be recorded. At the end of the novel, an unidentified young woman discovers six balls of paper wrapped in plastic, hidden in a foam pad in her own torture chamber. Each has Pato's name written on it. The young woman remembers one prisoner telling her about such notes, called "caramels" because they should be swallowed to be protected. The discovery of the names jolts her with exhilaration, pulling her out of her "amnesiac" (301) state and making her decide to survive. "Such a civilized act, writing one's name, a concrete act. It made her think she could leave a history of herself" (302). The names make the young woman believe that she might be freed, that it might be her purpose to survive and give them back to Pato's family. While the revealed names give her, for a time, miraculously renewed life, their power is most dramatically expressed in the terror they inspire, in what the young woman imagines as "the worst": "Pato dead, Pato gone, and she, carrying a message, his final and only link to the world, doing for him this good deed and, by accident—the accident of her own death—erasing his name from above" (302). When the young woman is killed—dropped from a plane into the Río de la Plata—the names are "swallowed up in all that dark" (304).

What these and other justice plots together seem to be modeling is a fictional equivalent to the concept of legal personhood developed in international human rights law. Article 16 of the International Covenant on Civil and Political Rights reads: "Everyone shall have the right to recognition everywhere as a person before the law."[38] Subsequent articles detail some of the freedoms contingent upon this recognition of personhood, including freedom of thought, conscience, and religion. Shortly thereafter, Article 24 establishes the fundamental duties required of each state to promote the dignity and worth of the children within its territory. What steps must states take to ensure the recognition of the personhood of their children? Section 2 of Article 24 reads: "Every child shall be registered immediately after birth and shall have a name."[39]

Lawrence Thornton's *Imagining Argentina* has a justice plot that organizes itself around the act of naming (as does its sequel, *Naming the Spirits*). Carlos Rueda is a director at a children's theater in Buenos Aires during the Dirty War. When the father of one of his young actors is disappeared, Carlos discovers he has the power to accurately "imagine" the fates of the victims of the junta. Carlos tells the boy his father will be released; the very next day he is. Carlos soon begins holding meetings with the Mothers of the Plaza de Mayo and other family survivors, revealing to those who join him in his garden what has happened or will happen to their missing loved ones. For all who come, the truth—however painful—is better than the agony of not knowing. Carlos's powers are triggered by names. The mystic sessions begin with the same queries: "What is your name, señora?"; "Give me more names"; "Now, give me more names."[40] When Carlos's own wife is disappeared, he cannot see her in his visions until his daughter participates in the ritual by telling the story of her lost mother, beginning with the name. "My mother is Cecilia Corazon Rueda. She was taken from our house by four men who came in a green Falcon" (46). As the stories of the disappeared accumulate, names become one of the only anchors of distinction. "The worst of it," the narrator says, "was my sense that they were all telling the same story. The names were different, the locations, but that was all" (57).

The contest between the junta and its victims is in key ways a contest over naming, a contest in which family members seek to stop their loved ones from dying "a second time" by becoming "numbers, statistics," rather than names (189–190). The contest reaches a climax at the midpoint of the novel, when Carlos manages to arrange a face-to-face meeting with one of the leaders of the junta, General Guzman. Together they perform a grotesque parody of Carlos's prophetic meetings with the family survivors. The general begins the session by putting Carlos's perpetual question back to him: "What is her name?" Guzman asks (106). But when Carlos replies, Guzman denies its existence. To the other names Carlos invokes, Guzman replies only, "Their names are not on the list" (107). After the meeting, Carlos conceives the idea for a play that will become a turning point in his own life. He calls it *The Names*. It begins with Carlos sitting alone on the stage, performing a plaintive song on the guitar as he speaks:

> This is a play about memory and desire, about words and the sounds we live in. Think of it. Argentina tells us where we are. Names make us known to family and to strangers. La Plata makes the river ours, allows us to know it from all the other rivers. Buenos Aires is the name of home. Calle Cordova, my street, is unlike any other because of its name. It is that way with your street, too. Names are the foundation of everything. Think of it. Names tell us about a life and the memory of that life. But

in Argentina names are not like they are elsewhere. Here, now, they are as easily erased as markings on tissue paper. Now the page of Argentina is clean of names that belong there, that have a right to be there. So this is also a play about history, how that happened. Argentina is full of names. Our memories are full of names. Names are as natural as trees, birds, breathing. They are the right of a person, but there are those who believe they can take the people and their names away, and this must not happen. Names must never, never be stolen again . . . This is a play about what we must do to keep the names alive. (121)

That night, after the first performance, security forces disappear Carlos's daughter Teresa; soon after, they kill her. The narrator imagines the moment when that decision was made as an act that approximates unnaming, as an inversion of Carlos's play and his evening sessions with the Mothers. "I am convinced they made their decision offhandedly, almost casually, making a joke of it. Perhaps, toward the end of the meeting, a list was passed around with a check in red ink beside a name. Perhaps the name was never spoken. That nicety would fit in perfectly with the scene as I envision it, somehow making it more terrible because of the silence" (162).

The contest between naming and unnaming continues throughout the book. When Carlos's friend Silvio is murdered, he repeats his own name over and over as an act of final defiance. A literature professor who is disappeared gathers the strength to survive his torture by repeating the names of his most cherished authors when asked to name fellow conspirators: Dostoevski, Koestler, Camus. "What saved Hirsch was his belief in the names even when the electricity was applied . . . [The torturers] did not understand when he said that those names opposed everything they imagined, that they had already pitted force against force, chaos against reason, death against Argentina. Hirsch knew, even when they beat and burned and carved away his flesh, that they could never touch his names" (160).

Against these acts of clear naming, the novel pits the alias. Fugitive Nazis who fled to Argentina meet with Guzman in secret and then "retreat to their anonymity, to the other names they have taken" (91). The spy who infiltrates Carlos's meetings, posing as the victim

Gustavo, is in fact a soldier named Mario Rabán, known to his fellow perpetrators by the nickname "White Angel" because of the way he descends upon his victims like a bird of prey. The narrator publishes attacks against the junta in a French magazine, but acknowledges with shame that he "lacked the courage" (17) to use his real name. He sees the same cowardice in his fellow citizens, whom he criticizes for "hiding inside themselves" (69) when they refuse to acknowledge the Mothers and the placards they carry: "WHERE IS RUBEN MACIAS? WHERE IS JULIA OBREGON?" (37). The name is most violently attacked, however, not by the alias, but by what Scarry would call the unmaking of the interior structure of the name, by the cruel logic of civilizational inversion—that is, the deliberate transformation of the fundamental institutions, objects, and practices of mutual care into sites of terror. Cecilia's torturers attempt to turn naming itself into a weapon during their sessions, forcing her to choose who among the security forces should rape her daughter. "Say his name" (155).

Throughout the novel, key plot points hinge on naming. Carlos is psychically reconnected to his wife when he encounters an elderly woman who recovered the shoe of someone she saw being disappeared, hanging it on a wall on the street afterward.

> "Do you remember what happened that night?"
> "She screamed, but all I heard was a name," the woman says. "Then she said a man's name."
> "Cecilia?"
> "Yes, that was it, Cecilia."
> "And the man's name?"
> "It has been a long time. Over a year. I put the shoe up in case she came back."
> "The man's name?"
> "Carlos, I remember. 'Carlos,' she said, 'it's Cecilia.'" (152)

After that night, Carlos is able to see Cecilia in his visions again. She has escaped, and is hiding at an *estancia* connected to the name Souza. At the climax of the novel, Carlos is at a parade in La Boca when he sees the name Souza on a sign above an office; when he rushes to it, he finds his wife. The novel closes with Cecilia watching the leaders of the junta as they are sentenced to prison. "As the generals were led off she said, "*Nunca más*, Videla. *Nunca más*, Guzman," and she named each and every one until they'd gone" (213). Names prevail.

Ariel Dorfman, who was forced to flee Chile after the 1973 coup conducted by Augusto Pinochet, has written widely across genres on the nature of tyranny. *Death and the Maiden* is perhaps his most widely known work about human rights abuses and the fight for justice through naming. While it is technically outside the genre as a theatrical production (later made into a film directed by Roman Polanski), the play has had a widespread influence upon human rights representation, figuring prominently in the establishment of patterns developing across genres. It merits extended attention here.

Death and the Maiden tells the story of Paulina Salas, a former political prisoner in an unnamed nation that has recently transitioned to democracy. Her husband, Gerardo, becomes acquainted with a man named Dr. Miranda after the latter rescues him when he is stranded on the road with a flat tire. When the doctor comes to visit Gerardo in his home, Paulina—who was blindfolded during her detention—immediately recognizes Dr. Miranda's voice as that of a sadistic doctor who participated in her torture and rape. Dr. Miranda denies the charge in shocked outrage, insisting that Paulina is disturbed and delusional. Gerardo, a stand-in for the intended experience of the audience, remains anxiously, almost unbearably, confused and uncertain. But Paulina is relentless. Imprisoning Dr. Miranda in their house and threatening his life, she forcibly extracts a confession from him.

Much of *Death and the Maiden's* high-tension plot revolves around the different moral functions of naming. It opens by highlighting the honorific function of naming when discussing Gerardo's appointment to the nation's truth commission. "'So the president named you?' *Brief pause.* 'He named me.'"[41] The politics of naming are thereafter a primary thematic. First, refusing to name is depicted as cowardice. When Dr. Miranda (whose identity has not yet been revealed by Paulina) initiates a conversation with Gerardo about the truth commissions, he expresses his enthusiasm for the idea that finally the perpetrators' "names can be published" (15). But Gerardo explains that the commission has been ordered to keep the names confidential—a concession to the army, which threatened the president not to let the commission push too far. As Dr. Miranda draws Gerardo out, however, the latter finally reveals the secret that the president believes "names will pour out like water," if off the record, as testimonies accumulate (17).

After that exchange, refusing to name is depicted as heroism. When interrogating Dr. Miranda, Paulina recalls with something like pride that she never revealed her husband's work in the resistance, "never breathed his name" (30). But in *her* interrogation, Paulina will get names. "I want him to confess . . . With all the information, the names and data, all the details. That's what I want" (41). Dr. Miranda attempts to use the personalizing quality of naming to protect himself in the makeshift trial that Paulina has prepared, asking Gerardo not to call him by his title but to "please" treat him with the "familiarity" of his first name, Roberto (42). Gerardo refuses the intimacy, saying that the formality of the title "will help me out" in his assigned role as lawyer in Paulina's trial (43).

One of *Death and the Maiden*'s main contentions is that lives turn on naming. Dr. Miranda is captured only because he recognizes who Gerardo is after dropping him off at his house—"I heard your name on the news" (13)—and on an impulse decides to return to visit with him and discuss the investigation. By contrast, Gerardo is not captured because Paulina protects his name. "Strange how things turn out," she says to Dr. Miranda. "If I'd mentioned Gerardo, he wouldn't have been named to any Investigating Commission, but would have been one of the names that some other lawyer was investigating" (30). And in the final plot twist, Dr. Miranda—who has persuasively maintained his innocence throughout—finally reveals himself when he makes a crucial mistake with names. In the course of the trial, Paulina feeds to Dr. Miranda an incorrect name, identifying one of the men who tortured and raped her by the nickname "Bud." "I never found out his real name," she says (60). But when Dr. Miranda gives his confession to Gerardo, insisting that he is only doing so under duress and only giving the information that Paulina has scripted for him, he accidentally corrects the false name "Bud" to the real name "Stud." With that, he sentences himself. Paulina points her gun at him. As the play ends, it is not clear if she has executed him or left him to live under the threat of exposure.

Daniel Alarcón's *Lost City Radio* is the story of an unnamed South American nation reeling in the aftermath of a bitter civil war. Like *Imagining Argentina*, it is a novel whose primary action is, in key ways, the act of naming. Indeed, the novel deliberately invokes *Imagining Argentina* with its stark premise. Norma is a radio personality whose husband, Rey, has been disappeared. Every Sunday evening, she hosts a show in which she reads lists of names of those who have disappeared and invites listeners to call in and give her more names. Her show is immensely popular, and people come to believe that she is, like Carlos, "mantic and all-seeing, able to pluck the lost, estranged, and missing from the moldering city."[42]

Norma's primary activity outside of the radio station is also name-tracking: she tracks down her husband by searching prisons. But it is a search doomed to fail, as one guard notes, because she only knows his proper name. Rey used a pseudonym in partisan newspapers, took an alias as a member of the resistance, and collaborated with insurgents who remained unnamed. Norma tracks down the stranger who abandons an orphan named Victor at her radio station by filtering through potential names in the phone book: "Twelve different Manau households, in nine different districts. No Elijahs or E. Manaus. He lived with his parents then" (153). In a brief mirror plot, Rey retreats into employment with the government after his capture and torture, taking a job ratifying land takeovers that requires collecting names on his clipboard. Finally, in the mid-novel's key plot line, Norma tracks down the name of the man who turns out to be, in a staggering convergence, the orphan's father: Rey, who she realizes lived another life with another woman by a different name.

From her very first meeting with Rey, Norma encounters his names as a series of mysteries to be investigated. He refuses to give her his last name and, in the first line of dialogue between them that the novel depicts, cryptically asks her, "You don't know who I am, do you?" (16). On their way home from that party, the bus the two are riding is stopped at a checkpoint. Rey is caught without identification and is taken away to what Norma later learns is a torture facility called the Moon. When Norma finally returns to her own home that night, bewildered, she finds Rey's identity card in her pocket: his picture, but with somebody else's name. Thirteen months later, after Rey's release, she encounters him by a bench at the university, but he denies knowing her. "I'm Norma," she says, holding up to his face the dangerous identity card that she has carried for so long. "Should I call you Rey?" (226). Later, when they are to marry, Rey's father warns her: "Our name is tainted, child . . . I promise you: you don't want it" (77).

Discovering that Rey is the name of Victor's father is at the center of *Lost City Radio*'s plot, but what connects the opening and closing pages, what provides the novel's primary emotional closure, is a different act of naming—one that is personal for the author. Discussing the background of his novel, Alarcón recalls watching a talk show in Lima in 2003 when his own uncle's name was read on air from a list of the disappeared.[43] *Lost City Radio*'s climax is a fictional reworking of this moment; it is the realization of Norma's primary desire throughout the book, the reason she agreed to host Lost City Radio in the first place: to hear Rey's name spoken aloud on the air.

Norma has long thought such public acknowledgment would be impossible. The government has forbidden the naming of suspected dissidents or guerrillas. As Norma explains to Victor when he asks her to tell him about Rey: "He's on a list they keep in the palace: his name can't even be said out loud. Every night on the radio—can you understand this—I want to talk to him. But I don't. If I let myself say his name, it would be terrible . . . arrests, investigations, disappearances" (104). Victor, however, was delivered to Norma because his village had a list of names that they wanted her to read, and Rey's name is on it. When Norma's producer sees it, he blacks it out with a felt-tip marker. "Norma gasped. What was worse: realizing Rey's name was there, that she had somehow missed it, or seeing it disappear again?" (99). The producer warns her: "The wrong name, Norma. I'm sorry, but the wrong name and we're dead. You and me both" (251). But Norma finds it impossible to stop herself. In the closing pages of the novel, in what will be her last show, she surrenders to impulse. "She has been talking now for a few minutes, and the realization scares her: the words are forming in her throat, not in her mind. The words are expelled and thrown into space before she has a moment to reflect on them. Rey. She's said one of his names already, and so there's no going back. *Rey Rey Rey*" (252). She invites Victor onto the live program to read the list he has brought from his village.

> And now she can't even hear the names. Norma has her eyes closed, and the war has been over for ten years. Let the boy read, let him, they won't do anything to him. Just send me to prison, they'll reopen the Moon for my benefit, and welcome me as they did my husband. It's the middle of the night, and no one is listening anyway. It's just us. He reads very well, and Manau should be proud of what he has taught the boy. The names mean nothing, not to Manau, not to Victor. One or another is familiar, a surname he has heard before, but most are empty. There is his father's name, and he nearly skips over this one altogether. Norma sits upright at the sound, as if someone has touched her. "Pardon me?" She says. "Could you repeat that last one?"
>
> Victor looks up from his list.
>
> "What a nice name," Norma says. It's all she can do not to scream . . .
>
> And now, it is time to wait. (253–254)

The alias, nickname, and lost name are all forms of the secret, protective covers for somebody who wants to avoid being targeted. The moral significance of this secrecy depends on who is doing the hiding: perpetrator or victim. As the wife of a general in the junta puts it when threatening Kaddish in *The Ministry of Special Cases:* "It's much easier in this country to get disappeared than to stay hidden. They are two very different things" (335). This binary—between disguising and denying, hiding and covering up—is a key thematic in *Ministry.* Kaddish's mother, a prostitute in the Society of the Benevolent Self, disappears her own name to protect her son from social stigma. Kaddish's first and last name are inventions designed "to give him the new start that she couldn't manage for herself" (22). Indeed, many in the Jewish community of Buenos Aires have the names of their parents chiseled off their gravestones in the Society, fearing that their scandalous pasts might draw further attention to them as scapegoats and targets. Meanwhile, the government gets rid of Pato's name. When Lillian files for a writ of habeas corpus, the bureaucracy concedes, but the forms they return to her declare that the person abducted from her home is a woman named Mónica Álvarez. Before she reports to the police station to collect the child, Lillian scratches out the false name and writes Pato Poznan on the forms. But the security forces adamantly maintain the state fiction.

> "You're Lillian Poznan and we've got a girl, sixteen years old, a Mónica Álvarez to release to you."
>
> "I don't want her. I want my son."
>
> The sergeant held one of the papers up to the light. "You can still see where it says Mónica," he said.
>
> "Where's my Pato?" Lillian said.
>
> Lillian opened her mouth to yell again and was silenced with a stare. The sergeant wouldn't have it. "Do you want the girl or not?" he said. "You can take her or leave her. Decide quickly before we scratch out her name on our forms too." (225)

The disguise / erasure binary is a key thematic throughout novels of human rights. At the midpoint of *A Constellation of Vital Phenomena*, Sonja's life changes when a disguise un-erases. She is interrogating Akhmed at gunpoint because he has addressed her by her full name, Sofia Andreyevna Rabina, which is information she has revealed to no one—a sure sign that Akhmed is an informer. But Akhmed saves himself by explaining—in one of the many coincidences that tie all of the novel's characters together—that a refugee at Havaa's hostel gave him those names when he inquired about the possibility of work in the nearby hospital. Sonja, who had despaired of finding clues about her trafficked and disappeared sister, reacts with fierce shock:

> "What was her name?" Sonja asked, eyes as fixed as constellations. She stood close enough for him to hear her teeth grind. There was so much of her, right here, in his face, and he would have stepped back, had a gun not pushed him forward . . .

"What was her name!" she demanded. He was afraid to answer, afraid even to exhale; the hope wrapped within the question was so small and flickering a breath could extinguish it.
"Was it Natasha? Was her name Natasha?" (165)

In *The Ministry of Special Cases*, Englander depicts the perpetrator
as one who need never hide his name, who is in fact tragic because
he cannot escape his name. When Kaddish meets the navigator who
had the job of tossing disappeared children into the sea, he is surprised that the man does not hesitate to give his name. "A guilty man
cannot get himself killed in this town," the traumatized navigator
says. "Only the innocent need to watch out" (263). There is no point
in hunting him down for his name or for the truth, the navigator
continues, because he is a drunk and a disgrace, "the man who tells
their secret and out of whose mouth it sounds like a lie" (265).

In novels centered on the lives of perpetrators rather than victims
and survivors, however, the search for true names and the truth
through names is determinative. The novel of rights, it could be said,
insists upon taking off Colonel Joll's sunglasses (Coetzee's iconic
image of the refusal to see or be seen). In Jonathan Dee's *The Liberty
Campaign*, Albert Ferdinand is a pleasant neighbor living quietly in
a small town called Belmont. Shortly after the narrator meets and
establishes a friendship with him, the media releases a story identifying Ferdinand's real name: Captain Joao Carvalho da Silva, a
former torturer in Brazil's military junta. To his victims, da Silva remains an all-powerful figure, even when under surveillance. One
evening, an unidentified survivor sneaks into the neighborhood to
catch a glimpse of the suspect. When his fears are confirmed, he becomes hysterical, begging the neighbor who finds him not to let da
Silva know he was there and running away in panic. But da Silva himself is also in fear for his life. Having entered the United States with
falsified documents when he fled Brazil, he will be subject to deportation and returned to his home country, where he is certain to be
murdered. Terrified, he makes plans to abandon the life of his alias
and flee once again.

In Edwidge Danticat's novel *The Dew Breaker*, the former torturer
for the Tonton Macoute takes an alias when he resettles in the United

States, disguises himself through extreme weight loss, and uses "coded utterances" when discussing a former victim whom he dare not name to his wife. In this way he is finally made equivalent in power to those whom he formerly terrorized, and who refused in fear to give their names to human rights investigators.[44] But the Dew Breaker is unable to hide from the scar his last victim gives him, the scar that "left a mark on him, a brand that he would carry for the rest of his life" (227). In the end, he is compelled by shame to explain this scar to his daughter, offering a confession about his true past— an existentially disorienting revelation that is prefigured earlier in his daughter's life by a chance encounter with a man her mother takes for a former perpetrator. "'I wasn't going to hit him,' the daughter said. 'I was just going to ask his name . . . Would it be so wrong, Manman, to ask his name?'" (80).

In Walter Mosley's GWOT torture allegory *The Man in My Basement*, a mysterious stranger hires the protagonist to secretly imprison and punish him in his basement so that he might atone for the "crimes against humanity" he committed while trafficking in conflict diamonds.[45] The perpetrator, who goes by the alias Anniston Bennet, suffers many indignities voluntarily. But when he is pressured to reveal his true name he immediately balks, insisting he no longer wants to participate and threatening the protagonist. In *The Tattooed Soldier*, the perpetrator takes the tattoo of a jaguar—the name of his battalion, which inspires fear in civilians and respect in soldiers—because he knows it will be "his forever" and "would still be recognizable" into his old age (241–242). In its brazen permanence, in other words, the tattoo promises that he will never need to hide his identity. But after he leaves his war behind, the soldier is recognized by his tattoo and murdered in revenge.

Each of these three perpetrator-centered novels is also a novel of aftermath. Here, privacy functions differently from the way it does in conflict-centered novels like *Breaking the Tongue* or *The Foreign Student*, where privacy is resistance. In perpetrator-centered novels, privacy can be an aspect of violence even when violence seeks to eliminate the possibility of privacy. That is, war's elimination of private space does not engender public space; elimination of secrets does not result in transparency. Viewed afterward, or from the outside, war is the process of violently converting all individual private spaces into a single, vast private space: the private space of atrocity.

At the sphere of the political, the quintessential literary example of the tyranny of the private is Adam Johnson's North Korea, a nation figured as an international secret and a grotesque impersonation of the inviolable home, where Kim Jong Il is the benevolent "fatherly leader."[46] At the sphere of the personal, the tyranny of the private is epitomized in Walter Mosley's secret basement. Here, the privative sense of privacy—that is, privacy as the staging ground for tyrannical unselfing—has its philosophic roots in the work of Hannah Arendt, who characterized the "shadowy interior of the household" of ancient Greek city-states as a site of unchecked patriarchal power. The private home was a place where women and slaves—those "not fully human" (38)—lived not as political agents but as subjects to the law of necessity.[47]

Privacy as privation also has its roots in contemporary trauma theory. Judith Herman has argued for recognition of psychic overlap "between rape survivors and combat survivors, between battered women and political prisoners, between the survivors of vast concentration camps created by tyrants who rule nations and the survivors of small, hidden concentration camps created by tyrants who rule their homes."[48] Such abuse is a dreadful perversion of the human rights novel's conception of home, which draws from Arendt's alternative description of the home as a "sphere of intimacy" designed "to shelter the intimate" (38).

This chapter began by tracking the topoi of violated privacy and the concomitant desire to protect it. But as these perpetrator-centered stories reveal, human rights novels also engage the ethical counterpressure to undo rather than to achieve privacy. In *A Constellation of Vital Phenomena*, Anthony Marra uses an especially peculiar device for developing this theme of restorative exposure, a device that calls attention to the ethics of "crowded" narrative. In depicting Russia's brutal invasion of Chechnya, *A Constellation of Vital Phenomena* reconfigures how minor characters accumulate in war representation. Conventionally, we see such characters only briefly or partially, with their troubling backstories hidden and their high-stakes futures occluded. They function as uninvestigated secrets, as typical instances of the tragedy of wartime's crowding interactions, where everybody hurtles to their separate, desperate fates too quickly to know one another, but closely enough to triumphantly help or permanently harm one another. In *A Constellation of Vital Phenomena*, by contrast, people at the margins are important not in spite of but because of their obscurity. From start to finish, Marra transforms his minor characters from unimportant narrative functions into opportunities for narrative transparency. He appends to their brief moments of visibility parenthetical omniscient views that flash out over the arc of their lives, revealing origins, final fates, and unforgettable, poignant details.

Describing the portraits Akhmed composes, for instance, Marra suddenly pivots, opening the inner psyche of one unnamed boy who "is tired of being the youngest and hopes his older brother will return for many reasons, not least so he will marry and have a child and the youngest brother will no longer be youngest . . . [and who] would have a smile on his face and the silliest thought in his skull a minute before the first bullet would break it" (139). Inserted like an accident into the description of Akhmed's wife's smile, Marra writes: "Twelve years earlier those incisors were beloved by the city dentist, a young man who plugged his most lascivious thoughts into the open mouths of young women; but the dentist died a virgin when a misaimed mortar shell landed on his practice and carried him to Paradise in an erupting gray cloud" (39). Such haphazard detailing is a decidedly quirky device that, because of Marra's insistent repetition, begins over time to feel like the expression of an ethical norm: namely, a refusal to let war hide what has happened, even in what might be called minor spaces, and to minor characters.

Throughout the above, the undoing of privacy seems tied into, rather than an alternative to, the prioritization of privacy insofar as it is an aspect of property-based, liberal individualism. But elsewhere the genre takes a different tack, showing how the fixation with privacy rights conceptually thins out the "human" of human rights. In *Maya's Notebook*, for instance, privacy is modeled as a key element of self-fashioning in the romantic coming-of-age narrative, but it is also depicted as an unbalancing form of lack. Allende portrays the survivor's retreat into secrecy as an act of self-protection that becomes pathology. Maya disappears herself both politically and personally, and Manuel's reclusion is so complete that he no longer needs locks or closed doors. His emotionally impoverishing privacy is not even hypothetically interruptible. Narrative desire in *Maya's Notebook* therefore inevitably arcs toward exposure: sharing of personal histories, opening of domestic space, and the revelation of trauma as the collective undoing of isolating violation. In other words, while many of the texts analyzed in this chapter do rely upon a liberal calculus of autonomy and self-determination, the genre also opens up space for the thematization of a communitarian ethos that resists atomistic reductions of rights discourse.

Movement

In domestic contexts, residence and free movement in public space function as primary expressions of citizenship through tacit consent: in essence, the iterative formation of a shared public identity. Tracking linked images of free movement in Western political philosophy, Scarry identifies freedom of movement as "the right that underlies all other rights," and therefore a right that entails obligations. In Plato's *Crito*, Socrates is awaiting his execution in Athens. When his distraught friend Crito comes to his prison cell to help him escape, Socrates refuses. He explains to Crito that he must accept his death sentence because he has accumulated deep obligations to the state in a variety ways—most notably, in the daily act of residing and walking freely within its borders, which most translations characterize as a "contract" and some as an act of "love." Scarry views residence and free movement as foundational concepts for the social contract in Hobbes, Rousseau, and others. But if there is a "single doctrinal location" for tacit consent through such concepts, she notes, it is in section 119 of John Locke's *Second Treatise of Government*. Here, Locke uses two primary images to describe possession of the state: taking residence in the territory and "traveling freely on the highway."[49]

The novel of human rights is about the breakdown of state legitimacy, about the undoing rather than the establishment of the social contract. In these novels, Socratic/Lockean conceptions of mobility and residence are overturned. Like photographic negatives of their idealized counterparts, free public mobility is depicted as a form of resistance to state-defined space and residency as a primary site of conflict with state power, a form of defiant secret-keeping. Key to this dual reconceptualization is the idea of translation. Etymologically, the word translation blends the idea of codebreaking with (through the Latin *trans* and *latum*) the physical act of *carrying across*, connecting revelation, meaning-making, and motion. Unsurprisingly, translators and acts of translation emerge as recurring, even dominant concerns throughout the novel of human rights. *War Trash*'s Yu Yuan is a translator. Jun Do in *The Orphan Master's Son* is a translator in multiple roles. June from Chang-rae Lee's *The Surrendered* is valued as an adoptee because she can translate for other Korean War orphans. Both Joy and Kraft from Richard Powers's *Operation Wandering Soul* are constantly translating across language and culture. José Luis from *Mother Tongue* works in the United States translating human rights alerts. Gen Watanabe is the center of all narrative lines in *Bel Canto* because only he can translate between the terrorists, the hostages, and the outside world, and the romance at the novel's center begins poignantly with Carmen's request that Gen teach her to read Spanish and English.

Corban Addison's *The Tears of Dark Water*, which I will discuss in detail later, is concerned throughout with translation. The Somali pirate who is its tragic protagonist is nicknamed "Afyareh"—"agile mouth."[50] Quentin, one of his hostages, loses executive function and, consequently, the ability to recall many words after he is shot, setting the stage for the novel's redemptive subplot: the process of rediscovering his ability to translate the world. In *The Ordinary Seaman*, Esteban's continual translations invoke linguistic and national border crossing, the concepts of legal and industrial property through the associated "convey" and "conveyance," and the possibility of that which remains untranslated, unidentified, and secret. Choi's Chang Ahn is a translator for USIS and Army Intelligence during the war. He is a conduit of secrets, debriefing spies and devising propaganda. The work of translation also defines his experience as a student in the United States, and his key memories of his father involve translating books together. Perhaps most important, to return to this section's primary concept, mastering languages makes Chang mobile. As Choi writes, Chang becomes a translator because he has "faith in its power to transport him," even "across the ocean to Sewanee" (219), where he discovers belonging and love by traveling freely on the highways hour after hour with Katherine.[51]

Throughout the novels I have discussed, free mobility is not simply a plot-driver; it is a primary thematic. Maya from *Maya's Notebook* escapes authority as a runaway and escapes her interior psychological lockdowns as a dedicated jogger. Rey from *Lost City Radio* is fundamentally defined by his movement back and forth between his different lives in the city and the countryside. Dave Eggers's *Zeitoun* is about restoring the possibility of community by creatively reachieving mobility, by escaping the imprisonment of flooding and of unjust government detention. As one critic writes, discussing Zeitoun's seaman father, "Water and mobility, rather than land and fixity, are the foundations of identity."[52] *The Orphan Master's Son* structures the sequence of its sections by progressive images of movement: from running in the dark to small motorboat, to large but dilapidated ship, to luxury car, to airplane. This development of vehicles matches the development of the protagonist's identity: from lack of identity as an orphan to hidden identity as a criminal, to celebrity identity as an imposter, to authentic identity through revelation and freedom. In *The Ordinary Seaman*, Esteban is an undocumented worker who can escape brutal working conditions on the *URUS* only by sneaking off the ship and risking deportation. Like a modern-day revision of Socrates, Esteban initiates his life in a nonstate, "illegal" community by wandering the city streets and, finally, finding love during an encounter on a public thoroughfare. This salvific union mirrors a previous love affair during the war in Nicaragua, which was consummated, significantly, in an abandoned moving vehicle.

At the same time that these escape plots celebrate free movement, they lament failed movement—immobility, forced mobility, asymmetric mobility. J. M. Coetzee's singularly influential *Waiting for the Barbarians* provides one of the most troubling images of damaged mobility in recent decades: the ankles and feet of the barbarian girl, which are broken during her torture by colonial special forces and then exploitatively nursed by a guilty colonial magistrate. In Richard Powers's *Operation Wandering Soul*, Coetzee's barbarian girl is the haunting shadow behind the Laotian war refugee, Joy Stepaneevong, who is being treated by a white humanitarian for bone cancer that begins in her ankle. And the central image in Ha Jin's *War Trash* is the leg injury that causes the protagonist to limp, which I read as a deliberate reworking of the broken ankles of the barbarian girl. Now, however, gender and power are reversed, as a woman doctor treats a vulnerable man's wound, and does so with a professionalized intimacy that sharply contrasts the magistrate's sexually exploitative relationship with the barbarian girl.

The dramatic contrast between free motion and constraint is a near-continuous structure in the novel of human rights. Emiko the windup girl dreams of escape but cannot run without dangerously overheating and cannot pass unnoticed in public streets because of her distinctively robotic, "herky-jerky" way of moving. When Maya achieves false liberty as a drug dealer, she moves continually but in pointless circles. In *Breaking the Tongue*, Claude cannot move freely or escape because he is burdened by Jack, who cannot walk independently, and together they cannot get on the boat to escape the sacking of the city. In *When the Emperor Was Divine*, the interned family is converted into a public secret when clandestinely transported on trains to the paralyzing internment camp. Here, the stripping away of mobility rights correlates with the stripping away of privacy rights. There is no safe domestic space in the camp: dressing and undressing, the physical indignities of illness, and sexual relations are all exposed. Chris Abani's *The Secret History of Las Vegas* juxtaposes the mobility restrictions of apartheid South Africa with the escape plot of conjoined twins involuntarily committed to a US psychiatric hospital. And Wideman's *Philadelphia Fire*—a lament over the author's own imprisoned son—returns frequently to images of exhausted or injured legs and feet. The novel uses as one of its central metaphors the work of Alberto Giacometti, who is most known for his sculptures of stretched-out figures locked in midstep, with heavy, disproportionately large feet welded to the ground.

In her memoir *Brother I'm Dying*, Edwidge Danticat tells the wrenching story of her uncle's death, which was, effectively,

manslaughter through immobilization. After fleeing conflict between UN forces and gang members in Haiti, Joseph Dantica re-
quested temporary asylum in the United States. He was detained
and jailed; his medicine was taken away; he was put in leg shackles.
When he had a seizure and began to vomit during his asylum interview, he was accused of faking. He died soon after.

Danticat's deep personal concern with constraints on movement
is a key theme in her fiction. In her torture novel *The Dew Breaker*,
survivors walk or take the bus while their torturer drives a car;
survivors lose their way while their torturer loses those who follow
him. In *The Farming of Bones*, Danticat's novel about Trujillo's genocide, exploited migrant workers are constrained by how far they can
walk before collapsing or swim before drowning—a stark contrast
to the unfettered mobility of their Dominican military patriarch. He
makes his first appearance at the opening of the novel when he reck-
lessly runs over a sugarcane worker walking by the side of the road,
refusing to stop long enough to identify the body. He makes his
final appearance at the end when he orchestrates the brutal truck
transports that will carry countless sugarcane workers to their mass
executions—again without identifying them, leaving them officially
disappeared. The novel's continuing metaphor for its violent, genocidal asymmetries is the parasitism of twins, which is most gro-
tesquely realized in the mobility-twisting image of a baby's two
small legs found lodged in a grown male cadaver.

The crime at the center of Danticat's *Breath, Eyes, Memory* is the
rape of Martine, which is committed by a Macoute as she is walking
home from school. This shattering memory, a reminder of the threat
women face when seeking to move freely in public space, is directly
contrasted to the description of the Macoutes that immediately precedes it. "They roamed the streets in broad daylight . . . They walked
naked in the night . . . They did not hide."[53] And finally, in *Krik?*
Krak!, the sinking refugee raft that swallows up child, mother, and
the narrative itself becomes the counter-symbol to the US literary
archetype that Bruce Robbins characterizes as the celebratory
"coming to America" refugee narrative. Danticat herself elaborates
in an interview: "In *Krik? Krak!*, many of the characters travel out
of necessity, for political or economic reasons. Then they find that

their lives are severed by that travel. A boat trip from Haiti to the United States is extremely perilous, and many Haitians who make that journey are imprisoned when they get to the United States, or are returned to Haiti . . . Our ancestors who were forced onto slave ships and brought to the Americas to enrich others—that kind of travel wasn't liberating, either."[54]

In US literature from *Moby-Dick* and *Benito Cereno* to *Huck Finn*, ships at sea and travel by boat have functioned both as symbols of "lighting out" for freedom and as settings to explore the permanent damage slavery has done to the democratic ship of state. The human rights novel explores this literary inheritance by depicting the ship as a vehicle of movement that never "arrives."[55] In Thomas Glave's Middle Passage short story "He Who Would Have Become 'Joshua,' 1791," death imagined as drowning is the only salvation available, the only way to not arrive with the ship heading to the auction block in Charleston. *The Ordinary Seaman*'s opening paragraph features an airport, sidewalk, bus, port town, and highway—hopeful movement that ends with a ship. But this ship is a derelict vehicle, even a prison. It can only move when it can crash. It is a symbol of violent stasis that contrasts the perpetual fluidity of global capital embodied in "flags of convenience," just as the crushing immobility of the *URUS* slave workers contrasts the effortless globe-trotting of the ship-owners, Mark and Elias.

In the escape plot, immobility is surrender. As Danticat puts it when explaining the importance of movement in *Krik? Krak!*: "When things are difficult, we often think of traveling, of physical as well as imaginary escapes. So that even before we take off on the physical journey, we have already traveled many times in our minds."[56] In the justice plot, by contrast, a refusal to move can be a refusal to surrender; immobility can be an expression of agency. The dominant pattern here depicts movement as a matter of returning rather than advancing: returning to one's homeland, returning to the scene of the crime, returning to the same sites in a circuit of investigation that increasingly narrows. Movement not only repeats itself, it also diminishes over time. Indeed, the most significant work of movement—the arrival of the protagonist from afar—typically occurs before the novel even begins.

If there is a summary image for the justice plot, it is not the car or train or ship that might plausibly define the escape plot. It is, instead, something like the chair by the window that closes Nathan Englander's *The Ministry of Special Cases*. The mother who sits there—actively waiting for her disappeared son, postponing trips of any kind lest she miss his impossible return—steadfastly rejects the calls of those around her to move forward with her life. The book closes with an image of her in the chair by her window, resolutely waiting for her son to appear—a shocking echo of the iconic closing of *Sister Carrie*, in which a childless woman sits by her window in perpetually futile hope for a happiness she will never feel. In key ways, the justice plot is aesthetically defined by the political examples of the Mothers of the Plaza de Mayo and the Saturday Mothers of Turkey, dissident groups that defied their governments by claiming a space and refusing to be moved.

Louise Erdrich's justice plot *The Round House* is an exemplary case study of resistance as stillness. The novel tells the story of Geraldine Coutts, a woman who has been violently raped on a reservation in North Dakota. Because her rapist, Linden Lark, is a white man, and because the crime is committed at jurisdictional borders where tribal sovereignty is compromised, he will likely never face legal prosecution. Lark commits the rape, in fact, precisely because he knows this. "I won't get caught," he says. "I've been boning up on law. Funny. Laugh . . . I know as much law as a judge. Know any judges? I have no fear."[57] A large part of the novel's great outrage is that Lark can still enter the community and wander through it at will, even after being identified as the perpetrator. Geraldine's husband, Antone, has a heart attack after a confrontation with Lark in a grocery store, and shortly thereafter Lark opens fire on a reservation gas station. As a white US citizen, Lark can move across borders with de facto legal immunity; his free mobility is unassailable. After Antone's heart attack, however, the narrative's grinding sense of helplessness turns to resistance in one of the novel's most quiet, most still, and most dramatic scenes. Geraldine sits down for a meal. "No," she says, seemingly out of nowhere. "I won't let him," she continues, after her son Joe asks what she means. "I will be the one to stop him" (248). Joe comments: "Her determination terrified me. She picked up her food and deliberately, slowly, began to eat. She didn't stop until she finished all of it, which also frightened me. This was the first time since the attack she ate all the food on her plate. Then we went back to the room, got ready for bed. My mother took a pill and fell asleep at once" (248).

At the broadest level of symbolism, Geraldine reflects the will of a community that will not again be pushed or moved, that will, in effect, be sovereign. The aim of sovereignty—which is the capacity to have a place to stand and, so to speak, to have standing—is the lifework of Antone, who spent years as a judge establishing precedents to claim limited jurisdiction over non-Indian persons and places. At the other end of the symbolic spectrum from his mother, Joe represents sovereignty as the capacity to put an end to the border-violating mobility of others. He executes Lark on a golf course—significantly, a space of mobility for the sake of mobility and, in Lark's case, a performance of impunity through mobility. These two central narrative acts are both about achieving stability in place, and they are bookended by narratives of returns to the center. The novel opens with the mother returning home after the assault, and it closes with the family returning home after Joe has nearly died in a car crash while running away from the reservation with friends (itself an echo of the novel's primary subplot, in which a woman with whom Joe is infatuated returns home after running away).

The concern with rights and mobility is perhaps nowhere more systematic than in the works of Susan Choi and Dave Eggers. In Choi's *The Foreign Student*, directionless driving and endless road trips offer Katherine her only chance for escape from the cruel small-town surveillance of Sewanee, which blames her for her childhood rape. Driving is intimacy and privacy for Katherine, a metaphor of unfettered self-realization. Her car is a "cocoon" (45), "fitting around her like a shell" (151), "warm inside, like a just-abandoned bed" (152). Chang's defining experiences of mobility in Korea, by contrast, include the lethal danger of military patrols and checkpoints on highways, the disruption of leftist rebels "dismantling bridges [and] felling trees to make roads impassable" (82), and the retaliatory detention of civilians in internment camps.

With this politicized binary, the novel seems to symbolically validate the image of the US as the guardian of a liberal subject dignified by privacy and free movement. Choi, however, develops a more complex model of the relationship between mobility and rights as the novel progresses. Mobility is an unrestricted freedom for Katherine, who is depicted crossing state borders over and over again with privileged unselfconsciousness. "It feels very private," she says (55). But when Chang attempts to travel independently, without her or the sponsorship of the Episcopal Church Council that occasionally sends him out to give talks about Korea, everything goes awry. At multiple points in the novel, Chang is depicted as a contemporary Robinson Crusoe, a castaway "marooned on an island" (167), invoking what Joseph Slaughter has characterized as the prototype of the self-inventing liberal subject of human rights. But Chang is permitted to be Crusoe only when he stays where he is meant to stay. When he unexpectedly leaves a job at a bindery in Chicago to find Katherine in New Orleans—significantly, on a public bus rather than in a private car—he is subjected to racial slurs. A child on a nearby seat stares at him and tells him "you can't tell the difference between gooks and chinks" (232).

Despite this reminder of his place in the United States, Chang begins to feel like a "fearless, invisible citizen" as he travels (274)—until he is detained in a New Orleans bus station in an act of racial profiling by Port Security Program officers on the lookout for Communists. To make matters worse, the very fact that Chang chooses to leave Chicago in the first place becomes evidence later to support a charge that he robbed the bindery. In the United States, when it comes to somebody like Chang, free movement is suspicious. Importantly, Choi is careful to emphasize that the social cruelty of such racism is not an anomalous moral failing. It is, rather, the necessary flip side of the kindness and "charity" the community in Sewanee shows him. "They thought of him as a romantic castaway, whose presence among them confirmed everything that was best about themselves" (145).

Locke's theory of tacit consent links free movement with residency, formulating a paradigm of liberal selfhood that continues to define Western conceptions of rights. Rights in this model are understood as claims to noninterference. They protect an individual whose movement is unfettered and who possesses cognate inviolable zones of privacy. Comprehensively examining liberal/Lockean conceptions of dignity, Choi cannily links her deconstructive plot of mobility to an equally complicated plot of residency. In my earlier discussion of Choi, I noted how she links the preservation of home and privacy with human dignity and, in supportive opposition, torture with the violation of home and privacy. In his first experiences in the United States, Chang is overcome with feelings of shame, of personal brokenness, because he is unable to take privacy as a natural given, like the privileged Sewanee residents who feel no need to lock their doors. But this reverence for private zones in Sewanee is also, simultaneously, the novel's enabling condition of violation and predation. It is precisely because Charles Addison can assume that nobody will look behind closed doors that he can sexually abuse Katherine as a child with such privileged confidence. Indeed, because a room in a Sewanee home is like an "impregnable island" (128), Katherine is not discovered when she slits her wrists with a razor, even as she does so vainly hoping that her mother will "burst in on her, horrified" (128). Katherine's house itself is directly implicated in the crime of sexual molestation. Years after she has escaped Sewanee and Addison, she is called back to her hometown by her father to look after the family house, which has stood empty for five years. And because Katherine comes back for the house, Addison finds her: significantly, when he spots her car near her house. She is right away pulled back into a toxically exploitative relationship.

Eggers's *What Is the What* is an exemplary case study in mobility, a book defined by the Lost Boys' imperative: "Run. Always run" (99). The novel begins with a home invasion. The book's first two paragraphs, as a setup for the robbery and also a thematic map of the book to come, meticulously examine the promises and challenges of movement:

> I have no reason not to answer the door so I answer the door. I have no tiny round window to inspect visitors so I open the door and before me is a tall, sturdily built African-American woman, a few years older than me, wearing a red nylon sweatsuit. She speaks to me loudly, "You have a phone, sir?"

She looks familiar. I am almost certain that I saw her in the
parking lot an hour ago, when I returned from the convenience
store. I saw her standing by the stairs, and I smiled at her. I tell
her that I do have a phone.

Eggers begins with "I have no," which he immediately repeats: "I
have no." Here, in short summary, is the arc of the book to come.
What Is the What is about a life of subtractions. What happens when
you take away a boy's childhood? His family? His village? His country?
His name? His language? (The book opens by emphasizing that Valentino doesn't know the word "peephole.") What is left of a person
after everything that makes a public self is removed? The answer
comes at the end of the second paragraph, when the repeated "I have
no" structure is inverted: "I do have." The word that follows this
promising affirmative—phone—is as disappointing as it is elaborately
positioned. "Phone" is the closing word of its paragraph and the final
term of a classic three-part repetition. It is the novelistic equivalent of
an English sonnet's final rhyme. What is left when everything you
have is taken away? What Valentino has is only a mobile phone.

In *What Is the What*, however, the mundane mobile phone becomes
a critical lifeline, even an existential answer. Because of the US government's "scatter approach policy" to refugee resettlement, in-
coming communities are deliberately broken up and separated so as
to "diminish the impact on any one resettlement site."[58] In the United
States, therefore, Valentino's defining moments almost always involve using a phone. His deepest relationships are enabled by phone.
He speaks to his girlfriend, Tabitha, seven times a day by phone, and
he is connected, sometimes suffocatingly, to 300 other Lost Boys
who regularly call him—with news, offers of assistance, requests for
help. What do the Lost Boys have left when everything has been
taken away from them? Where do they go when every hoped-for safe
place, every place to which they have fled (Ethiopia, Pinyudo, Kakuma, United States) ends in violent death? What safe space is there?
For these war refugees resettled in pockets across the country, the
imagined community of the phone is the only unburnable village. It
is the one place those who have survived may gather without fear. It is
community as a constantly moving target.

The other important repetition in the opening is the word "door." Significantly, it is "the" door rather than "my" door, a dis-possessive that reveals how lightly Valentino is tethered to his home. To think about doors is to think about entries and exits, about transitional spaces. Indeed, as in the opening of *The Ordinary Seaman*, the architecture of *What Is the What*'s first two paragraphs offers up *only* transitional spaces, spaces designed so that bodies will pass through them as fast as possible, without leaving a mark: a door, a parking lot, a convenience store, stairs, a shared apartment in a quick-turnover complex. These spaces are each, so to speak, the architectural equivalents of running, prose elaborations of the fleeing boy imprinted on the spine of the book's first hardcover edition. The door with which the novel opens, then, is not only the old literary symbol of entry, but also a new literary symbol of final subtraction. A life of doorways is a life of escapes, but perpetual escape is homelessness.

In a life defined by temporary spaces, what does it mean for somebody to be, as the narrator describes the woman he meets, "familiar"? Familiarity for most connotes some degree of depth in time. A woman is "familiar" rather than "remembered" or "known" because she comes from long enough ago or far enough away that her identity has begun to blur. Or she is familiar because she is encountered frequently in a social life that is stable enough and rich enough in relationship opportunities to promise repetitive encounters with large clusters of people who might, individually, remain unfixed as identities. But here, for the refugee, "familiar" means somebody he saw once, briefly, one hour ago, by the stairs by the parking lot by the convenience store, somebody he smiled at because he didn't know any better, because he didn't know that in this, once again, new environment, smiling at a stranger would make him a home invasion target. For a person who has spent his life running, that is what it means for somebody to be "familiar." Just as the idea of secrecy discussed above reverses its function when moving from wartime to postwar recovery, then, so does mobility. Mobility as self-preservation becomes mobility as existential impoverishment. Mobility as control becomes mobility as helplessness. The very first words spoken in the novel grammatically encode such undoing of agency. The assailant's "You have a phone, sir?" is simultaneously an interrogative and a declarative. It is a supplication that disguises a command.

The problem of the "familiar" will return over and over again in *What Is the What*. In Eggers's depiction of refugee experience, information veers wildly between its opposed experiential poles, poles that represent the extreme mobility and immobility of information: hyperinformation and hyperredundancy.[59] The former describes situations with too much new information, where things move too quickly. The latter describes situations with too little new information, where things move too slowly. In both cases, the management of meaning is threatened; the capacity to hierarchize data and conceptualize relationships is compromised. Information overload can disorient, and information scarcity can stifle. At their extremes, the unique and the familiar meet. Eggers thoroughly examines this cognitive merging in the novel's two primary settings: the overcrowded refugee camp at Kakuma, which is both frighteningly chaotic and relentlessly predictable; and Valentino's apartment during the robbery, which is a site of both confused bewilderment and enervating boredom.

In what Valentino believes will be his final escape—getting out of Kakuma to be resettled abroad—Eggers connects physical mobility with mobility as a metaphorical frame for understanding information and identity. Valentino knows that many will never get to leave the camp. To be selected, all applicants must first submit autobiographies to the United Nations High Commissioner for Refugees (UNHRC):

> We knew that those who felt persecuted in Kakuma or Sudan would be given special consideration. Maybe your family in the Sudan had done something to another family and you feared retribution? Perhaps you had deserted the SPLA and feared punishment? It could be many things. Whichever strategy we applied, we knew that our stories had to be well told. (431)

Many insist that it is essential to "embellish as often as possible" (438), especially to claim that all of one's family and known relatives had been killed. Valentino struggles with his narrative. His subsequent interview, which is quick and formulaic, leaves him "puzzled and depressed" (439). "Certainly that was not the sort of interview that would decide whether or not a man traveled across the world and became the citizen of a different nation" (439). When the UNHCR attaches to his nine page file a passport photo—the international key to mobility—Valentino stares at it for hours, "debating with myself whether or not this picture, these words, were truly me" (432).

Discussing such refugee narratives, Gillian Whitlock explains how the global infrastructure of human rights and humanitarianism has turned the refugee into a narratable identity only by way of restrictions and exclusions. "Asylum-seekers must master the codes and conventions of the acceptable narrative in the performance of their testimony," she explains. "They are required to match their subjective life experiences to the objective parameters of asylum policy to achieve credibility within the asylum determination procedure."[60] The core problem of familiarity in *What Is the What*, then, is how a person processed through the international humanitarian regime can even recognize himself. Valentino recalls, in a distant echo of US slave narratives, how the Lost Boys are first processed by the UNHCR at Kakuma. Aid workers assign their ages as a best guess, and give them all January 1 as a birthday.

Endings are returns to the beginning, but with a difference. The third to last paragraph of *What Is the What* recalls the critical *I have*'s of the opening passage by beginning, "Today I have options." In the cascade of sentences that follow in this closing mirror paragraph, Eggers offers a catalog of conflicting motions: "drive," "drive on," "swim," "drive the other way," "drive all day and night," "walk," "walk," "walk barefoot" (474). Valentino is now an American, and Americans "have options," including most prominently the option of upward social mobility. But one option he does not have is stillness. In these final pages of the book, after a lifetime of seeking, the narrator has no place where he can safely stop moving. Or perhaps mobility itself has become a form of stillness, a false promise of forward progress, much like the treadmills that figure centrally in the novel: the treadmills Valentino hears from the check-in desk at the gym where he works, swiping in people who can exit and enter when they choose; and the treadmill that kills one of his only US friends, the filmmaker Bobby Newmyer, whose promised documentary about the Lost Boys offered early hope of the possibility of acknowledgment and forward movement in US culture.

"Today I have options." In *What Is the What*, the options of US freedom are little different from the hyperinformation and hyper-redundancy of the refugee camp. The paragraph's final word, which echoes a series of "ma" words throughout the paragraph, is "mad-ness." The novel, in other words, uses mobility's hectic limitlessness together with its inherent forward momentum, its metaphoric tele-ology, to achieve three dualities. First, the novel simultaneously vali-dates Valentino's life narrative—his running *matters*—and refuses any easy plot of "coming to America" redemption. Second, it simul-taneously reifies the Lockean model of tacit consent—in the United States, Valentino can choose when to move—and destabilizes its promise of stable belonging. And third, it simultaneously sweeps us along in empathic, identificatory suspense—we can't help but feel for Valentino's feelings—and guards against the narcissistic identification that makes us think we can feel, rather than feel for, his feelings.[61]

Family

What Is the What is a dramatic example of another recurring con-cern in the novel of human rights: the lost child. Children are uniquely vulnerable targets who are nonetheless, as Jacqueline Bhabha notes, insufficiently theorized in international law as agents and bearers of rights. This inadequacy is especially important for au-thors based in the United States, where the Convention on the Rights of the Child (CRC) remains unratified.[62]

Children have ambiguous status as agents. Their rights to privacy and free movement are both fiercely defended and radically curtailed; their autonomy is both liberally nurtured and autocratically re-stricted. Article 14 of the CRC enshrines this paradoxical status by guaranteeing to children the right to freedom of thought, conscience, and religion, while at the same time guaranteeing to parents the right to direct their thought, conscience, and religion. Children are, in many ways, emblems of the paradoxes of rights I discuss throughout this book. For this reason, they function as resonant, even synoptic symbols in the human rights novel. In this closing section, I will focus on the way authors use children to represent damage to the family.

Miscarriages and dead or endangered infants are persistent points of narrative focus in the genre. In *Krik? Krak!*, Célianne holds onto her dead baby for days before finally throwing it overboard, drowning herself immediately after. In *The Brief Wondrous Life of Oscar Wao*, Beli is beaten by security forces sent by Trujillo's sister, known as La Fea, and injured so seriously that she miscarries the child she conceived with La Fea's husband. *The Secret History of Las Vegas* emphasizes the physical pain of a primary character's abortion and concludes with the shocking realization that another lead character—a conjoined twin named Fire—is in fact a brain-dead miscarriage ventriloquized into life by his twin, Water. *The Tattooed Soldier* centers on the murder of the protagonist's wife and their baby by security forces. In *Mother Tongue*, Mary suggests that her premature baby survives only because she emotionally offers it up as a symbol for all the other "mothers whose children are disappeared" (147). In *In the Time of the Butterflies*, Trujillo's wife tries to stab one of his pregnant mistresses, Mate miscarries in prison, and Patria's baby is stillborn—the last of which Alvarez connects, significantly, to images of the home: "I was an empty house with a sign in front, *Se Vende.*"[63] *A Constellation of Vital Phenomena* introduces the hospital that is its primary stable setting with the tragedy of malnourished newborns who are, it is implied, born of wartime rape. Later, in an inversion that reinforces the narrative norm, traumatized Natasha is psychologically and emotionally reborn by staring into the eyes of one of the hospital's surviving infants.

Older children and young adults who are lost also function as structuring plot points in the genre, as with Choi's *A Person of Interest* and Lee's *The Surrendered*. If the miscarriage or the dead infant represents damage to the family at its most intensely private, the lost child represents damage to the family at its most agonizingly public. Families are torn apart and children disappear in the civil conflict of *The Ministry of Special Cases*, *Imagining Argentina*, *Philadelphia Fire*, *When the Ground Turns in Its Sleep*, and Graciela Limón's

In Search of Bernabé (the latter a story of one mother's search to recover her son, who disappeared during the tumultuous aftermath of
Archbishop Romero's assassination).

At the other end of the spectrum of damage to the family, the orphan is a figure of almost obsessive concern in novels of human
rights. Amabelle from *The Farming of Bones* is an orphan; Jun Do
from *The Orphan Master's Son* is an orphan; Reza from *The Age of
Orphans* is an orphan; Gabo from Castillo's *The Guardians* is an orphan; Victor from *Lost City Radio* is an orphan; Simba from *Philadelphia Fire* is an orphan; Flor from *The Long Night of White Chickens*
is an orphan; Havaa from *A Constellation of Vital Phenomena* is an orphan; and the eponymous protagonist of Chris Cleave's *Little Bee* is
an orphan. The violations at the center of Louise Erdrich's *The Round
House* involve two abandoned children. *Tales from the Blue Archives*,
the third book in Lawrence Thornton's Argentina trilogy, is the story
of a grandmother who seeks to recover two orphans kidnapped by
the security forces that killed their mother. Patricia McCormick's
war crime novels *Never Fall Down* and *Purple Heart* center on the
plight of orphans—in the former as an escaping protagonist and in
the latter as the murder victim of a justice plot. In Corban Addison's
The Garden of Burning Sand and *A Walk across the Sun*, the plots are
organized around the rape of young orphan girls. In the latter novel,
the orphans are saved by an FBI agent who was an orphan himself.
They become explicit stand-ins for the protagonist's own child, who
died in infancy, and for the ninety-one children who were killed due
to the negligence of a coal company he legally represented. The list
could go on.

Danticat's *The Farming of Bones* is a study of damaged families.
Tracking Amabelle's search for her lover Sebastien, lost during the
genocide, the novel opens with a relentless series of lost children: the
death of Valencia's newborn son, imagined as a "sacrifice" for his
"darker" twin, who is cared for by the elder servant Juana (who is
childless after her own miscarriage) and midwifed by the orphan
Amabelle (who as a child watched her parents drown in the river that
becomes both the primary site of the impending genocide and the
narrative double of Valencia's water breaking). Danticat has said that
the "quest for family" is essential to the novel.[64] Reflecting the way

the genre continually presents human rights violations as best understood through the family as a unit, *The Farming of Bones* structurally juxtaposes images of childbirth with the passage of bodies across borders through ethnic cleansing. The novel does so first in the opening, with Amabelle worrying over the violation of Valencia's physical privacy during childbirth, even as Haitian workers like her—the targets of the coming genocide—must live by necessity, having children in the fields. The novel does so again at the conclusion, when Amabelle ambiguously conflates rebirth and suicide by immersing herself in the Massacre River that separates Haiti and the Dominican Republic. Here, Danticat invokes the conclusion of Kate Chopin's *The Awakening*, which is perhaps the seminal US story about individual rights and children as sites of emotional devastation.[65]

At this stage in the development of the genre, it is no exaggeration to say the novel of human rights defines itself through the heteronormative family. Arguably, human rights law has as well. Language prioritizing the family as the necessary organizational unit for conceptualizing rights permeates the UDHR. Article 16 in particular declares, "The family is the natural and fundamental group unit of society and is entitled to protection by society and the State." This narrative privileging of historically heteronormative sites of empathy even maps onto US asylum and immigration law, which continues to privilege the legal / biological family. As Chandan Reddy observes of US immigration procedure: "Policies such as family reunification extend and institute heteronormative community structures as a requirement for accessing welfare provisions for new immigrants by attaching those provisions to the family unit. In sum, the new federal structure has increased immigrants' exposure to and structural dependence on heteronormative and patriarchal relations and regulatory structures."[66]

When Danticat invokes Edna Pontellier's self-delivery through drowning, as Thornton also does in *Imagining Argentina*, she does so to represent grief over the damaged family and its lost children. In the original novel, however, family is a prison for women; children are, in Edna's words, "antagonists who had overcome her; who had overpowered and sought to drag her into the soul's slavery for the rest of her days."[67] The tension between these two different representations of family mirrors broader tensions within human rights representation more generally. Human rights work is often riven by competing ethical demands. Examples include the tension between the need to illuminate atrocity and the duty to avoid obscene exposure, and between the need to amplify the immediate scope of appeals through clarifying simplification and the duty to avoid long-term harm through the pernicious exclusions of generalization. Few if any of the novels I have discussed in this book have achieved such elusive balances. Perhaps in principle they cannot.

The Orphan Master's Son, for instance, exposed human rights violations in North Korea to an unprecedented audience, winning the Pulitzer Prize. The *Daily Beast* described it as "the best way to understand the country."[68] In an interview with the *Paris Review*, Johnson expressed the deep moral urgency he continues to feel about the work. He cited his horror over Yodok prison camp, where entire families are disappeared, as one of his inspirations for writing the novel. But reviewers who have praised *The Orphan Master's Son* for the breadth of its social function have also expressed significant discomfort with the very thing that made the book so popular: the novel's Jun Do / Sun Moon love story. The *New Yorker* denigrated it as a "wish-fulfillment romance" that fits poorly with the grim realities of rights violations.[69] The *Daily Beast* lamented that the novel "hammers a 'love conquers all!' theme to mawkish effect in the final act."

Such reviewers offered their critiques as aesthetic matters. The salvific heterosexual romance formula was a problem because, in their view, it overlapped clumsily with the book's own internal aesthetic imperatives. I believe, however, that their dissatisfaction comes from something deeper. I believe their criticism shares moral borders with concerns my own students have raised when reading *The Orphan Master's Son* in my human rights seminar. The novel plays to the lowest common denominator of emotional appeal, they argue, by depicting nonbiological caregiving as a lack and heterosexual union as climactic fulfillment. In this way, the novel participates in the cultural sidelining of other ways of loving and of being a family. At the very time of the book's publication, arguments over what counts as a family, and what kinds of families merit rights, were matters of legal dispute in the United States.

Dave Eggers's *Zeitoun* is an especially painful example of the problems embedded in the tropes of family so frequently used in rights writing. The publishing history of the novel reveals, indeed, the terrible risks of acting forthrightly and with moral courage, as Eggers has done with his writing. With *Zeitoun*, Eggers helped illuminate the human rights catastrophe of Hurricane Katrina; moreover, he donated all author proceeds to rebuilding efforts in New Orleans (just as he took no money for *What Is the What*). Not only did the novel win the American Book Award, it also received a rave review from the pop culture magazine *Entertainment Weekly*. It would be a gross simplification to reduce the novel's broad appeal to any single narrative pattern, but certainly a good deal of it came from the power of its love story. When Zeitoun is unjustly detained and separated from his family in Camp Greyhound, his family is broken. As Zeitoun and his wife Kathy told Amy Goodman on *Democracy Now!*, their separation was the most difficult part of the Katrina aftermath. Kathy and the children were distraught—the youngest stopped eating and started losing her hair.[70]

What happened after the book was published is no discredit to Eggers, who worked with professionalism and integrity. Unforeseen crises and unintended consequences are inevitable in human rights work and are not the personal moral failings of the workers who sacrifice health, wealth, and emotional well-being to aid strangers in need. What happened afterward is best understood, rather, as an agonizingly painful example of the way the dominant narrative patterns of human rights can screen as much as they can reveal. In 2014, Kathy received a permanent restraining order against her husband after he was charged with attempting to beat her to death with a tire iron and with offering a fellow inmate $20,000 to murder her. Kathy emphasized that she did not reveal information about abuse to Eggers, asserting in one interview that it started later. But when Kathy finally began to speak openly about domestic violence in court, she explained that it predated Katrina.[71] Arendt's "shadowy interior of the household" is resistant to even the most ethically engaged narration.

Precisely because of this, authors in the genre are increasingly working to pressure the narrative primacy of the heteronormative family, focusing on families of choice rather than biological families. As Danticat said in an interview about Haitians and the Haitian diaspora, the idea of family is "something that's constantly being redefined as people find more and more ways to be a community . . . I think it's a constant effort, and each family decides for themselves what it means to be a family."[72] In *The Greatest Performance*, for instance, Elías Miguel Muñoz links a reimagined concept of family to a narrative of flight from human rights violations against the LGBT community in Cuba. In many of the novels already discussed, the emotionally primary bonds are affiliations beyond kinship. Prime examples include Choi's *The Foreign Student*, Danticat's *The Farming of Bones*, Goldman's *The Long Night of White Chickens*, and Loh's *Breaking the Tongue*. Englander's *The Ministry of Special Cases* refuses to romanticize the heterosexual, biological nuclear family even as it relies on the iconic lost child for its tragedy. Part of what makes Pato's disappearance so traumatic is that the relationship between the father and son is so chronically bitter and dysfunctional. Kaddish's last words to Pato are harsh, but not unexpected: "Fuck you . . . I wish you'd never been born" (116).

Thomas Glave's short stories deserve attention in this study of novels because of the unique way they reimagine the tropes of rights writing. Throughout the stories collected in *The Torturer's Wife*, Glave uses reconfigurations of heteronormative narrative patterns to mount broader critiques of US human rights exceptionalism. The narrator of Glave's title story, "The Torturer's Wife," is driven mad by her marriage to a prominent torturer. She can only conceive of an escape by cutting the throats of their children—the two "with His flesh and face"—and by drowning herself in the sea.[73] Here, Glave is offering readers the quintessential example of what counts in US popular culture as a human rights violation: systematic, state-authorized torture against civilians committed by another nation. As discussed in Chapter 1, the US focus on physical integrity violations abroad frequently functions to cover up the continuing history of rights violations at home. But Glave invokes this sequestering trope only to blend it back into US historical self-conception. "The Torturer's Wife" is a narrative palimpsest that overlays patriarchal torture by imagined others onto classic US literary depictions of trapped women. "The Torturer's Wife" invokes Edna Pontellier's suicide (she, like the torturer's wife, is narrated through images of the moon), and recalls Toni Morrison's Sethe, who seeks to protect her children from future evil by cutting their throats.

Glave juxtaposes the "The Torturer's Wife" with "He Who Would Have Become 'Joshua,' 1791." The latter is an emotionally shattering story about the death of two boys in the Middle Passage. Slavery, like torture, is one of a small number of crimes included in the international legal concept *jus cogens*—that is, laws considered so basic and universal that no derogation is permitted under any circumstances. The Middle Passage as a crime against humanity, however, is often excluded from the origin stories of human rights. The typical explanatory history asserts that the UDHR emerged when it did because the atrocities committed in Europe during World War II were unprecedented in global history. As Wole Soyinka characterizes the view, European genocide "placed the first question mark" on modernity and European humanism. But this view, Soyinka protests,

> merely provides further proof that the European mind has yet to come into full cognition of the African world as an equal sector of a universal humanity, for, if it had, its historic recollection would have placed the failure of European humanism centuries earlier—and that would be at the very inception of the Atlantic slave trade. This, we remind ourselves, was an enterprise that voided a continent, it is estimated, of some twenty million souls and transported them across the Atlantic under conditions of brutality that have yet to be beggared by any other encounter between races.[74]

In "He Who Would Have Become 'Joshua,' 1791," Glave grounds atrocity of unthinkable scope in the tragic deaths of two innocent and beautiful lost boys. Glave invokes this familiar literary device, which reaches as far back as Shakespeare's *Richard III*, in order to revise it. The boys are special not because of their presexual innocence and vulnerability, as is typically the case, but rather because of their spiritually liberating, transcendent sexual relationship. The same revisionist impulse defines Glave's home invasion story "Out

There," in which the violated family—so often the centerpiece of empathy in human rights narration—is composed of two gay men. Glave's work evokes only to undo the binaries of straight/gay, home/abroad, and present/past that form the blinkered conception of atrocity in US popular culture.

Glave's stories merit attention for many reasons. What I want to highlight here is a claim implicit in his work that will provide a theoretical through line for Chapters 3 and 4. Illuminating the hidden gaps of rights discourse, Glave's stories demonstrate that the vital project of human rights is incomplete and should be expanded. But his brutal and lyric reconfiguration of our human rights imagination goes beyond amelioration. Glave also reveals that sometimes the very work of expanding rights—that is, pursuing strategies deemed most effective for maximizing scope—can hinder rather than promote human flourishing. In other words, chasing the urgent can sometimes mean sacrificing the important. Transitioning to Chapter 3, then, I want to emphasize how important it is to keep the contested concepts of privacy, mobility, and family centrally in view as we consider the representation of gender in US novels of human rights. I will not argue, however, that these concepts in their liberal formulations must either be reified or subverted, judged guilty for furthering narrowly construed subjectivities or celebrated for undoing them. Instead, I want to borrow a formulation from Fiona Wright and call for a "less purist, and perhaps therefore less gratifying" analysis of human rights representation; for an acknowledgment of moral irreconcilability, uncertainty, and loss no matter what choices are made; and for the requirement to live responsibly within the anxiety that doubt produces.[75]

CHAPTER 3

Ethical Concerns in
the Novel of Human Rights

THE NOVEL OF HUMAN RIGHTS has deep historical roots, roots that precede the modern articulation of a human rights movement. Rachel Ablow contextualizes representations of torture in post-9 / 11 television and film by providing an aesthetic and philosophical history of the Victorian "humanitarian narrative"—a nineteenth-century form that, in Thomas Laqueur's words, "relies on the personal body . . . as the common bond between those who suffer and those who would help."[1] Ablow explains that the humanitarian narrative emerged from a range of cultural and political pressures, including abolitionism, marketplace changes and the bureaucratization of charity, and the rising role of women in social reform. To her list I would emphatically add the birth of international humanitarian law with the inception of the International Committee of the Red Cross (ICRC) and the first Geneva Conventions, which were summoned into being by the electrifying effect of Henri Dunant's *Un Souvenir de Solférino* (1862), an account of the horrific conditions facing soldiers wounded in battle. Imbuing the Victorian novel with urgent social mission, humanitarianism also produced a set of recurring sentimental tropes that should by now seem familiar. "The dead children, fallen women, and virtuous but abjected or misunderstood workers that littered the Victorian novel," Ablow explains, were part of what prompted modernism's reaction against sentimentality.[2] Ablow cites Oscar Wilde's quip, "one must have a heart of stone to read the death of little Nell without laughing," to summarize this turn of the century aesthetic disdain. But as Ablow points out, citing current trends in popular culture alongside the mailing campaigns of Human Rights Watch and Amnesty International, the humanitarian narrative surges today despite the efforts of many twentieth-century novelists and critics to "ring the death-knell" of sentimental social mission in literature (1152).

In this chapter I will examine in detail how these inherited humanitarian tropes of perceived-vulnerable populations have been reconfigured in contemporary rights novels. Lauren Wilcox has argued that the focus on violated bodies in human rights discourse today produces classes of persons defined by their vulnerability: "subjects to be saved."[3] The cultural production of such identity categories poses an intractable problem for rights workers and authors. On the one hand, serious work against violence requires that we identify specific vulnerable populations and focus on their unique realities—their risks, capacities, needs, and resources. On the other hand, the identification of vulnerable populations can veer dangerously close to rendering such populations equivalent to their vulnerabilities—and worse, of reifying classes of absolute identity defined by their opposition: the invulnerable and the vulnerable, the able and the unable, the autonomous and the constrained. In the pages that follow, I analyze how this problem of "subjects to be saved" works itself out in the novel of human rights. My primary aim is to scrutinize the representation of violence against women, along with its ideological counterpart in the novel of human rights: the representation of safe, heteronormative union. My central concern throughout will be the grave ethical implications of using women as allegories of justice and injustice.

In Chapter 1, I discussed the criticism Isabel Allende has received for the "soap opera" romance exemplified in the flight of the beautiful, vulnerable Maya of *Maya's Notebook*. I also described the patterns of desire that make Flor's beauty one of the defining facts of *The Long Night of White Chickens*. Works like these are representative in the genre rather than exceptional. In my human rights and literature seminars, for instance, students often note that *In the Time of the Butterflies*, an account of revolutionary women who helped topple a monstrous tyrant, seems to invoke the narrative structure of *Little Women*. Patria, Minerva, Mate, and Dedé function like Meg, Jo, Amy, and Beth, respectively. The two novels share tropes of womanhood and gender that include depicting the heteronormative family as the primary indicator of national health and subordinating female politicization to heterosexual romance. Mate, for instance, joins the national underground to be "worthy of" a man she has a crush on (142). Lynn Chun Ink argues that *In the Time of the Butterflies* reifies patriarchal nationalism by reinforcing the gendered public/private divide between political participation and personal romance. "The novel confirms that their participation in the national liberation struggle inevitably entails the breakdown of the domestic sphere."[4] In much the same way, while *Philadelphia Fire* has been praised for its unflinching depiction of US racism, it has also been criticized for sidelining autonomous female characters. Cudjoe's narrated sexual desire could be interpreted as an act of resistance to the US criminalization of the black male heterosexual gaze, but it seems more often to have been charged with reinforcing "a gender system that generates relations of domination."[5]

In the end, I think it's safe to say that literature and human rights classes run a nontrivial risk of overloading students with plots of beautiful women rendered vulnerable. In *The Orphan Master's Son*, a range of brutal violations are highlighted, but the novel's subplots center most often on the violation of beautiful women. At the start of the novel, Jun Do and Gil kidnap an opera singer, choking her, binding her hands and covering her mouth with duct tape, and wrestling her into "submission" before tying her up in a sack (30). Later, the North Koreans kidnap a "brawny, beautiful American"—the Girl Rower, who tried to row a boat around the world (it is repeatedly emphasized that she rows naked) but ends up shackled in a North Korean prison cell, as helpless as a "giant child" (330, 350). And at the center of the novel is the romance plot of the ineffably beautiful Sun Moon. Jun Do is a hero because he sacrifices himself to protect her from the Dear Leader's predatory desire. In *A Constellation of Vital Phenomena*, the devastation of human trafficking is depicted through the story of the victim Natasha, whose defining feature is her "swan-like" beauty (167), by contrast to her physically plain but intellectually wondrous, nonvictim, tough-as-nails sister Sonja (the narrative assures us, though, that even though Natasha chose to become a secretary rather than go to university, she "wasn't stupid" [171]). How much does the narrative need Natasha to be beautiful for her sexual violation to fully matter? Describing the useless leather boots, cashmere sweaters, and silk gowns Natasha chooses to preserve during the war, the novel declares that "beautiful things were so rare it seemed wrong to leave them behind" (179).

Bob Shacochis's *The Woman Who Lost Her Soul* and Paolo Bacigalupi's *The Windup Girl* take all three of the above terms—violation, beautiful, and woman—to painful extremes. Bacigalupi does so in an effort to imagine the nightmare consequences of our current wealth asymmetries, corporatocracy, experiments in genetic modification of food, and refusal to address global climate change. Windup Emiko is bioengineered to be a superlative example of a particular conception of woman. She is as compliant as a dog (genes spliced from a Labrador) and her skin is as beautiful as ivory (her pores have been designed to be inhumanly small). Both features make her vulnerable. Her inability to sweat keeps her perpetually on the verge of dangerous overheating, and therefore always needful—ice and climate control are scarce resources. And her compliance makes her a uniquely desirable commodity to sex traffickers. She is repeatedly and brutally raped on stage and in private sessions and, because of the way men programmed her, she enjoys it despite herself. Emiko's genetically designed vulnerability makes her almost irresistibly alluring to the men around her, including Anderson, who plays the role of her noble rescuer.

Emiko's *aesthetically* designed vulnerability presumably also appealed to many readers, including those who—in an exaggerated enactment of the rescue fantasy staged and critiqued by Goldman in *The Long Night of White Chickens*—imagined themselves as rescuers like Anderson.

The novel was a breakthrough success. It won both the Hugo and Nebula awards and was ranked the ninth best fiction book of 2009 by *Time* magazine. The *Guardian* noted that the book "generates real poignancy out of [Emiko's] degradation" but concluded that it did not achieve the right balance "between critiquing Emiko's sexual objectification and simply reproducing it."[6] Some bloggers more openly characterized the novel's violent scenes as torture porn.[7]

The Windup Girl is an extreme, clarifying example of a cross-genre problem that some writers address explicitly. Chang-rae Lee's science fiction dystopia *On Such a Full Sea* is a powerful critique of the global immiseration of the working class, originally sparked by his observation of young women working under harsh conditions in a Chinese factory. The novel—a picaresque echo of *Light in August*, in which a young woman escapes home-as-prison by chasing after her lover—relies for its effect upon a series of threats to the fetishized protagonist, Fan, who travels alone through a gritty, frightening, Mad Max landscape. An indefatigable heroine as well as a mother-to-be, Fan is nonetheless repeatedly described as childlike. She is, significantly, more spoken-for than speaking throughout the novel. But for Lee, staging Fan as an object of regard is the whole point. The novel is an examination, rather than exploitation, of the cultural work of fantasy. It is precisely about how we project our needs and desires onto each other. The novel, as Lee has explained, is about the workings of a community's consciousness.[8]

Shacochis's *The Woman Who Lost Her Soul* (2014) is an ambitious, 700-plus page attempt to illuminate the global war on terror. Shacochis, a former Peace Corps volunteer, reaches back to the Cold War and the collapse of Yugoslavia, via Haiti and Turkey, to show how it came to be that the United States is where it is today: in endless war. Shacochis depicts the clichés of contemporary Hollywood political thrillers—secret agents, assassinations, sexual intrigues, covert operations—not as revels but as laments, as, in his words, "a continuous waste of the nation's treasure and blood."[9] Widely celebrated for his morally serious critique of US foreign policy, Shacochis was a Pulitzer Prize finalist and won the Dayton Literary Peace Prize. National Public Radio described *The Woman Who Lost Her Soul* as "the first Great American Novel of the twenty-first century," and the

Los Angeles Review of Books called it "the last Great American Novel." The book is a disturbing read on three levels. First, it is an unsparing critique of US militarism that reveals an underbelly of morally troubling black ops missions and democracy-subverting military cabals. Second, it is an unflinching representation of sexual violence repeatedly visited upon a female US intelligence agent. Third, it uses the latter to intensify the former. I will explain why that final point is disturbing at the end of my discussion; first, a broader look at the book.

The Woman Who Lost Her Soul begins with a familiar formula. Tom Harrington, a human rights lawyer who documented war crimes for a Truth Commission in Haiti, is enlisted to investigate the death of a beautiful woman abroad. Disillusioned by the failed US intervention in Haiti—"the magnificent pantomime of redemption"—Harrington is drawn to the individual justice plot precisely because he feels incapable of addressing the collective needs of a nation that, in his words, "remained an infant and still required breast-feeding."[10] The many twists and climaxes that follow revolve around the exploits of the assumed-to-be deceased intelligence agent Dottie Chambers, known also by the aliases Jackie and Renée. The novel begins from the perspective of the embittered, fatigued, and sexually frustrated human rights lawyer, and it closes from the perspective of his apparent structural opposite, a loyal, indomitable, and sexually transcendent Delta Force soldier. In between, the reader sees the world from the perspective of Dottie. Importantly, however, her primary narrative perspective is not that of an adult, as it is with the male narrators, but rather of a vulnerable adolescent. Throughout the novel she is more often a mysterious object of sexual regard than an actualized person.

> Her beauty seemed to be the source of profound discomfort and unending satisfaction, the American ideal, the girl every boy dreamed of courting and winning, the girl who made every one of them crazy in high school and wretched in college, their universal torture queen, blithe collector of tormented young hearts, the first and last girl to occupy their beautiful self-told lies of perfect love, perfect companionship, the one they could never stop needing and never stop hating and never get out of their minds. (32)

In a familiar cultural formula, Dottie/Jackie/Renee embodies dominant, perceived-masculine traits (violent, dangerous, emotionally rugged, and verbally sharp) only to be repeatedly punished for it. In each stage of her life and each section of the novel, she is brutally sexually assaulted. In the end, when she is fatally injured in a terrorist explosion, she is reduced to a grotesque infancy, "swaddled mummylike in bandages from head to waist, her face hidden and misshapen, a breathing tube snaking into a mouth hole" (683).

The *New York Times* declared that the novel was successful *despite* the "annoyance" of the "gilded, pornographic . . . fantastical siren at its heart."[11] But I think the novel succeeded *because* of its pornographic gaze. Human rights representation in all its forms—from photography to novels—always faces the choice of pornographizing for spectacular appeal. Indeed, Shacochis openly frames his book by way of this hazard. Harrington is at a bar talking to a Hollywood director who wants to set a soldier movie in Haiti. The director wants to loan "his celebrity to Haiti's cause" because his heart has been broken by "the brutalities of the tyrants, the blood of the innocents" (26). Meanwhile, Harrington sees Dottie and tries to chat her up. Harrington looks back at that evening later as a "sixty-second charade of voyeurism and desire" (33). Here, he is describing not only his flirtation with Dottie but also the empathy of the Hollywood director (who quickly forgets about Haiti and the movie idea), which is itself a stand-in for the fleeting ethical investments of the international community. The following morning, Harrington shares a farewell breakfast with a group of humanitarian journalists and photographers. Suffering in Haiti persists, but it is time to move on, time to go somewhere fresh. "The story was dead, the Haitian people were becoming invisible again, imaginary creatures, right before the magnifying eyes of the international press and there was nothing the *pep* could do about it" (45–46).

I want to contextualize Shacochis's narrative choices with two examples that may seem, at first glance, relatively distant. Not long ago, I was in a working group with a psychologist who had been involved with the South African Truth and Reconciliation Commission. At one point, he shared with our group a series of posters that had been distributed in local communities to get people to participate in the commission as it was starting its work. The posters were striking. They delivered a series of messages in horror movie font—grainy, all-caps, block letters—above requests to visit commission offices or attend commission meetings. "IF YOUR MOTHER WAS TORTURED FATHER MURDERED AND CHILDREN ABDUCTED WOULD YOU BE SILENT." "SOME OF THE CRIMES OF OUR PAST: MURDER ABDUCTION TORTURE. ONE OF THE CRIMES OF OUR PRESENT: SILENCE." "REVEALING IS HEALING." Effective at the time in getting people's attention and drawing them in, the posters in retrospect seemed to the psychologist troubling in two ways. First, they were emotionally coercive, implicitly equating the desire to keep trauma private with apartheid crimes. Second, they advertised a process of psychological healing that was often not realized. Psychosocial support, counseling, and follow-up were simply inadequate, and many survivors were left only with reopened wounds. Nonetheless, he emphasized, the moral compromises of representation were at the time perceived to be small compared to the larger value of overcoming apartheid silence.

Anecdote two. Years ago I spent time with the communications manager of the New York office of Doctors Without Borders (MSF). He explained that his organization knew very well that spectacular depictions of violated, vulnerable bodies were the most effective way of generating short-term infusions of support, money, and interest. Nonetheless, MSF chose to reject this method of representation. Such "human rights porn," he explained, is ineffective as a technique for generating long-term commitment to issues and regions. It attracts easy and therefore necessarily shallow-rooted interest. Worse, it perpetuates deleterious cultural stereotypes that harm vulnerable populations. The images of abject, helpless "others" that circulate so widely in US popular culture spark instant sympathy but also train spectators to believe that those others will ultimately never be able to take care of themselves. They are perpetual sufferers; their natural state is therefore misery.

I believe a plausible argument could be made for a parallel to both of these dynamics in the reception of *The Woman Who Lost Her Soul*. Shacochis chooses to maximize immediate appeal and impact. The benefits are the awards, the sales, and the blurbs pasted front and back on the novel, all of which translate into amplified distribution of his messages. And his messages certainly aim at high moral values: high-lighting the often hidden violence of contemporary US foreign policy and, as I'll discuss shortly, decrying systemic violence against women. But there are costs, too. First, as the MSF case shows, sensational visibility does not reliably translate into enduring attention. Taking the novel's self-conscious narrative frame as evidence, I'm willing to wager that Shacochis was quite aware of the "now versus future" trade-off he was making. Second, I believe that the images perpetu-ated in *The Woman Who Lost Her Soul* are harmful. They undercut what I take to be Shacochis's own deep values. And this brings me back to my claim above that it is a troubling choice for the author to use sexual violence to amplify our discontent over US foreign policy.

Like *The Windup Girl, The Woman Who Lost Her Soul* founders on the problem of representing sexual violence without reproducing it. On the one hand, there is real moral value in depicting violence against women in fiction. Rape and murder of women amount to a centuries-long, slow-motion genocide that has been denied for too long, that has, indeed, been a taboo even to speak about, hidden in the "shadowy interior of the household." And Shacochis, to his credit, takes pains to represent sexual violence as systemic rather than incidental, a distressingly predictable consequence of cultures of militarism and toxic masculinity. In this way he is a writer much like Goldman, whose *The Long Night of the White Chickens* tells a sequence of stories about violated women, including Flor, a sex slave who is rescued by Roger's father, and Roger's great-grandmother, who was a child bride.

On the other hand, there are real moral dangers in depicting vio-lence against women in fiction. *The Woman Who Lost Her Soul* does not simply represent the sexual objectification of Dottie; it *depends* upon the sexual objectification of Dottie; it invites male voyeurism. Granted, this can be difficult to avoid in some contexts. Even Cath-erine MacKinnon—one of the world's leading feminist thinkers and a lawyer at the front edge of the movement to identify rape as a weapon of war and to prosecute it as a crime against humanity—was accused of licensing "the pornographic gaze" for the dramatic way she brought attention to mass rape during the war in Bosnia.[12] But because Shacochis is less focused than MacKinnon on the manifold complexities of the ethics of representation, there is rather more to worry over in his text. Indeed, *The Woman Who Lost Her Soul* is structured around an aesthetic device that I and others see permeating systems of real-world violence against women: namely, using a violated female body as a resonant emotional symbol for a violated nation. But before unpacking what is at stake in that claim, and why it is so concerning, let me be very clear. The point in what follows is to understand how the text functions, not what the author intended. This is an argument about the cultural circulation of a text, not about the soul of a writer.

The woman of *The Woman Who Lost Her Soul* is both the vulnerable heroine Dottie and the equally vulnerable United States. "Our soul as a nation," Shacochis declared in an interview, making explicit the allegory of the title, has been "outcast into a wilderness of fear."[13] The parallels between the two women are explicit. Dottie and America are both betrayed by those closest to them: Dottie by the men who rape her, and America by the men who rule her; Dottie by Steven Chambers as father, who sexually violates her throughout her childhood, and America by Steven Chambers as intelligence agent, who violates the principles of his nation as part of a shadowy military cabal. The parallels are meant to intensify our outrage over each. The political is made visceral by the personal (feel the betrayal in your body), and the personal is elevated by the political (the betrayal is not just to one body). But as with all human rights representation, the strain to create instant, coercive affect has consequences. My claim is not simply that it is unsettling to use a woman's body to dramatize political claims. It is that doing so in particular ways can play into larger patterns of violence against women.

I have spent a fair amount of time taking testimony from war criminals who used rape as a weapon of war. I, like many, have come to believe that such wartime rape is not a product of male sexual desire but rather a product—at least in part—of globally and historically pervasive symbolic systems. Ruth Seifert explains the dangers inherent to this woman-as-nation trope:

> Thus the rape of the women in a community can be regarded
> as the symbolic rape of the body of this community. Against this

background, the mass rapes that accompany all wars take on new meaning: by no means acts of senseless brutality, they are rather culture-destroying actions with a strategic rationale.[14]

In other words, when the female body becomes a symbol of the body politic, it also becomes a target. It is important to emphasize here that the distance between our storytelling practices and the horrific violence Seifert references is great. But it is also important to acknowledge that rape culture is a spectrum of practices that reinforce one another, and the idea that women's bodies are symbols for male use is essential to many, perhaps even all of them.

Shacochis, I must emphasize again, writes with a clear and brave moral purpose: to dramatize the moral derailment of US politics in the global war on terror. His work tackles the US descent into temporally and geographically unbounded war; political corruption in the military-industrial complex; ham-fisted military interventions that destabilize regions and generate violent blowback; and equally ham-fisted humanitarian interventions that only solve the problem of the guilty conscience. Shacochis's aims are consistent with human rights and humanitarianism broadly conceived, including the self-reflective critiques human rights and humanitarianism struggle with internally. Part of what his work demonstrates, in other words, is the way the clarion call of human rights can transform focused attention into a variety of unseeing. Just as civil and political rights violations abroad historically functioned to obscure domestic violation of economic and social rights, Shacochis's various urgencies function to obscure key aspects of women's rights.

Here's another case study. Corban Addison is a morally serious attorney and best-selling author who markets his novels first as human rights works—what a Victorianist might think of as the international social problem novel. His work is particularly useful for examining the way the novel of human rights links identity, gender, and nation. Addison rose to international attention with *A Walk across the Sun*. The novel, which tells the story of two Indian girls orphaned by a tsunami and abducted by human traffickers, is organized around a particular form of narrative desire. It begins with the details of the brutal violations committed against the older sister, Ahalya, who has been sold to a brothel. With this as the harrowing background, the novel sets in motion a suspenseful contest between Washington, D.C., attorney Thomas Clarke and a network of criminal traffickers. Will Clarke find and save Ahalya's younger sister Sita before traffickers sell her to the highest bidder for her virginity?

Scrupulously avoiding the pornographic, *A Walk across the Sun* nonetheless relies upon the sensational power of depicting innocent young women threatened by rape, much like *The Windup Girl* and *The Woman Who Lost Her Soul*. In fact, in Addison's work as a whole, rape is perhaps the primary narrative concern. *A Walk across the Sun* opens with Clarke witnessing the abduction of a young woman in North Carolina by sex traffickers, and moves forward by tracking the many sites of sex trafficking, including brothels, nightclubs, parking lots, online videos, and exclusive chat rooms. In his second novel, *The Garden of Burning Sand*, Zoe Fleming, a rape survivor, is a human rights attorney investigating the rape of a young Zambian woman with Down syndrome. During her investigations, Fleming is sexually assaulted. Several other characters are raped in the novel, in service of one of the novel's primary messages: that rape in sub-Saharan Africa is a systemic human rights violation requiring international attention.

Addison's third novel, *The Tears of Dark Water*, reconceptualizes the status of rape in human rights. The novel is based on the media-saturated 2011 hijacking of an American yacht, the *Quest*, in which four US citizens were killed by Somali pirates. As Addison explains in an author's note, piracy offered "a narrative framework to explore not only how a hijacking and hostage crisis could end in tragedy but also how the breakdown of social order on land could inspire young Somalis to take to the ocean" (442). The bulk of the novel is about Ismail, a pirate who has been captured and put on trial in the United States. In this variation on the justice plot, investigators seek to un-cover the truth of Ismail's story. Did he murder his hostages or was he coerced? Is he guilty or is he sacrificing himself to protect others? Behind Ismail's courtroom drama, however, is the original escape plot of his sister Yasmin. During the breakdown of order in Somalia, Yasmin is abducted and raped by an al-Shabaab leader. Ismail be-comes a pirate only so that he can raise money to rescue her. The ordering here is very important. With this embedded narrative frame, *The Tears of Dark Water* reconfigures the historical priorities of human rights. In, for now, crude shorthand, the first priority of the international human rights regime—piracy—is revealed to be secondary to its last—sexual violence.

Let me step back to unpack that last sentence. Origin stories for the history of international human rights law often begin with the Dutch jurist Hugo Grotius, who laid the foundation for the concept of universal jurisdiction—that is, the idea that certain crimes may be prosecuted no matter where they are committed—in his seminal work, *De Jure Belli ac Pacis* (1625). Universal jurisdiction is a critical concept for all of international law, and for human rights law in particular. It lays the groundwork for the concept of crimes against humanity, first legally prosecuted in the Nuremberg Trials, and contributes to the concept of *jus cogens:* namely, the still-revolutionary idea that certain legal norms exist that bind sovereign states and from which no derogation is permitted. Notably, for Grotius and those following him, piracy was a central animating force for developing these concepts. The high seas were a site of true lawlessness, a realm where state sovereignty could not securely extend. Pirates were, in the words of Cicero, "hostis humani generis"—enemies of all mankind—who could and indeed should be prosecuted by all nations because their crimes were a threat to the international order as a whole. In short, as a historical matter, human rights law began with piracy.[15]

Rape, by contrast, has a complicated history of neglect in international law. The Lieber Code (1863) was the first international document to codify the prohibition of rape in war, but as Kelly Dawn Askin notes, rape was rarely prosecuted and typically considered an inevitable by-product of wartime violence, a secondary rather than a standalone crime. At the Nuremberg and Tokyo trials, she writes, "war crimes against women were essentially ignored." During the Vietnam War, American rape of South Vietnamese civilians was "punishable by court-martial . . . but not a war crime." And even by the 1990s, initial debates in the Yugoslav Tribunal about prosecution of rapes concerned "whether or not rape was even a war crime." Publishing one year before the trial of Jean-Paul Akayesu by the

International Criminal Tribunal for Rwanda, in which rape was for the first time defined as a crime of genocide under international law, Askin concluded, "Gradually, grudgingly, women have achieved increased status in international law."[16]

Over the long history of international law and human rights, in other words, rape and piracy have anchored the opposing poles of invisibility and visibility. *The Tears of Dark Water* is modeled upon this binary. It depicts the crime of piracy as a matter of dangerous visibility. Authorities must struggle to keep the media and other onlookers at a distance. It depicts rape and sexual violence, by contrast, as secrets to be unraveled. The midpoint of the narrative arc is defined by the defense attorney's attempt to unlock the secret of Yasmin's abduction. Its end point includes the painful, cathartic revelation of a secret that has shaped the life of the murdered hostage's surviving wife: her own mother, who had been forced by poverty into prostitution, had been raped for years by her father. Rapists in the novel are hidden perpetrators, perpetrators who go unpunished, even as they precede pirates as "hostis humani generis."

In Addison's novels, however, it is unclear—just as it is with *The Woman Who Lost Her Soul* and *The Windup Girl*—whether sexual violence against women functions primarily as an acknowledgment of its real-world pervasiveness or as an easy device for generating powerful emotions in the reader. The didacticism of Addison's novels appears to support the former interpretation. Addison is explicitly interested in educating his readers about a range of human rights issues, from human trafficking to female genital mutilation (FGM). His novels include multiple "information dumps" when characters or the narrator explain the historical, political, or medical contexts for each concern. And his various afterwords include specific proposals for addressing sexual violence, including recommending the establishment of DNA labs in every African country to assist in prosecution of rapes, and instructing readers to make private donations to antitrafficking organizations.

Moreover, Addison's novels carefully avoid two common moral failings in the representation of rape. First, he does not depict rape and sexual violence as exceptional crimes committed only against tragically targeted main characters. Secondary characters throughout his novels also survive sexual violence. Thomas Clarke's contact at the FBI, for instance, lost her sister to sex traffickers as a child. And *A Walk across the Sun*'s strong concern with FGM reinforces the thematic of institutionalized violence against women. Yasmin is a rarity in Somalia because "she had never been cut," and Vanessa's work as a physician brings her to painful encounters with Somali refugees suffering from medical complications due to FGM.[17] Second, Addison attempts to contextualize his depiction of sexual violence in India and Africa through parallel narratives of sexual violence in the United States or by Westerners. Kuyeya's mother is sexually exploited by a doctor from Doctors Without Borders; Sita is most imperiled when she is trafficked to the United States. And Clarke, in his conflicted, colonializing arrogance, becomes the author's self-conscious emblem of the dangers inherent to human rights volunteerism. In a conversation with his alienated wife's father, who resents Clarke for "stealing" his daughter away from India, Clarke is forced to confront a challenge to his self-concept.

> "Ah," he exclaimed, "yet another Westerner who thinks he can fix all that is broken in India. My friend, you are neither the first nor the last to carry the white man's burden."
>
> Thomas simmered. He could handle the accusation of stealing Priya, but to be called a racist was infuriating. He considered walking out, but he knew it would be a defeat.
>
> "What is broken here is broken everywhere," he countered.
> (202)

However, there are also many moments in Addison's novels when sexual violence seems less an ethical concern and more a narrative ploy. Sexual predation sometimes quite clearly functions as a transparent and clumsy device to guide readerly emotion. *A Walk across the Sun* permits the happy reunification of all characters—Thomas and his wife reunite at the end along with the orphaned sisters—only after returning to the abducted young woman from the opening of the novel. Addison is struggling here to achieve the tragically tempered balance appropriate to human rights novels (as I have written elsewhere, rights novels often eschew the closure of uncomplicated, successful endings).[18] The kidnapped girl, it is noted in an aside, is found in a shallow grave near a trailer park. The reader is appropriately chastened and thus permitted to take measured satisfaction from what will follow. "'So the story goes on,' Thomas said" (423).

In a more obvious narrative stumble, Addison's attempt to use Clarke as a transitional figure—that is, somebody "like us" who gains access to a world we could never see and could never understand without his guiding perspective—turns Clarke into a near-voyeur, obsessed with having the chance to see the details of sex trafficking from all angles. When he is told that his presence in a Bombay courtroom could endanger a case against traffickers because of local sensitivity to signs of foreign interference, Clarke pleads to be permitted to watch anyway, promising to be "a fly on the wall" (190). When he is told that it will not be safe for him to accompany investigators from the antitrafficking nonprofit he has joined, CASE (Coalition against Sexual Exploitation), on their mission to arrest a suspected trafficker, Clarke nonetheless insists on coming so that he can see them "take him down" (239). Later he asks to "tag along" (317) during a more dangerous operation against a group of brutal eastern European traffickers—but here he is, finally, turned down. Ever persistent, he complains again later—"I wish I could go with you"—and is rewarded with permission to come "visit the scene after the property is secured" (394). When investigators discover a group of minors bound and gagged in the basement, they invite him to look. "You guys deserve to see this" (415).

Addison's intentions are, so to speak, merely technical. He feels he needs Clarke to guide the responses of readers throughout, and therefore must insert such scenes to justify Clarke's implausible, Forrest-Gumpy omnipresence. The overall effect is nevertheless ethically disconcerting. Indeed, the language around Clarke's desire to see strikes an even more jarring note than his compulsive tagging along. He complains that as a lawyer for CASE he has to push paper while the investigators "get all the sexy work" (105). He admires "the novelty" of the "dramatic" (236) sting that CASE performs against a local brothel trafficking in sex with minors. He says he wants "to see what the investigators see" and is rewarded with "a glimpse" (106) by way of a tour of the largest red-light district in Bombay. The tone of exploitative visual desire raises unsettling questions about what it means to be drawn to such work—both for the character and for the reader. One reviewer for USAToday.com objects to the novel on just these lines, if somewhat hyperbolically: *A Walk across the Sun* "leaves a reader pondering the question: How different is a novel that relies on the abuse of children for its 'entertainment value' from a predator who exploits them for sex?"[19]

Addison responds to these concerns in a blog for the *Huff Post*. Disarmingly, he acknowledges his own thoughtful anxiety about the "ethical line in fiction between realism that reveals and sensationalism that exploits," and emphasizes the effort he took to avoid appealing to "prurient interest."[20] Addison is unfortunately less self-conscious about the way his novels enact the "damning metaphor" identified by Makau Mutua as a threat to the success of the international human rights movement: namely, the "savages-victims-saviors construction."[21] As Mutua characterizes the political narrative of human rights, subjects to be saved produce subjects who are saviors. Savages—purportedly corrupt, antidemocratic states—commit unspeakable crimes such as FGM against "powerless, helpless, innocent" victims (203), who are then dignified by the actions of white saviors. These saviors are defined by "the pathology of self-redemption," that is, by the project of validating their own lives by "'defending' and 'civilizing' 'lower,' 'unfortunate,' and 'inferior' peoples." As Mutua argues, so long as the global human rights narrative hews closely to this deeply alienating formula, it "will ultimately fail." "In order to prevail," he argues, "the human rights movement must be moored in the cultures of all peoples" (208). It cannot depend upon a narrative whose primary psychic payoff is the volunteerist's self-satisfaction and expanded experience of agency—an experience in a zero-sum relationship to the agency of survivors.

The blurb featured on the front cover of Addison's *The Garden of Burning Sand* declares, "If you like stories of good people struggling to do right in the world's forgotten places, there is no one better suited to take you on the ride of your life." This dismissive characterization of Africa as forgotten is matched on the other end of the spectrum of attention by the novel's hungry interest in Africa as a symbol of, in the narrator's un-ironic words, "exoticism and fecundity."[22] Fleming and her mother, it is frequently noted, "had fallen in love with Africa" (145). As Mutua might note, their appreciation and care is a straightforward extension of colonializing desire. In one particularly resonant moment, Fleming characterizes Zambia in a legal brief much like a developing child in need of benevolent guidance. She explains to the African courts that the use of DNA in court cases is "de rigueur" around the world, and declares encouragingly that Zambia is also finally "ready for it" (186, 125).

In *A Walk across the Sun*, Clarke goes to India less to fight trafficking than to serve himself. Surveying his failed marriage and deadening legal career, Clarke concludes in the spirit of one purchasing a self-help book or enrolling in Outward Bound: "Something needed to change: he needed a new horizon. He didn't know exactly what, but the status quo was no longer an option" (48). In language evocative of the undergraduate engaged in the project of self-realization, he decides to take what is described as an "internship" and "scholarship" at CASE (68, 72). The kidnapped children he encounters turn out to be effective vehicles for the renewal of his personal and professional life. Helping children is, in the language of the novel, one of the "perks" of the job (110).

The Garden of Burning Sand is little different. Here, Zoe Fleming achieves self-enhancement by rescuing the most vulnerable of victims: Kuyeya, a child with Down syndrome who has been raped and rendered mute from trauma, and who also has developed a life-threatening spinal instability that requires advanced surgery unavailable in her home country of Zambia. While the prosecution of Kuyeya's rapist drives the main plot, it is emotionally sidelined at the novel's climax by the subplot of Fleming's effort to privately fund the surgery that will save Kuyeya. This shift is notable for two reasons. First, the charity plot is the final step in Fleming's coming of age, a parallel to the self-development plot of *A Walk across the Sun*. As Fleming discovers at the end of *The Garden of Burning Sand*, her mother left her with a multimillion-dollar trust to "train" her to be "an instrument of good," and deliberately put a crotchety and conservative trustee in charge as a way of educating Fleming through adversity. "I wanted you to learn the traditional rules of philanthropy," her late mother explains in a letter, "so that when you have gleaned their wisdom and been frustrated by their rigidity you will know exactly how and when to break them" (398).

Second, the suspenseful philanthropy drama—will Fleming succeed in raising the money? will she fail?—shifts attention away from the court case, which is the expression of community agency, toward the entirely private agency of the white savior. Fleming's heroic fight against the system to pay for Kuyeya's surgery is a high-stakes adventure in "charity" and "generosity"[23]—words that, unlike the philosophical concept of duty, highlight the superior character of the donor. In an afterword that praises the rise of "smart, innovative private giving" over public investment in development, Addison emphasizes, "What matters is that we in the developed world maintain the spirit of magnanimity that has defined our relationship with the developing world for generations" (402). Addison returns to this message in the afterword to *A Walk across the Sun*, when he calls human rights work "a gift" (462). Africa in these novels is a site where white humanitarians can perform their generosity. As Fleming's mother Catherine explains in a Trump-like flattening out of cultures and peoples in *The Garden of Burning Sand*: "Their children are starving; their daughters are being assaulted; their sons are being slaughtered. They see our planes, our doctors, our supplies, and they remember how to hope" (209).

Gillian Whitlock has pointedly written: "Humanitarian storytelling has the power to create spectators of suffering who engage empathetically with terrible events. It generates compassion and benevolence, and elicits donor support. At the same time, it can be called to account for the part it plays in representing communities and people as inhabitants of a 'developing world,' and as subjects of 'distant suffering' offered for Western benevolence and spectatorship."[24] Despite these and other blind spots, however, Addison's novels do make a sincere effort to avoid reproducing uncomplicated narratives of Western moral generosity and international repairmanship. *The Garden of Burning Sand* criticizes the United States for retrenching on AIDS relief in Africa, and *The Tears of Dark Water* critiques both the death penalty and the disastrous US intervention in Somalia. The novels are, moreover, self-conscious about the combined dangers of ignorance and narcissism in human rights work. In *The Tears of Dark Water*, a Somali man named Mahamoud surfaces a range of critiques while helping Megan in her investigation of Ismail's past. "You are American," he tells her when they meet. "When you think of Somalia, you think of Black Hawk Down and pirates and starving babies and al-Shabaab. Your perspective is incomplete" (295). Later, he confesses to her, "I thought you were just another rich American trying to soothe your conscience by helping a poor Somali" (312).

In the end, Addison's characters prove they are better than such critiques—indeed, better *because* of such critiques. But this is a particularly worrying proclivity in human rights self-representation generally, insofar as it reveals a strategy of transforming fatal criticism into moral inoculation. Certainly for Addison's United States and his human rights volunteers, accepting small doses of human rights skepticism is an effective means of defanging critics and proving worthiness. Because, in the end, they *are* worthy. The United States is for Yasmin a source of "goodness" and "gloriously disorienting" "manifold blessings" (423, 425). Clarke wears a *rakhi* bracelet that makes him a "brother" to the trafficked sisters, as authentic a rescuer as King Porus, who spared Alexander the Great in the Punjab (223). He is "noble," leaves people "inspired" and "honored" to know him, and bears the burden of those who have "urged the impossible upon him" (273, 331, 442, 339). Like the protagonist of the much-criticized film *Avatar*, he is an even better and braver defender of Indian citizens than the Indian police, physically catching the criminals they are incapable of nabbing in more than one chase scene. And finally, the novel seriously undermines the criticism that human rights is a form of US cultural imperialism by repeatedly attributing it to non-Western sexual predators and their defense attorneys, who use it to worm their way out of prosecution.

As has perhaps become increasingly clear, Addison's characters and their paths of personal development function as allegories of larger political patterns. Any claim of this sort, of course, would do well to begin by reckoning with Fredric Jameson's highly influential and disputed claim that all "third world" literature should be read as "national allegories." Jameson's view is that, in a postcolonial context, the lives of individuals necessarily function as emblems of the state of the nation. In his words, "the story of the private individual destiny is always an allegory of the embattled situation of the public third-world culture and society."[25] For many years, this argument has been criticized for its Eurocentric attempt to define much of the non-Western world by way of a single characterization. Even worse, Imre Szeman explains, the "technologies" Jameson ascribes to the literary work of the "third world" are those now considered intellectually outmoded or morally suspect in the West: allegory for its "naïve mode of one-to-one mapping," and the nation for the devastation wrought by "the virulent nationalisms of the twentieth century."[26] Reassessing such critiques, however, Szeman offers a framework for understanding Jameson that is especially useful when thinking about the novel of human rights. In Szeman's interpretation, national allegory is complex, fluid, and suggestive rather than prescriptive and simplifying. And, moreover, it isn't even really *national* at all. For Jameson, he argues, the nation names

> the possibility of new social relations and forms of collectivity not just "other" to neoliberal globalization, but the possibility of imagining these kinds of relations at all. Such forms of collectivity are not to be found in some actual national space . . . The nation is the name for a frankly utopic space that designates "whatever programs and representations express, in however distorted or unconscious a fashion, the demands of a collective life to come, and identify social collectivity as the crucial centre of any truly progressive and innovative political response to globalization." (820–821)

To return, then, to Addison's novels. While they crystallize many of the patterns we have seen in works discussed earlier, they illuminate in their formulaic clarity an additional pattern to be discerned in the genre. The novel of human rights reconceptualizes national allegory according to a utopian vision of a world without borders, a single nation of humanity. Significantly, it does so by extending the representational logic of its by now familiar gendered script. The threat of sexual violence in novels of human rights amplifies the perceived urgency and priority of protecting safe, heteronormative pairing. The use of violence against women to highlight the realities of injustice, that is, has as its ideological counterpart the use of safe, heterosexual union with women to highlight the possibilities of justice. Caren Irr has identified the reunion of separated couples as a critical aspect of national allegories.[27] In Addison's novels, reunion is a repeated plot line that reinforces conceptual configurations of global rights utopianism. Narratives of repair performed upon damaged US families are interwoven with mirror narratives of repair performed upon more deeply violated families abroad, and these together ultimately function as allegories of international healing and utopian borderlessness.

It is important to note that this structural pattern is, so to speak, morally neutral. For writers like Addison, the international allegory is invoked in the service of a savages-victims-saviors model of human rights. Narratives of redemptive, dyadic interpersonal connection symbolize the triumph of global human rights, but do so by relying upon absolute categories of identity: the broken and the fixed, those who need saving and those who save. By contrast, for writers such as Demetria Martínez and Dinaw Mengestu, whom I have already discussed, or Richard Powers and Chang-rae Lee, my next two case studies, the international allegory is a narrative and ideological pattern that is useful precisely because it is self-consuming, because it lays bare otherwise hidden values and assumptions that can then be scrutinized and, sometimes, rejected.

But before I develop what is at stake in Lee and Powers, let me show how generous, well-intentioned, un-ironic global utopianism works, and how it might go wrong. In *A Walk across the Sun*, Clarke saves his marriage by saving Sita. Initially he goes to work for CASE to rescue his marriage—it is the only way he can get close to Priya after she has separated from him and returned to her family in India. When Clarke rescues Sita, he re-earns Priya's admiration, heals the shared wound of their own lost infant, and proves, in the words of an ex-lover, that he can "stick with it" (431). Moreover, by saving Sita he bridges the gulf that separates him from his father-in-law, who had before perceived Clarke as a betrayer who stole his daughter away to the United States after being denied permission to ask her hand in marriage (an inoculatory trafficking parallel by the author). "This is the way of things in the West," Priya's father charges, inviting the reader to the task of bridging cultural divides. "The young have no respect for their elders" (201). What Clarke finally learns is not only how to repair his marriage—a union that would suffice to symbolize movement toward unity in a national allegory—but also how to reimagine his pursuit of Priya as something more than a matter of "wooing her back to the United States" (249), as something that helps him transcend his identity as a US citizen. This is the step needed for an international allegory. When the couple reunite at the end, they commit themselves to leaving the United States for good and, in the novel's final substitution, they conceive a child together whom they name Sita.

In a similar formula in *The Garden of Burning Sand*, Zoe Fleming repairs her damaged US family through her rescue work in Africa. She is doubly alienated from her father. When she was an adolescent, he refused to support her accusations of rape against the son of an influential colleague. Later, as a presidential candidate, he adopts policies that challenge Fleming's deepest values, cutting aid to Africa significantly. Achieving justice for Kuyeya leads ultimately to their reconciliation on both matters in a climactic, substitutive moment when Zoe's father travels to Africa and meets the young survivor of rape in a hospital. Watching them hold hands, Fleming reflects that "it was a scene she could never have predicted in a hundred lifetimes, a vision of the world that could be, the world of the possible" (389). As with Clarke's reunion plot, however, US family repair is only a partial step. Fleming must also heal another allegorically freighted family. She persuades Kuyeya's father, a distant MSF doctor who left Kuyeya's mother before her birth, to take responsibility for and establish a relationship with Kuyeya. Finally, Fleming fully realizes the international allegory of global reconciliation when she achieves the emotional clarity needed to commit herself to a long-distance, bicontinental relationship with an HIV-positive Zambian police officer.

In *The Tears of Dark Water*, pirates, who are described in the novel as "hostis humani generis"—that is, as the nightmare of borderlessness that produces human rights—are poised against "mariners," who symbolize the flipside utopia of borderlessness in human rights ambition. "These weren't just any Americans at risk; they were mariners. And mariners were family. Military, civilian, American, Indian, Russian, Chinese, the rules established on land were superseded at sea by a code of honor known to every sailor—that humanity was the highest dignity, and that transcended all" (84). The three families featured in the novel all begin broken and scattered, aching for connection. Ismail is separated from his family by the shame of his piracy. Vanessa loses her husband emotionally before he is murdered—they are, in a heavy symbol, "like islands shifting apart" (169). She also very nearly loses her son, Quentin, who returns from his fateful voyage traumatized, suffering from amnesia and damage to his language skills and "executive functioning." Meanwhile, Megan and Paul, Ismail's lawyer and hostage negotiator, respectively, are struggling to reconcile themselves to their brother Kyle's suicide.

All of these divisions, in the logic of the novel, are tied together and cannot be solved independently. Ismail cannot be reunited with his sister and family until he learns to trust Megan. Vanessa is overwrought and cannot connect emotionally with the world until she is able to overcome her rage at Ismail. And Megan and Paul must unravel the mystery behind Ismail's choice to pull the trigger because of their shattering confusion over their brother's choice to do the same. In a heavy parallel typical to Addison, both Kyle and Ismail, it turns out, are characterized as having been forced to pull the trigger: Ismail at gunpoint by another pirate, and Kyle at the abuse of his father. *"You made me do this!"* (190).

The gulf separating all is vast, but in the end the international allegory prevails and divisions are bridged. Quentin begins to recover his memory and communication skills, and falls in love with an Australian named Ariadne. Vanessa and Paul fall in love, and Paul—"homeless" because of his itinerant career—learns what it means finally to have a home. Yasmin, after escaping her captors in a scene that deliberately echoes Eliza's famous river escape in *Uncle Tom's Cabin*, begins a new life in the United States. And Ismail escapes the death penalty, serving his life sentence in a prison accessible to his family and leaving his piracy money to a relative to fund education in Somalia.

The idealistic and individualistic lesson hammered home in each novel, ultimately, is that a sincere effort to understand another's perspective—even if only through reading a novel—is an essential first step in healing a divided world. Addison's novels repeatedly stage acts of self-transformation through recognition of the other, most often through the simplest model of empathy: "like me" analogism. When confronted by difference, characters find a single, personal point of similarity that helps them imagine the suffering of another as if it were their own. "You know," an FBI agents says to Sita in a typical moment, "I have a daughter about your age" (442). While seeing one's own child in another is the most common trigger, there are variations on the "like me" device. In *The Tears of Dark Water*, for instance, one hostage realizes with a click of sympathy that "if he had been born in Somalia, he could've ended up just like [Ismail], stealing other people's money" (177). And Megan, Ismail's attorney, learns to empathize with Ismail because she too lost her brother to violence. "She tried to keep Ismail's story separate from her own, but she found it impossible" (297). It is here, I think, that the admirable and energetic hopefulness of the international allegory gets into worrisome territory. It's not just the imperializing win-win Mutua diagnoses. It's the conceptualization of human rights as the product of narrative empathy.

The best starting place for synopsizing this complex issue remains, in my view, Rousseau's 1758 concerns over theater:

> In giving our tears to these fictions, we have satisfied all the rights of humanity without having to give anything more of ourselves; whereas unfortunate people in person would require attention from us, relief, consolation, and work, which would involve us in their pains and would require at least the sacrifice of our indolence, from all of which we are quite content to be exempt. It could be said that our heart closes itself for fear of being touched at our expense. In the final accounting, when a man has gone to admire fine actions in stories and to cry for imaginary miseries, what more can be asked of him? Is he not satisfied with himself? Does he not applaud his fine soul? Has he not acquitted himself of all that he owes to virtue by the homage which he has just rendered it? What more could one want of him? That he practice it himself? He has no role to play; he is no actor.[28]

He continues:

> I hear it said that tragedy leads to pity through fear. So it does;
> but what is this pity? A fleeting and vain emotion which lasts
> no longer than the illusion which produced it; a vestige of natural
> sentiment soon stifled by the passions; a sterile pity which feeds
> on a few tears and which has never produced the slightest act of
> humanity. Thus, the sanguinary Sulla cried at the account of
> evils he had not himself committed. Thus, the tyrant of Phera
> hid himself at the theatre for fear of being seen groaning with
> Andromache and Priam, while he heard without emotions the
> cries of so many unfortunate victims slain daily by his orders.[29]

Addison's promise of post-innocence harmony, his international
allegory, depends upon the sort of lazy privileging of narrative empathy that worries Rousseau. The fiercest criticism one could make
is that works of this sort (whether literature, film, or other media)
function as moral commodities, assuring their consumers that the
experience itself is enough, that consumption is absolution, and that
individualizing solutions can solve institutional crises. By allowing
readers to imaginatively rest in the familiar power of one-to-one
tenderness, in the cocooning certainty of our feelings of care for
specifically realized others, such works promise resolution to vast
networks of suffering through the sheer accumulation of sentiment. If enough individuals experience this feeling, this intimacy of
empathy, then how could we not overcome all our differences?

The answer, of course, is that there are many ways we could fail.
Rousseau worries over the disconnect between empathy and action.
The contemporary psychologist Paul Bloom adds the concern that
even when empathy promotes action, it is a failure. Empathy, he argues, leads us astray.[30] It causes us to pay special attention to what
one might call narrative suffering (highly visible, attractive victims
that we feel have some kind of relation to us), and thereby to ignore
statistical suffering (faceless victims to whom we are not connected).
We squander our attention on Baby Jessica who fell into a well (one
of Bloom's prime examples), while ignoring all of the yet-to-exist babies who will be born into the eco-apocalypse caused by our reck-

less global warming. We generously donate time and money to the victims of spectacular catastrophes even when more time and money are not particularly helpful—as with the 2004 tsunami, a disaster for which MSF stopped accepting money, pleading instead for donations to less media-friendly crises. Meanwhile, we stingily withhold resources that could make critical differences for the vast population suffering from the invisible, slow tortures of poverty, violence, and disease.[31]

While Rousseau's and Bloom's arguments against empathy may be a tad too forceful, they are nonetheless useful perspectives with which to conclude consideration of Addison's empathy-saturated international allegories. Because beneath all the problems raised so far in this chapter—beneath the troubling tendency in human rights to sensationalize violence, restrictively categorize vulnerable identities, and promise reconciliation through narrow behavioral norms—is a problem at the very heart of the contemporary model of human rights: the assumption that empathy *works*. Lynn Hunt argues that our modern conception of empathy, which emerged with the birth of the novel in the eighteenth century, is the foundation of the evolving human rights movement. Just so in our contemporary culture of human rights, empathy is viewed as the enabling condition of effective international action. But as we have seen over and over again in the examples discussed so far, the play toward empathy in complex systems involves sacrifices, risks, and sometimes dangerously unquestioned assumptions. I've written at length elsewhere about the problem of empathy in human rights, so I will restrict myself here only to highlighting it as a broad theoretical concern as I now begin to shift perspectives. Wrapping up this chapter, I will move away from authors who endorse, with great moral earnestness, the narrative patterns I have identified toward authors who treat such patterns with deep suspicion.[32]

I have focused so intently on Addison because his work provides a transparent template for clarifying the international allegory in the novel of human rights. One could just as easily, for instance, track similar structures in Scott Turow's novel about war crimes and the

International Criminal Court, *Testimony* (2017). Looking for more complicated and self-conscious examples in the genre—examples that can open a range of new aesthetic and ethical issues—I will turn to Lee's *The Surrendered* and Richard Powers's *Operation Wandering Soul*.

Before moving to these two novels in detail, though, a quick summary of where we've been and what's next, as the argument over the final pages of this chapter will get a bit twisty. I began by analyzing the reliance on and simultaneous worry over the spectacular representation of violated women in human rights. I then moved to the formally opposed but ideologically parallel fixation on repaired heterosexual relations as a way of imagining utopian borderlessness. It was my claim that in both cases, the effort to write against violence plays into the fetishization of perceived ideal or norm-reinforcing bodies, a fetishization that accelerates the othering that drives violence in the first place.

My next authors, Lee, Powers, and Abani, are aware of this moral double bind. Their novels are in key ways organized around the problem of subjects to be saved in human rights writing. First, I will show how Lee reconfigures the international allegory as a suspicious critic rather than an Addisonian booster. After that, I will look beyond the international allegory to see how Powers disrupts narratives of reconciliation more generally in order to put humanitarianism itself into question. As a particularly focused case, I will analyze Powers's treatment of Henrietta Lacks, whose story functions as both a celebration and a critique of missions of global goodwill in *Operation Wandering Soul*—and also, importantly for Powers, as an introduction to the thematic of the grotesque, which defines the aesthetics and ethics of his novel. With the grotesque's inversions as a theoretical backdrop, I will then circle back to gender and the international allegory in *Operation Wandering Soul*, showing how Powers includes within that frame other categories of identity, including childhood and disability, as a way of drawing attention to the pervasiveness of the problem within human rights of subjects to be saved. I will conclude with Abani as a synoptic case study.

So, to the texts. When Lee won the Dayton Literary Peace Prize with *The Surrendered* in 2011, he closed his acceptance speech by emphasizing that expressing "forceful moral or political statements" was secondary to his desire as an author "to engage an aesthetic idea."[33] Nonetheless, *The Surrendered* was written with moral purpose, as he elaborated in his written comments about the award:

> History shows that all nations eventually decline, governments shall fall, great structures will crumble to dust; yet literature endures. Why? Because in order to thrive we need our own voices to tilt against intolerance, ignorance, callousness; to make ourselves vulnerable to the difficult and beautiful truths of our humanity; to remind us we are one.[34]

Keeping in mind that Lee is writing here in grandiose award-ese, it is nonetheless telling that he emphasizes the goal of international reconciliation in his comments.

The Surrendered is a lyric account of war, trauma, and memory that blends grim realism with myth and fantasy. Governed both by the numbing predictability of leftover, middle-age life and by the alarming unpredictability of life-changing accident, the winding novel is ill-served by plot summary. Nonetheless, a quick, clarifying synopsis can illuminate the unique ways Lee employs the now recognizable tropes of the human rights novel. In that spirit, I would begin by noting that the novel echoes basic structures of his earlier work, *A Gesture Life*, in which an adopted Asian orphan becomes a father's psychic stand-in for a comfort woman he violated decades earlier. (I have discussed this novel elsewhere.)[35]

The Surrendered is a book of homelessness and escapes. It tells the intertwined stories of June, a refugee from the Korean War, and Hector, a US veteran suffering from PTSD. Hector is separated from his unit and ultimately discharged after he assaults two fellow soldiers for torturing a young boy who served as a bugler for the North Korean army. June is orphaned after her father is executed by South Korean soldiers and her mother is killed while trying to stop June from being raped. Fleeing with her younger brother, June is eventually forced to abandon him when he loses his foot in a train accident. Hector later finds June alone, near death, on a countryside road. He rescues her and brings her to a nearby orphanage, where he takes on the job of a builder, designing and repairing its various shelters. At the orphanage they meet and fall in love with Sylvie, a beautiful missionary who will define the rest of their emotional lives, becoming a substitute for both of their lost families. "She was exalted and flawed, someone who required as much grace and succor as she herself readily offered, someone both he and June desperately needed, a mother and a lover and a kind of child, too."[36]

Like Hector and June, Sylvie has no surviving biological family. Her marriage is a sham from the start, and she has given up on having children after five miscarriages. Like June, she is a war orphan. Japanese soldiers raped her and killed her parents during the Second Sino-Japanese War in China, where they had been stationed as humanitarian field-workers. Sylvie processes this childhood trauma through an obsession with Henri Dunant's *Un Souvenir de Solférino*—an obsession June soon shares. In the cascade of events that follows, June sets fire to the orphanage, inadvertently killing Sylvie; Hector and June flee to the United States, marry, and quickly separate; and June conceives a child without telling Hector. Many years later they meet again when June hires a private investigator to find Hector and enlist his help. Dying of cancer, June is homeless once again, having sold her apartment so she can spend her final days tracking down her bitterly alienated son, who has run away—as if in a retributive reenactment of the way she ran away from her dying younger brother— staging "a perpetual series of departures that would never quite lead him back home" (42). In the course of their international search together, Hector learns that the boy has died, but he does not tell June. Instead, he coerces a young man into impersonating her son in order to effect a fraudulent reconciliation. Shortly after, in June's dying moments, he rushes her to the chapel at Solferino to offer her the truer resolution of symbolic return to Sylvie. It is here, finally, that the emotionally homeless pair find their home and the international allegory is realized. "*It is beautiful,*" he whispers to her as she dies. "*This is our place*" (483).

But this is no Addisonian close. On the one hand, June, who is now blind, has been brought to Solferino through deception by a man she doesn't love to celebrate a woman neither of them fully understood. On the other hand, however spare and conflicted their union is, it is one they have freely made for themselves outside the confined, given structures of the bio-legal heteronormative family. As an ideological construct, in other words, the allegory persists as its own double, matching each assertive state with its negation. Indeed, *The Surrendered* is governed throughout by a cycle of contrasts and repetitions that aesthetically echoes trauma's dual logic: both the temporal loops of trauma's perpetual psychic returns and the polar oppositions of power that make it possible in the first place. Hector is physically invulnerable, an embodiment of Greek warrior myth and the model, quite literally, of idealized Western citizenship (he is featured in a national World War II war bonds poster). June, by contrast, is vulnerable and endangered. As a child she is the embodiment of the racialized other that humanitarianism figures as the needy recipient of Western aid. At middle age, dying of cancer, she is the antitype of Hector's everlasting health, the terminal image of a disabled body. For June, the plot doubles avoidances and escapes; for Hector it doubles acts of rescue. As a young girl, June escapes by abandoning her baby brother to die alone. As a mother, she emotionally abandons her child in myriad ways, finally refusing to take an emergency phone call from a hospital in England where he is dying. Hector, by contrast, physically rescues June as a child when she is escaping the war, and again when she is surrendering to cancer as a middle-aged woman, yearning for a final return to the one she loved.

This model of oppositions, however, is matched by its own opposition. Just as Hector's final rescue is rendered ambiguous by its proximity to June's false reunion with her son, so is Hector's role as agentic white savior. In the novel's final pages, it is revealed that June saved Hector from the orphanage fire as he was, in unthinking despair, allowing himself to burn to death. "The girl," the novel concludes, "was inordinately strong" (476). Indeed, throughout the novel, June is depicted as unbreakably resilient, while Hector is quietly desperate, fatigued, and emotionally surrendered. June is wealthy and successful, and her choices drive the arc of the novel's plot. Hector is impoverished and directionless, reacting to rather than controlling the events and people around him. Accident rather than choice defines his life. Hector's days "played out in a circle no larger than the carry of a human shout" (104), while June as a character is defined by linear, purposeful motion. As the novel proceeds, Hector's indestructibility begins to resemble something closer to a curse than an ideal, a parody of the concept of normative health that seemed to exclude June. If the two protagonists are bound together in an international allegory, as I believe they are, it is one that is written against the readerly desires Addison caters to: against the comforting but false clarity of binarized classes of persons, and against the guilt-relieving ideals of seamless union and stable resolution. Instead, *The Surrendered* dramatizes the irreconcilability of our moral ambitions and our realities, and our duty to live responsibly within the anxiety that irreconcilability produces.

Powers's National Book Award finalist *Operation Wandering Soul* is equally ill-served by summary. It is less a plot-driven novel than a fugue. The through line of the novel takes place in a hospital in a near-future dystopic Los Angeles. Richard Kraft is a surgical resident at Carver General working himself to breakdown. He is and has always been symbolically homeless. "Veteran repacking campaigns left him a quiet child."[37] An international wanderer who has throughout his life moved between annual leases, he often chooses to stay at a motel near the hospital rather than return to his apartment. Soon, however, he meets Linda Espera, a physical therapist, and they fall in love. Here the novel invokes the genre's familiar promise of hope through a cross-cultural heterosexual union—Linda's racial "foreignness" (65) is one of Kraft's recurring erotic fixations. Together they create what is simultaneously a hopeful simulation and a tragic parody of family as they work to care for a range of desperate, hopeless children in the pediatric ward. Their patients include a range of victims of neglect, abuse, and catastrophic disease: a boy with progeria, a boy with no face, and, most centrally, a Laotian war refugee, Joy Stepaneevong, who triggers Kraft's traumatic memories of a young woman he saw killed by a mine in Thailand when he was a young man. Throughout the couple's emotionally freighted but spare encounters, Powers weaves a series of myths and historical accounts of lost children, from Peter Pan and the Pied Piper to the Children's Crusade and the London evacuation—tales of "children adrift, out of doors too late at night, too far from home, migrating, campaigning, colonizing, displaced, dispersed, tortured loose, running for their lives" (163).

Like *The Surrendered*, *Operation Wandering Soul* is a novel about the traumatic aftershock of war, and it reprises many of the same tropes and concerns. Both take place in what are, effectively, orphanages; both feature a morally compromised white savior; both center their tragedy on the suffering of a vulnerable, non-Western girl; and both are defined by the desire to escape. "We must be headed *somewhere. Somewhere unprecedented*. He would never escape the need to unravel, extend, be *off*" (264). Both novels, finally, are fixated on damaged mobility. Like many of the books discussed in this study, they participate in a centuries-long literary tradition that uses feet and mobility as primary emblems for representing vulnerability in wartime. As classics scholar Thomas Palaima notes, two-footedness has throughout history often functioned as a symbol of what makes us distinctly human, and the binary of fleet-footedness and injured feet—feet that enable both escape and heroic action but that also put us on the ground and make us vulnerable—has defined the "essence of war" from Homer to Tim O'Brien.[38]

For Lee and Powers, images of compromised mobility are especially useful because they disrupt the neat binaries of personhood that seem to permeate human rights writing, binaries like the damaged and the whole, the healthy and the sick, the normal and the abnormal, the saving and the saved. In *Operation Wandering Soul*, everybody is compromised. The novel begins with a long description of the false mobility of Los Angeles traffic, the "dream of free agency" (8) that compels everybody to frantically cut lanes and fill empty spots on the highway, to anxiously fill "the otherwise-idle nano-second" (6). "The curve of mobility," Powers writes, "will sidle up ever more intimately to asymptote until that moment at decade's, century's, and millennium's end when the last living road-certified creature not yet on rolling stock will creep out onto the ramp in whatever vehicle it can muster, and poof: perpetual gridlock" (8). The novel's defining traumatic symbol, its summation of adult failure, is the loss of a child's foot. Joy will have her foot amputated and then, soon after, will die from the cancer that is spreading up from her ankle into her leg bones. Against such inevitability, Powers

pits Richard and Linda's defiant effort to achieve hope. At the
midpoint of the novel, they try to teach the children to dance,
taking them on a field trip to an Arthur Murray class, embar-
rassing the instructors with "the army of child cripples who have
come" (206).

Damaged mobility is, likewise, the center of Lee's novel. June's
brother will have his foot amputated and then bleed to death. Lee
has explained in interviews that this scene is a fictionalized attempt
to work through a traumatic event from his own father's life, and was
the conception point of the novel. Invoking not only the *Iliad* but
also *Philoctetes*, Lee makes foot injuries a recurrent, almost obsessive
concern in *The Surrendered*. Hector's father limps from a "right foot
turned permanently sideways at birth" (62). Hector's lover Dora is
mortally wounded when a car crushes her leg. Min from the orphanage nearly dies when he accidentally injures his foot with an ax,
a crisis that recalls Hector's haunting failure to save another soldier
after his foot had been "blown off by a friendly shell" (120). And in a
plot point that publicly reveals the illicit emotional intimacy between
Hector and Sylvie, the latter twists her knee and Hector pushes
everyone aside to handle her leg "with great tenderness" (442). The
novel ends with June's delirious memory of her barefoot escape from
the war, when she abandoned her brother. The final sentence, as she
is dying: "She was off her feet, alive" (484).

Both novels depict a world of pervasive vulnerability. While *The
Surrendered* offers a chastened consideration of reconciliation and
healing closure, *Operation Wandering Soul* is relentlessly despairing
about such possibilities. Kraft cannot save Joy from cancer and retreats into traumatized emotional isolation. Espera realizes that her
relationship with the older Kraft is an unhealthy traumatic return
to her own childhood abuse. And the children, in a fantastical repetition of the novel's lost children tales, inexplicably escape from the
ward. The international allegory is most fully realized in its negation, in the elimination of the very possibility of family—what Kraft
describes as a "genocide" of children (342).

The novel doesn't just reject redeeming allegorical closure, however.[39] It verges on rejecting narrative itself. The novel's title refers
to a propaganda campaign Kraft's father participated in during the

war in which US forces broadcast sham spirit messages at night to Vietcong soldiers, hoping to make them flee their positions. "Our babies," the spectral voices call out. "Our offspring! *Have you forgotten us?*" (231). As the fugue-like novel continues to weave together narrative after narrative, the propaganda campaign begins to resemble an act of nighttime storytelling, not unlike Linda's bedtime ritual at the hospital. Her stories, also, can haunt. Just after Linda describes storytelling as "therapy, the reading cure," "the best way to keep from dying in midfable," and "our one moral obligation" (79), she puts the children to bed by telling them the story of the Leech Child, which concludes with the "children of Europe" finding a "surefire escape." "They can leave home. They start to pile into boats, whole families, whole countries of them" (89). Joy, who is listening, escaped atrocities as what was then referred to as a "boat person," not a child of Europe finding independence but a refugee struggling to adapt, "still pitching from months on the sheet of corrugated tin that took her six hundred miles across the South China Sea" (27). "*But that's not, that's not how* . . . ," Joy interrupts. Linda emotionally flinches: "Oh God. Joy. I'm so sorry. I wasn't thinking. I completely forgot. Oh, child, forgive me. It's only a story" (89).[40]

The book is throughout concerned with the injury inflicted by blind humanitarianism. As an adolescent Kraft spearheads an unlikely project to build a school in Nam Chai during the Vietnam War. "The boy with the beautiful idea" (309) soon sees from the inside, however, the self-serving quality of international do-goodism. The school is built with the support of the "self-appointed international ambassadors of goodwill" (297); a television reporter who "wanted allegory, Little Eva or Nell" (301) comes to cover the story, asking if he can get "a good cross-section of *color*" (299); and the headmaster in charge christens the project, to young Kraft's horror, "Operation Santa Claus" (293). As it turns out, the purportedly humanitarian project is made possible only because the military "was in urgent need of PR" and wanted at least "one good report on foreign philanthropy in the region" (292). "The whole project felt suddenly cruel," Kraft decides (203). "Operation Santa Claus" culminates with the death of two children in a mine explosion and the quick exit of all do-gooders.

Similar concerns are developed in *The Surrendered*. In the novel's climactic emotional confrontation, Hector belittles Sylvie's copy of *Un Souvenir de Solférino*, calling humanitarianism "worthless" because it promises everything and changes nothing. Its workers have no stake and no enduring connection to the objects of their care; they can "come and go" as they wish (430). In the end, humanitarianism is surrender, in that it—like Hector and Sylvie both—accepts failure as a given, seeking not to end suffering by addressing its deep causes but rather only to prolong our ability to endure it.

Early in *Operation Wandering Soul*, Kraft invokes the story of Henrietta Lacks, an African American woman whose cancer cells were removed from her cervix for research in 1951, becoming the world's first immortal cell line. Since then, it is estimated that scientists have grown more than fifty million metric tons of her cells and used them in tens of thousands of studies, helping countless people suffering from a range of diseases.[41] Kraft depicts the HeLa strain as the "favorite cell strain of researchers the world over" (52). In an uncharacteristically optimistic moment, he describes HeLa as the "dream of one world," of people united from "the coast from Baja to Livermore and on into the wilds of BC, shooting out across the Aleutians into central Asia, down to the polyglot Indonesian archipelagoes, into the Indian subcontinent, reversing Alexander back to Our Sea and up into Europe, over the Atlantic to North America again." Henrietta Lacks, as Kraft imagines it, "is the modern world's oversoul" (52).

As Rebecca Skloot reveals in her study *The Immortal Life of Henrietta Lacks*, however, Kraft's dream of progress and unity is actually a story of race, exploitation, and science's outpacing of ethics. Lacks's cells were removed without her consent; her family's privacy was violated when health records and genetic information were revealed; and fortunes were made without a thought of compensation. As Lacks's daughter Deborah commented, discussing her own medical history with Skloot:

> When people hear about my mother cells they always say, "Oh y'all could be rich! Y'all gotta sue John Hopkin, y'all gotta do this and that." But I don't *want* that . . . Truth be told, I can't get mad at science, because it help people live, and I'd be a mess

without it. I'm a walking drugstore! I can't say nuthin bad about
science, but I won't lie, I *would* like some health insurance so I
don't got to pay all that money every month for drugs my mother
cells probably helped make. (256)

Powers published *Operation Wandering Soul* long before Skloot's
study exposed to the broad public the profound divisiveness behind
HeLa—certainly part of the reason he rehearses HeLa's uncomplicated symbolic pan-humanism. But even though most who knew
about HeLa then viewed it first and last as a research miracle, Powers
nonetheless incorporates into his rhapsodic catalog of the strain's
meanings a sense of suspicion and even exploitation. The lessons of
"Operation Santa Claus" and "the boy with the beautiful idea"—
lessons about moral blindness in the pursuit of a particular conception of progress—are lessons not just for Kraft but for Powers. Powers
closes his vision of the desire to heal the world through HeLa by
suddenly dismissing it as a lie, a phony "backwater neon come-on insisting WE DO IT ALL FOR YOU." He then moves into a description of
a different kind of unity. Kraft "hears Helen's breathing on the semi-
arid air" (52) as he watches "all the proverbial races, colors, and
creeds" (53) driving to the impoverished neighborhood of his hospital to buy illegal drugs. As with HeLa, the privileged will get what
they want from others who pay the mortal price.

The ethical vector of Kraft's vision of HeLa—the move from
cliché to complication—governs *Operation Wandering Soul*'s relationship to the tropes of the human rights novel. Powers invokes genre
patterns to simultaneously endorse and disrupt them; he writes a self-
consuming book. I will develop this claim in a moment, but first
want to provide a bit of theoretical background. *Operation Wandering
Soul* is, quite self-consciously, a Bakhtinian grotesque. In German
Romanticism, the word "grotesque" referred to a unique genre of
writing. The literary grotesque is marked by the disruption of stable
borders and categories, like the freakish creatures of ornament from
which it takes its name (the *grottesche* of the Italian Renaissance).[42]
In literary theory, the touchstone work on the grotesque is Bakhtin's
Rabelais and His World. For Bakhtin, the idea of the grotesque is understood primarily through acts that open the body. The grotesque

body, he writes, "is not a closed, completed unit; it is unfinished, outgrows itself, transgresses its own limits. The stress is laid on those parts of the body that are open to the outside world, that is, the parts through which the world enters the body or emerges from it, or through which the body itself goes out to meet the world." Bakhtin argues that the aesthetic grotesque echoes the social practice of carnivals that release chaos through humor and, in so doing, disrupt traditional forms of social order.[43]

Operation Wandering Soul references both Rabelais and the ornamental grotesque, the latter in a scene described as a "carnival" (143, 149). Powers draws upon the grotesque both as a cluster of literary tropes and as a metaphor for the instability of the adult world of meaning. The grotesque is the analogue at the level of scene and image of the broader epistemological confusion generated by trauma. *Operation Wandering Soul* turns its own clichés inside out just as it continually turns physical bodies inside out. Kraft, traumatized by the relentless butchery of his job at the aptly named Carver Hospital, cannot help seeing beneath the skin of people around him, to the tissue and fluid and pathologies within. "He can see beneath, to the hideous, fatty slabs just dying to squirt out all over. Beneath the pretty sausage casing, webs of nerve niagara in spraying veils. He has peeked beneath the packaging and become hardened, like a kid disabused of Adventureland by accidentally glimpsing the motor underneath the talking puppet Plasticine" (96). Scene after scene of surgery culminates in the final attempt to dig the cancer out of Joy's leg:

> Up here, at organ level, it seems a stash-stuffed haversack, an elastic, single-sheet hyperbolic solid lashing with surface tension a vitreous humor that would otherwise spew jelly all over the cavity . . . And this rubbery, slittable resistance, midway between failed tapioca and a chewed-up gum eraser: here is the prime pornography, the stuff of all prurient fascination. Tender obscenity spreads itself just a micron of latex away from his fingers. He must wade into lewdness up to the hip. (267–268)

In *Operation Wandering Soul*, opposites blend. Surgery becomes injury. Doctors become perpetrators. And, in the novel's central inversion, adults become confused children while children become world-weary with adult wisdom and foresight. Nico inverts the structure of the children's ward, initiating a carnivalesque disorder in which the children, the "freaks," usurp the authority of the adults (149). Such instability of authority and borders is literalized in the figure of the refugee, whose disruption of national borders is highlighted in the character Joy and the novel's through line myth, the Children's Crusade—itself a disruptive epistemological puzzle of history and legend about children in Europe who became refugees before the concept of the refugee was conceived.

Powers's grotesque disruptions target the emerging norms of human rights representation, upending expected values. The novel, for instance, invites us to prioritize the angst and emotional suffering of the white humanitarian who must bear the burden of his knowledge, guilt, and sacrifice. It then invites us to interrogate that priority. Just so, *Operation Wandering Soul*'s spare plot line is, from the start, an invocation of the international allegory, of redemption through cross-cultural heterosexual union. But the relationship fails. Linda tried to love Kraft, she realizes, precisely because she realized he was broken, because she needed to prove something by trying to fix him. "She needed little Ricky's infirmity for her own private ends." Her love was "charity," and charity "can be only a kind of belated revenge" (277). For his part, Kraft—who frankly acknowledges that "he needs her otherness" (133)—is a hero much like Addison's, a complex portrait of Mutua's "pathology of self-redemption." As a young man Kraft has a vision of the children of the non-Western world that provides a life mission for him and all his peers, the advantaged "offspring of UN relief agencies, intercontinental traders, lifer servicemen, or covert advisors" (265). The wretched are all around us, Kraft tells his privileged schoolmates, wasting away, and "calling out to this international class—this *us*—to come this way. Come save them" (266). As an adult Kraft remains compulsively driven by "something inside him" to "service, sacrifice, and salvation" (50). But the novel worries about his true motivations, depicting his concern for others as a form of self-regard, a way to "keep him from backsliding" into "existential aloneness" (67). In the end, the novel depicts Kraft as a false sacrifice, emphasizing that he is thirty-three

years old at the same time that it tells the horrific story of the Ana-
baptist leader John of Leiden, whose delusional Messiah complex
proved devastating to those who trusted him.

In what appears to be a bleak promise of unceasing repetition,
the failed Linda / Ricky dyad is mimed in the relationship between
the children Joy and Nico. Nico is figured as Western and older
because of both his progeria and his social dominance in the ward.
Joy is perceived as a younger, vulnerable racial other eager to please
those who need her. But just as with the adults they model themselves
upon, the power dynamic they share inverts as the novel proceeds.
Ultimately, both children come to see that they are using each other
to fill their own needs. Such failed childhood innocence is central to
Operation Wandering Soul because childhood innocence is the most
powerful and pervasive of clichés. The novel relentlessly uses children
as the most extreme embodiment of human vulnerability: lost
children; homeless children; sexually assaulted children; children
with disabilities; abandoned, murdered, and trafficked children. Foreign children are a special site of empathic focus. Joy is "a walking
Red Cross ad" (32), and the girl Kraft watched die in a mine explosion
has an "Oxfam face" (306).

Powers plays to the needs and desires of a reading public that seeks
"stories of good people struggling to do right in the world's forgotten
places." For this he earned lavish praise from, among other places,
USA Today, which characterized the book as a kind of rescue campaign for children:

> If you have children or will have children, if you know children
> or can remember being a child, dare to read *Operation Wandering
> Soul* . . . Like the stories read to children, this intensely caring
> novel can help prevent the nightmare it describes, children out
> too late at night, far from home, lost, the wandering souls of the
> future, our future.[44]

As hard as *Operation Wandering Soul* works to generate this readerly response, however, it also lambasts itself for doing so. Over and
over again, the novel stages interior criticisms of its own primary
narrative devices. It uses suffering children to elicit individual com-

passion, but worries over both desensitization and deindividualized othering. In repeated scenes of traumatic recall, Kraft blends the identities of the suffering children he encounters. He substitutes Joy for the "indistinguishable" (276) Asian girl he saw killed during the Vietnam War; this girl for the iconic image of a young girl fleeing a napalm attack in Vietnam; these three together for the hospital children; and all these together for the missing children on his obsessively accumulated milk cartons. To take a phrase and concept from John Rawls: humanitarian narrative, in part because of the utilitarian ethics undergirding it, fails to "take seriously the distinction between persons."[45] Discussing Joy's tragic life story, a stereotypical emotionally dead surgeon comments: "Doesn't she have to get raped by Thai fishermen first? Don't they always get raped by . . . ?" (92).

Later in the novel, Linda reflects on the way we use children to manipulate each other. She sees it as a lie through and through.

> Anyone who has exploited prepubescence for any campaign, however well-meaning, anybody who has ever trotted out pasteurized, freckled, fairybook simperers to pitch their wholesome radiance, has forgotten the lay of the land. Traveled too far in the interim. *Remember the children. What of the children? Doesn't anyone care about the children?* Rubbish, all of it. For Linda's money, these sales reps confuse innocence with lack of opportunity. Purity is an adult bill of goods. The sweet-meaning child is just an icon. (190)

In an even more explicit meta-textual moment, Nico, who adopts for himself the cliché behaviors of an old man, concocts a scheme to get Joy in the *Guinness Book of World Records* as the "recipient of the most get-well cards of all time." Encouraging her to act out her cliché role as the "little Asian girl" languishing "in the charity hospital," Nico explains: "Come on. They love this kind of pathetic kiddie crap. Capture the regional imagination. Feel-gooder campaign. Courage in the face of keeling over. Vote with your stamps. The whole bullshit waterworks. What d'ya think?" (195).

Such representation, the book asserts, is not only cliché and pandering but also cruel and exploitative. As the novel reaches its climax,

Nico begins a campaign to persuade the adults to let the children stage
a theatrical production of *The Pied Piper*. Most of the children see
Nico's plans as "yet another load of Eurocentric, racist, imperialist,
hegemonistic, queer-ball, degrading eco-exploitation" (238). But they
participate anyway, desperate for purpose. Parts are distributed; plans
begin in earnest; and in a moment that stands out as painful in a
novel defined by emotional brutality and physical butchery, Nico tells
Joy what her part in the story must be.

> Her turn for appalling compromise now. "What part?" she asks
> again, head down. Having bestowed him with executive powers,
> she must bend to whatever role those powers assign her. "I can
> make the costumes," she bleats. "I could whisper the lines. I
> could look up the different versions of the story. There must be
> an awful lot." Stress scatters her cantering accents wildly through
> the syllables. "I could print the programs. I'm a very careful
> printer." Better than any of her peers born into twenty-six
> letters. The advantage of the late starter.
>   "Well, yeah, fine. I'm sure you print just great. Only, you see,
> we've got that base covered already. What we really need now
> is . . ." He frets at the row of plastic sizing holes at the back of
> his cap band. He cannot bring himself to spell it out. It. What
> we really need.
>   "What part do you make me play?" The words rustle like raw
> silk, that raw silk that refuses to burn. . . . "Nico?"
>   He will not tell her what she already knows.
>   "I'm the lame one, aren't I?"
>   "You're the crip," he agrees tersely. "You're the gimp." He
> flares his beak of a nose at her, flashes the *so sue me* look.
> Showdown slides off into a shrug . . .
>   As the pair falls to arrangements, the details of set and
> stagecraft, the boy's gravelly, senescent voice goes low, half
> sympathetic. His subdued countenance turns away from her
> over their daring plans. Perhaps he even feels, just this once in
> his compressed, accelerated life, the shape of guilt, the pitiless
> cameo he places in her hands. (241)

Nico, here, is Powers. The novel *Operation Wandering Soul* sees itself as much a matter of "inventive derangement" (271) as the military propaganda campaign "Operation Wandering Soul." Whether one finds this self-reflexive critique effective or not depends upon a moral judgment: Is it more alienating to ignore one's moral complicities, or to dwell upon them, as if trying to generate surplus empathy through the very fact of one's guilt?

Powers uses disability as aggressively as Nico throughout the novel, thrusting forward society's most derogatory frames for understanding difference. Nico is repeatedly described as a "freak" and he, in turn, describes the children on the ward as "sickos, freaks, and illegals" (239). The narrator shares this vocabulary: "Monsters, freaks of gene or accident or pathology, race up and down these hallways in relays, in fifty-yard dashes leading to no medal, no record, nowhere" (137). They are "dwarfs," "midgets, mites, pygmies, Lilliputians" (237), victims of the "'congenital' heap, the fuck-ups in the master switches twisting the body this way and that like hideously abused raggedy Anns and Andys" (134). Joy is in particular a postmodern Tiny Tim, an extraordinary body that epitomizes vulnerability and demands pity: "All four of her limbs would have fit comfortably inside a third-grade lunchbox" (28).

David Mitchell and Sharon Snyder have used the term "narrative prosthesis" to describe the pervasive role disability has played in literature. "Disability," they argue, "has been used throughout history as a crutch upon which literary narratives lean for their representational power, disruptive potentiality, and analytical insight." As an "opportunistic metaphorical device," disability in literature functions to contain difference. It displays and compartmentalizes pitiable abnormality to reinforce the reader's sense of and investment in the normal. But Mitchell and Snyder also argue that, in many works, disability is used as subversion rather than containment, "as a metaphor and fleshly example of the body's unruly resistance to the cultural desire to 'enforce normalcy.'"[46] Mitchell and Snyder point out that *Operation Wandering Soul*, with its "highly experimental" and "self-questioning" narration, progressively reappropriates exclusionary language around disability by depicting the children's ward

as an "alternative family circuit that embraces its members and con-
tests their attendant devaluation by the able-ist adult world beyond
the hospital walls" (177). Disability, indeed, is figured as a temporal
norm in the novel. According to the Japanese creation myth of the
Leech Child that Linda shares with the children, "the first infant
who laid eyes on the world was born deformed" (81).

It is worth noting that here, as before, Powers and Lee run parallel.
The Surrendered is fundamentally a novel of disability. "'The normative
position of the nondisabled,'" Stephanie Hsu writes of the book,
"has all but been eradicated from the cast of characters." For Lee,
disability functions entirely differently from the way it does in the
novel's interior touchstone text, *Un Souvenir de Solférino*. According
to Hsu, in much humanitarian discourse protections are premised
on the idea of disability as an "exception" that ultimately valorizes
able-bodied norms of citizenship. In *Un Souvenir de Solférino*, for
instance, "the disabled are grouped with the dead and dying." In
The Surrendered, by contrast, disability models ways of being that rest
neither "in the fold of national belonging nor under the protection
of the state," ways of being that—as in *Operation Wandering Soul*—
develop alternative family circuits that challenge ablenationalism.[47]

If Powers challenges perceived norms with this affirmative model
of community, he pushes them toward a breaking point with his negative alternative: the "Holocaust of children" (122). Nico believes,
and convinces his peers, that the adults are planning to kill them. "I
swear on my last sheet of toilet paper, they're trying to deep-six us . . .
They don't like our kind, case you haven't noticed" (239–240). Scanning history and literature, Kraft acknowledges a generalized "baby
genocide" (342), but what he fails to see is that Nico is naming a more
specific set of targets: not children, but disabled children. Ruth Hubbard has argued, when discussing disability rights, that prenatal tests
for disability should be contextualized within the rise of Nazi eugenics and US sterilization laws. She writes:

> I am not arguing against a woman's right to abortion. Women
> must have that right because it involves a decision about our
> bodies and about the way we will spend the rest of our lives. But
> for scientists to argue that they are developing these tests out

of concern for the "quality of life" of future children is like the [eugenicist] arguments about "lives not worth living." No one can make that kind of decision about someone else. No one these days openly suggests that certain kinds of people be killed; they just should not be born. Yet that involves a process of selection and a decision about what kinds of people should and should not inhabit the world.[48]

Historically, eugenics has often relied upon arguments about humanitarian progress. Some of the earliest coded law—including Rome's Twelve Tables, which are often loosely included in documentary histories of human rights[49]—required the killing or exposure of infants born deformed. Indeed, it has been argued that because human rights rhetorically ground themselves in an ideal of the unviolated body, they reinforce norms that deny sociopolitical membership based on disability.[50] As Arlene Kanter writes, discussing the 2006 Conventions on the Rights of Persons with Disabilities (CRPD):

> Scholars of international law are not alone in ignoring the plight of people with disabilities. Until the CRPD, even the United Nations had essentially ignored the rights of people with disabilities as a matter of international human rights law. Although the UN had adopted what are referred to as nine "core human rights treaties," prior to the CRPD, only one of these treaties, the Convention on the Rights of the Child (CRC), mentions people with disabilities as a group worthy of international human rights legal protection. And even the CRC does not recognize the general right of children with disabilities to international human rights protections on an equal basis with children without disabilities.[51]

Operation Wandering Soul worries about the way ideals of the "dignified" reinforce exclusionary norms. The novel is infused with anxiety around the ideas of equal protection, lives not worth living, and medical progress. On the one hand, Kraft endorses the prenatal testing that will eliminate the possibility of children like Nico. He describes a family who refuses to abort a child with a predicted "severe mental handicap" as ignorant victims of a "love" that is a "severe handicap all its own" (318). On the other hand, the novel also continually meditates on the menace of eugenics. Invoking the memory of Anne Frank, it characterizes Kraft's vision of screening and treatments as a matter of "gene-weaponry" (134). The book climactically closes with the fulfillment of Nico's escape plan. The children decide—correctly, the book's tone suggests—that they can protect their right to exist as a class of persons only by fleeing the medical establishment that is meant to save them.

I want to conclude this chapter, and point to what follows in Chapter 4, by focusing on Chris Abani's *The Secret History of Las Vegas*. The novel synopsizes many of the issues discussed so far. Like Powers, Abani amplifies and exposes the devices of the human rights novel to complicate their effects. *The Secret History of Las Vegas* interweaves an escape plot and a justice plot, both featuring orphans rendered homeless. The former concerns the conjoined twins, Fire and Water, who seek to escape imprisonment and malign experimentation in a psychiatric hospital. The latter concerns the secret crimes committed by Sunil, a South African psychiatrist living in exile after collaborating with the regime to induce confessions without torture. Abani uses primary and secondary characters as narrative prostheses to examine discrimination in all forms and, in the spirit of Bakhtin's grotesque, the moral status of bodies that defy normative categorization. These include Sunil, a mixed-race child of apartheid; Fire and Water, self-identified "freaks" working in a sideshow; and White Alice, a woman exiled to Soweto after hyperpigmentation from Addison's disease, in her words, turned her black. In one of several meta-textual moments, Fire makes Abani's narrative ambitions clear: "Circuses are about entertainment and juggling and animals and all that shit. Sideshows are about freaks, about people and the limits of acceptability. We push those limits. If a circus is an escape . . . a sideshow is a confrontation" (131).

Literalizing Powers's metaphorical concern with the freak, Abani dramatizes the idea that human rights representation is, at its heart, both defined and distorted by the concept of freak. He invokes

Powers's concern over the idea of lives not worth living; Anker's claim that our norms of dignity are defined by pernicious contrast to perceived-disfigured bodies; and Lee's ambivalence about the morally urgent mission to identify vulnerable bodies to protect. To this concatenation Abani adds his own concern with citizenship as a system of classification that defines, parses up, and grants or denies rights-bearing personhood. "All empire is about classification," Sunil says, discussing the principles not only of apartheid but also of the Zulu Kingdom (133).

Fire and Water defy classification physically and bureaucratically. Water is a stereotype of the perfect male body, "beautiful," "muscular" and "perfectly proportioned" (14). Fire, by contrast, is "little more than a head with two arms projecting out of Water's chest." His distorted features are, significantly, described in the language of both injury and noncitizenship: his eyes and nose are swollen, as if they have been "punched," and he looks "alien" (14). The twins also have no fixed residence and no IDs. "We live off the grid," Fire explains when they are discovered near a crime scene. The police define that as "a problem" (15) and detain them. Throughout the novel Fire loudly insists that they have rights that must be respected, that they cannot be held indefinitely, but he is ignored. Indeed, he is rendered essentially invisible by the investigating detective who refuses to look at Fire when he speaks, keeping his eyes locked on the uncommunicative Water. "You're really going to pretend I'm not here, Fire asked" (18). Ultimately, the twins are symbolically demoted from citizens to animals, given an MRI in a zoo medical facility because, it is argued, animal equipment would better fit their bodies.

In *The Secret History of Las Vegas*, invisibility impairs our ability to possess our rights, whether it is the physical invisibility of imprisonment or the social invisibility of collectively averted gazes. As the novel emphasizes over and over again, there are certain things we wish to see, and certain things we need to look away from. Returning to South Africa for the first time after apartheid, Sunil is astonished at the "amnesia" of Cape Town, where races now intermingle, but with no sense of restitution. Talking on the beach to a stranger of indeterminate race who describes the atmosphere as "restorative," Sunil counters, "I imagine all the whites lying here during apartheid, the breeze and the water making it possible for everything to seem good" (217). Back in the United States, Sunil tries to describe the collective blindness of apartheid to Salazar, the police detective who detained Fire and Water.

> I was thinking about Cape Town, about the time I went back. I was having a coffee in this café and I saw Robben Island from the window. I said to the old waiter serving me, if the island was visible every day how come they pretended nothing was going on? He smiled and said, It was often quite foggy in those days, sir, the island was rarely visible.
>
> It's a skill, Salazar said. Like witnesses who can't remember anything at a crime scene.
>
> Selective blindness made Sunil think of White Alice. (219)

Like Powers, Abani consistently invokes the cliché patterns of rights representation to undo them. The most wrenching atrocities represented occur under apartheid, and the most dramatic villain of the novel is a monstrous South African death squad leader and torturer, Eugene, who co-opts Sunil into conducting experiments on African captives to make them more pliable during interrogation. Abani, however, refuses to allow the intensity of atrocity abroad to function as a distraction from atrocity at home. The parallels between contemporary US society and apartheid are relentless. Just as in South Africa, there is in the United States a "Dr. Mengele" (303) figure who puts Sunil to work on vicious and lethal psychiatric experiments, this time on untraceable homeless victims. Fire, whose black grandfather was shot to death by a policeman for holding a pipe, explicitly describes his detention as a form of "apartheid" (131). Sunil explains to Salazar that telephone poles only caught on in US society "when someone discovered they could lynch blacks in the middle of town using the poles" (164), and he reflects often upon economic inequality in the United States, wondering when it will lead to the "big and violent rifts" that occurred under apartheid (187).

> Vegas is really an African city, Sunil thought . . . And just like in every major city across Africa, from Cairo to his hometown of

Johannesburg, the palatial exteriors of the city architecture barely screened the seething poverty, the homelessness, and the despair that spread in townships and shanty-towns as far as the eye could see. But just as there, here in Vegas the glamour beguiled and blinded all but those truly intent on seeing. (30)

The novel's most dramatic metaphor for failing to see involves the nuclear weapons tests conducted in the region, which inflicted a range of injuries upon US residents living downwind from the blasts, including cancer, fetal malformations, infertility, and blindness. In a narrative echo of the Afrikaner refusal to see Robben Island, Salazar declares of the harm done to those referred to as "downwinders": "I'm still not sure I'm buying this Mulder and Scully crap about the government and nuclear tests that can harm its own people . . . I mean, this is America, for fuck's sake" (205). While *The Secret History of Las Vegas* opens with the story of downwinders, recounting the lethal radiation poisoning of Fire and Water's mother, the bulk of the novel sets its ethical attention elsewhere—that is, until the final pages, when the downwinder plot reemerges as the novel's ascendant concern. Water reveals that he is part of a direct action group committed to "eradication of dangerous military research in Nevada, Arizona, and Utah" (287). He murders the lead psychiatrist holding him in custody and blows up the facility, killing everyone inside.

With this twist, *The Secret History of Las Vegas* tells its predominantly US readership a series of three counter-stories. The first counter-story challenges the popular US self-concept that it is the world's guardian of humanitarian values and the bearer of international charity and gifts. (The book pointedly notes that in German the word "gift" means poison [220].) Abani instead depicts the scope of US violations of human rights as, quite literally, unsurpassed in global history. As Water would argue, US weapons of mass destruction are a threat to all. Because they are in principle indiscriminate they erase the distinction between friend and enemy, military and civilian, and war and peace. And as scholars and lawyers are arguing with increasing urgency, the US policy of maintaining nuclear weapons permanently ready and aimed at civilians is, straightforwardly, a policy of holding the world population hostage as a way of maintaining global political heft. As of this writing, the United States continues to refuse to adopt a "no first use" pledge.

US policy flagrantly violates international humanitarian law, which is based upon the moral and legal principle that civilians are hors de combat and must not be directly targeted in war. It is a policy that makes the United States in key ways an outsider to global order. Indeed, the United States became a signatory to the 1977 Geneva Protocols only after attaching the following, self-blinding reservation: "It is the understanding of the United States of America that the rules established by this protocol were not intended to have an effect on and do not regulate or prohibit the use of nuclear weapons."[52] Even with this gutting reservation, however, the United States has refused to ratify the protocols. (174 other states have ratified them.) In 1996, the International Court of Justice formally corrected the US "understanding" by clarifying that nuclear weapons violate the principles of international humanitarian law. Richard Rhodes, Pulitzer Prize–winning historian of nuclear weapons, summarizes the hypocrisy of US moral exceptionalism: "Why our elected leaders continue to believe that such genocidal weapons are legitimate and moral in our hands, but illegitimate and immoral in the hands of our enemies, rather than eradicating them from the earth, as we did smallpox, is yet another mystery."[53]

In its second counter-story, *The Secret History of Las Vegas* uses the downwinders plot to push back against representations of terrorism that have pervasively influenced US film and literature since 2001. Terrorism is a matter of targeting civilians—the very nature of US nuclear weapons—and the terrorists in the book are domestic rather than international.

Abani's third and final counter-story addresses the role of gender in rights representation. The beautiful body in need of rescue in *The Secret History of Las Vegas* is the body of Water; the indomitable person who engineers his escape is a woman. Elsewhere, Abani employs the trope of the beautiful female body under threat in order to subvert it, just as he uses the trope of US outrage at rights violations abroad to draw attention to its hypocrisy. Amplifying the contrast between bodies we cannot bear and those we cannot resist, Abani interweaves into the primary plot line a character who could very well have come from Shacochis or Bacigalupi: Asia, a rivetingly beautiful prostitute with a secret, painful past who, beneath her stern façade, yearns for love. As the assassin who beats her and considers murdering her puts it: "Asia had something that got under your skin very quickly, and not just because she was beautiful and could do things sexually he never knew were possible. There was a vulnerability to her that brought out the protective instinct in men. In a way he understood Sunil's fascination with her; too bad it felt like such a fucking cliché" (192).

Abani embraces the cliché. The vulnerable, beautiful female body is the origin and driver of narrative desire in the novel. In Abani's meta-textual setup, the criminal investigation that makes the story possible starts with a beautiful girl. Detective Salazar is tasked with looking into a series of homeless corpse piles—a crime that will likely be left as a cold case. But then he discovers a hauntingly lovely teenager in one of the piles. Salazar is driven, like the imagined reader, to follow her story and, in his heroic self-conception, to put her delicate, needful soul to rest. But as Abani points out through the voice of Salazar's therapist, his "desire had nothing to do with putting her to rest . . . It was really all about him" (101).

Abani closes the novel with Asia's ruminations on the way men like Salazar and Sunil use women's bodies as symbols and fantasies:

> Some johns come to empty themselves in your mirror, to peel away their own loss, until finally they see what they truly are . . . This kind of john can never love you back. Not in any real way, because not even you, with all the true gifts of the courtesan, can live for any length of time in the illusion that he has of you, wants of you, and even demands of you . . . The deeper danger, though, with this kind of john, is that the monster he sometimes glimpses in the mirror of you is so far away from what he can accept of himself . . . When the saint glimpses the monster, if his will is too weak, he turns not into the enlightened one but into the worst kind of violent man—the kind who will burn the world down. (311)

Asia's voice dominates the close of the novel. This choice seems, at first, discordant, given her relatively small share of narrative focus in all that comes before. But the questions Asia raises here—questions that, in Abani's depiction, Asia has unique insight into—are not only the primary underlying concern of *The Secret History of Las Vegas* but also, perhaps, of all human rights work. What is it that turns normal men into violent perpetrators? What makes a monster? Is there any way we can prevent it from happening?

Abani's answers to these questions tie together the key concerns discussed in this chapter, including the insistent and vivid representation of injured women in human rights, the imagination of global unity through triumphant cross-border heterosexual unions, the fetishization of norm-reinforcing bodies, and the discursive production of subjects to be saved. Discussing the latter, Wilcox argues that the category of the dependent, vulnerable subject functions to produce the autonomous, invulnerable (presumptively male) subject who "speaks on behalf of the human." This identity, in turn, produces "a constitutive other, an 'inhuman' subject": the perpetrator.[54] Abani's decision to end with Asia invokes this essentializing triptych of rights subjects, but only to destabilize it by undoing the strict segregation of "saint" and perpetrator. Abani's answer to the question raised above—How are monsters made?—defies any such simplifying identification of moral classes of persons. Abani offers instead individualizing, psychologistic models of identity that emphasize the possibility of multiple, conflicting, and even unconscious interior selves. This approach to understanding the other of the perpetrator is among the most common and powerful approaches used today to make sense of seemingly senseless violence. But as we shall see in Chapter 4, psychologism is most useful when it is contextualized through what is sometimes perceived to be its methodological opposite: structural and organizational analysis.

CHAPTER 4

Perpetrators in the Novel of Human Rights

THIS CHAPTER IS about perpetrators. That will make it somewhat unusual. Remarkably, perpetrators are less frequently the subject of analysis in human rights work than one would expect. Not long ago I was part of a public debate sponsored by a human rights network about "*whether, when,* and *how* to engage with perpetrators of human rights abuses."[1] I was first surprised by the "*whether,*" and then surprised again by the negative reaction I received from some who found offensive my proposed ideas for connecting and communicating with perpetrators. If we are to mitigate or prevent violence, I believe, it is essential for us to understand in the deepest possible way those who do violence. And it seems to me that what the novel offers, what it has always offered since Richardson's *Pamela*, is the opportunity to experience other minds in ways more complex and intimate than almost any other form of human communication and representation—more intimate even than many of our daily, real-world relationships. What I've learned from novels about perpetrators is as important, in its own way, as anything I've learned from my personal relationships with such men. So I want to make sure that my proposal that we take seriously the study of the human rights novel does not conclude without a serious look at the character of the perpetrator.

All that said, I will not begin with perpetrators just yet. I will explain why I'm starting aslant later, but for now I will just assert: before talking about perpetrators, it is important to talk about the nature of moral mistakes more generally.

Elaine Scarry has explained that there are two competing models for understanding how the discovery of moral wrongs can affect us. On the one hand, the shock of discovering we were blind to injustice in one place can dramatically increase our attentiveness to injustice in all locations. On the other hand, moral outrage can be exclusionary: sincere and intense focus on one category of violation can sometimes have the perverse effect of reducing our sensitivity to injustice elsewhere.[2] There are many real-world examples of such moral collateral damage. In her study of human rights and life narratives, Gillian Whitlock offers several dramatic cases, including a 2007 report on the welfare of children in the Northern Territory in Australia, *Little Children Are Sacred*, which prompted forceful intervention and policing of indigenous communities. "The trope of the suffering child," she writes, functioned "to legitimate intervention as well as reconciliation" and was readily appropriated into Australia's neocolonialist "campaigns to 'manage' indigeneity."[3]

The publication history of Ishmael Beah's *A Long Way Gone* is another example of the way moral focus and misdirection tend to pair—one uniquely important for US readers because it reveals how close to home this problem is, as close as the nearest coffee shop. *A Long Way Gone*, an autobiographical account of Beah's experience as a child soldier in Sierra Leone, has been rightly praised for its tremendous contribution to raising global awareness of child-soldiering. As Dave Eggers comments, Beah "finally brought the experience of child soldiers to mainstream America."[4] But the novel was able to do so only because Starbucks contracted to feature the book in its shops in a win-win trade arranged by Beah's agent. The book received instant global attention, turning Beah into the kind of international celebrity who could effect real change. And Starbucks's association with the ultimate virtuous cause—the protection of vulnerable children— distracted consumers from years of bad press alleging tax avoidance, anti-union campaigns, mistreatment of workers, misleading fair trade claims, and monopolistic bullying.

The end result remains morally complicated. Beah is an effective lobbyist for a range of international human rights organizations, from UNICEF to Human Rights Watch. He has also launched his own foundation, which has helped sponsor the education of more than 150 former child soldiers. Meanwhile, *Time* magazine reviews Beah's work by describing the child soldier as "the most sexy category" of war victim, and the "weaponized child" as a "great scene setter" for a Hollywood with a "weapons-grade crush on Africa."[5] As Katja Kurz writes:

> In an entertainment industry that targets "lost boys" for popular consumption, and where charismatic Beah is the "literary-humanitarian equivalent of a rock star," however, reality for the majority of former child soldiers often looks bleak, as many of them remain "hidden in plain sight" and overlooked by the media and by Hollywood due to their lack of education and cultural capital.[6]

As case after case in human rights writing reveals, even the most ethically urgent and internally self-conscious work must often make moral compromises if it hopes to reach broad audiences. In previous chapters I showed how the novel of human rights makes such compromises and also thematizes the process of making them. In Alarcón's *Lost City Radio*, for instance, Norma's radio program is able to maintain its strategic pressure against tyranny because of the populist power of its high ratings. To maintain these high ratings, however, the producer needs a steady supply of satisfying drama, which he can only reliably achieve by hiring actors to deliver "melodramatic" (69) false testimony and by staging fake reunions with the disappeared. The reunions help maintain national focus on the crisis of the disappeared, but they are nonetheless ways of quite literally not seeing, of putting somebody else in the place of the injured. Notably, Alarcón's next novel, *At Night We Walk in Circles*, begins with a quotation from Guy Debord, best known for his treatise *Society of the Spectacle*. As popularized by Greil Marcus, *Society of the Spectacle* has become a touchstone reference for anxiety over the way ideas and persons are commodified and falsified by large-scale media's market of desire.

One of the most dramatic examples today of this moral collateral damage can be found in US representations of torture. In 2004, CBS's *60 Minutes II* broadcast a report revealing now notorious images of US torture in Iraq. Shortly after, Seymour Hersh published his detailed article on US torture in the *New Yorker.* That same year, Edwidge Danticat published *The Dew Breaker,* Walter Mosley published *The Man in My Basement,* Vyvyane Loh published *Breaking the Tongue,* Susan Choi's *The Foreign Student* was reprinted, and Ha Jin published *War Trash*—all US books essentially worrying about torture. This was no coincidence. By 2004, US military forces had been aggressively prosecuting the global war on terrorism for three years; Guantánamo Bay had been up and running for two years; and popular media coverage of US torture had been available for at least one year. The year 2004 was in some ways one of the acutest periods of US anxiety around detention and torture, a moment when stories that might otherwise have been minimized or ignored became irreversibly visible.

In 2012, however, the literary marketplace registered a significant shift with the publication of Kevin Powers's *Yellow Birds.* A fictional account of the war in Iraq written by a US Army veteran, *Yellow Birds* was a sensation. It was a finalist for the National Book Award, it won the PEN/Hemingway Award for First Fiction, and it won the Guardian First Book Award. It was celebrated in a range of reviews as the first great novel to come out of the US Gulf Wars and was compared to Hemingway's war novels, *All Quiet on the Western Front*, and even the *Iliad*. Reviews and discussions of the book focused on the way it captured the new mood of the nation, articulating the United States' rising and much-deserved guilt over its neglectful treatment of veterans from its overextended, all-volunteer army. That same year, the Department of Veterans Affairs released its devastating *Suicide Data Report.* "Suicides Outpacing War Deaths for Troops," the *New York Times* announced. "22 Vets Commit Suicide Every Day," *USA Today* reported.[7]

In a review of Powers and his contemporaries, Roy Scranton argues that the "trauma hero" they collectively depict serves a secondary "scapegoat function." It alleviates "national bloodguilt by substituting the victim of trauma, the soldier, for the victim of violence, the enemy." "By focusing so insistently on the psychological trauma American soldiers have had to endure," he writes, "we allow ourselves to forget the death and destruction those very soldiers are responsible for."[8] But the psychological need Powers fills goes deeper even than that. What went unspoken in all the discussion around *Yellow Birds* was torture, despite the fact that the tragic center of the novel is an act of torture—notably, not of an Iraqi prisoner, but rather a US soldier. In *Yellow Birds*, the tortured US soldier displaces the hooded Iraqi detainee. Sincere, overdue, and morally grounded attention to the injured veteran draws upon and then reconfigures torture sentiment, directing it inward, toward the United States as victim. Just like torture images did in 2004, *Yellow Birds* was able to catch the imagination of the public in 2012 because it articulated a major shift in collective cultural self-perception. But now, the shift was a reaction *against* the images that saturated 2004, a shift away from guilty introspection about our responsibilities to noncitizens.[9]

Perhaps not coincidentally, the other major literary sensation of 2012 was *The Orphan Master's Son*—another book prominently about torture. While the victim in this case was not a US citizen, the perpetrator regime, North Korea, was the symbolic, axis-of-evil opposite of the United States. The same characterization is true of Dalia Sofer's successful debut in 2007, *The Septembers of Shiraz*, which focuses on torture committed during the Iranian Revolution. Sofer's account of abuses committed against the Jewish population during and after the revolution is lyrically powerful and, by any standard, morally necessary. But as Michael Richardson comments, all telling involves a certain kind of untelling:

> While American novelists have written books during the war on terror that deal with torture, they have largely focused on past events in other nations—Korea, China, Haiti, Latin America. Few have sought to address the post-9/11 US detention and torture . . . For the writers of mass-market thrillers, the war on terror has simply become the backdrop for action and intrigue, much like those of earlier decades used the Cold War to provide weighty scenery and the appearance of moral depth. So too the genre of "human rights bestsellers"—books such as

Khaled Hosseini's *The Kite Runner* (2003) or Ayan Hirsi Ali's autobiography *Infidel* (2007)—which reaffirm humanitarian ideals,
Western values, and liberal subjectivity, rather than critiquing
or questioning their constitutive role in the war on terror.[10]

Richardson notes that one of the few novels to have dealt centrally
with US-sponsored torture in its global war is Janette Turner Hospital's *Orpheus Lost*. The novel, as Hospital has explained, is about
what happens when ordinary people get caught up in extraordinary
political events. Leela and Mishka, a couple living in Cambridge,
Massachusetts, become targets of US counterterrorism networks
after a terrorist bombing in the subway. Leela is interrogated and
threatened. Mishka, through a complicated series of events, is detained
and transferred to Baghdad, where he is brutally tortured. Hospital is unsparing in her critique of US GWOT violence, offering
harrowing accounts of mass torture of non-Western citizens. Emphasizing that she is a member of Amnesty International, Hospital
in one interview explains that the novel is inspired by a moral question: "How do you balance human rights with legitimate means of
maintaining national security? To me there's a line you just don't
cross. Although we feel as an individual we can do precious little on
a world scale, I feel every human being is accountable for decisions
made in our name by a government. To me that is a passionately personal question, not just a big social one."[11]

The primary narrative focus of *Orpheus Lost* is the disappearance
and torture of Mishka and, perhaps just as significantly, the suffering
this causes Leela. Leela is the novel's emotional transition figure.
White US readers, it is hoped, will empathize with the beautiful white
US citizen. In turn, it is hoped that this empathy will help them identify with Mishka, the Australian of Lebanese-Hungarian descent,
whose father became a jihadist. And ideally, these two connections will help readers identify with the masses tortured in Baghdad.
While not quite a Starbucks compromise, this chain of affect is nonetheless a narrative tactic that plays to the lowest common denominator of moral imagination. It runs the same risk that so many of the
texts previously discussed run: after the book is put down, some
bodies will be remembered and some won't.

I signaled at the end of Chapter 3 that I would focus here, at the close, on perpetrators of crimes against humanity. The possibilities of moral misdirection I have been tracking above no doubt seem distantly related to this aim. But from the very first moment I started writing this chapter, I felt it was important, if only for myself, to begin by thinking about the ease and even the felt virtue of falling into moral blindness. Soon, I will be discussing a protagonist as horrific as any in recent literary history, the SS officer Maximilian Aue. Thinking about the men he represents, I feel it is important to affirm the moral conviction that made Arendt declare, when imagining passing judgment on the Nazi bureaucrat Adolf Eichmann: "We find that no one, that is, no member of the human race, can be expected to want to share the earth with you."[12] At the same time, I want to be careful not to allow singular instances of monstrosity to create for us a Manichaean dichotomy of us, the well-intentioned, versus them, the perpetrators.

I have spent much time talking with, and written at length elsewhere about, those who have committed crimes against humanity. I do not wish to excuse what is typically, and quite justly, described as their evil. But I have also come to believe that the steps toward such atrocity are often ones that begin with our virtues: our desire to make things better, to shelter the people and ideas we love, and to belong to something bigger than our petty selves. As Kazuo Ishiguro allegorizes it in his rights / fantasy hybrid novel *The Buried Giant*, our capacity for love and peaceful coexistence is separated only by a thin veil of mist from the resentment and fear that drive genocide. The monstrosity of the perpetrator shouldn't blind us. Most of us, under the right circumstances, are capable of becoming the moral others we collectively despise. I have at times been a touch overinsistent in my public writing with this claim (and have, ironically, received my fair share of physical threats from readers who found it offensive). Nonetheless, I believe that keeping such cautions at the front of our collective consciousness may be one of the best ways of preventing them from coming true. Often—not always, but often—the last people to think of themselves as perpetrators are perpetrators. This is as true for us as for others.

So to return, as promised at the end of Chapter 3, to Abani, and to his investigation into what turns men into monsters. *The Secret*

History of Las Vegas offers more than one way of making legible the psyche of monstrous moral others. The first is through something of a stock character. Eugene is an intellectually self-aware apartheid torturer who explains at length, and with sociopathic lack of affect, that he does what he does in the service of a greater good. Responding to Sunil's charge that he has been manipulated into doing apartheid's dirty work, Eugene declares:

> Unlike men like you and even Dante here who have wandered into the dark forest of error unknowingly and who now desperately want to return to their joy, kept from it by your own demons, your ferocious beasts of worldliness, I came here to this hell by choice. Those beasts that are your terrors are my constant companions, sometimes my pets, sometimes my leaders, but never ever the source of terror. I have no terror, you see. I'm not like Dante, who has come upon the sign that asks all who enter to abandon hope. I came here to find hope. I know that I have done bad things, that I must continue to do bad things, but I do so for the ideal. For the utopia that this land was and will remain—we drove the blacks from it and we drove the British from it, and I will be damned if I let any Afrikaner destroy it. Do you understand? (243)

Eugene has a parallel in the United States, Doctor Brewster, who appears briefly to justify his programs of murder and torture in the name of scientific pursuit. "In my experience," he says, "men of science—true men of science, mark you—are like unto the gods" (24). Eugene and Brewster embody two important and common psychological features of perpetrators. They see their actions as serving a greater good, and they have a narcissistic sense of their own importance. But these men are also clearly, for Abani, the least interesting cases to examine. Abani is much more interested in the hidden monster, the monster we never saw coming, the monster that is perhaps latent in each of us.

The Secret History of Las Vegas closes with a truly surprising revelation. Water has been pretending for his entire life that his conjoined twin Fire is highly intelligent and articulate while Water is severely austistic, when, in fact, Fire is brain-dead, a nightmare carnival ventriloquism act. Sunil reacts with instant alarm, concluding that if Water could live behind such a façade for his entire life, he must be a dangerous psychopath. No other personality structure could maintain such deep deception for so long a time. But as Asia emphasizes in her final reflections on the johns who see themselves as saints, who hide the "monster" (311) inside with performances of shallow kindness to the women they pay, many men live by denying the truth of what they are. Indeed, Sunil's characterization of Water's performance of identity bears important similarities to his own. He wishes to be the saint who loves and protects the vulnerable woman, but he can maintain this façade for himself and the world only by forever hiding the most important facts about who he is and what he has done.

Sunil, arguably, has lived a lie as long and as disassociating as any imaginable. When he began his collaboration with the apartheid regime, he did so hoping he could reduce its barbarity and maintain his integrity in the process. But by the end, Sunil is morally emptied out, defined by an act of complicity so appalling that it determines everything else that follows in his life. In one of the novel's most brutal scenes, Eugene explains to Sunil's lover, while Sunil sits next to her, how she will be tortured using a medieval device called the Pear. The passage that follows relies heavily upon the exploitative device of imagining desirable and violated female bodies:

> You see, it's quite ingenious really. You insert the pear into someone's mouth, and then you twist the bottom here until it begins to open. You keep twisting it and pretty soon it breaks the teeth, dislocates the jaw, even begins to rip the cheeks apart. Of course, the trick is to do it little by little, pausing occasionally to let the victim catch their breath while you wait for the confession you want . . . If you go at it long enough, you will eventually kill the victim, but only after a very long time and pain that is unimaginable, even for me. Now, the great thing about this, as I found out once, is that it works on any human orifice. Any. (229–230)

"How Sunil gets to be the hero of this story is the novel's most complicated tension," the *Washington Post* asserts in its review. "He's an odd man to root for, his hands soaked with blood as they are."[13] Abani's concern with the evil done by good men like Sunil (or, at least, "ordinary men," in Christopher Browning's phrase) has been a point of furious contention ever since Arendt declared in 1963 that the lesson she learned from the trial of Eichmann—who boasted that he would "jump into my grave laughing" knowing he had helped organize "the death of five million Jews"—was the lesson of the *"banality of evil."* "One cannot extract any diabolical or demonic profundity from Eichmann," she explained. "The trouble with Eichmann was precisely that so many were like him, and that the many were neither perverted nor sadistic, that they were, and still are, terribly and terrifyingly normal."[14] Arendt's claim, then and now, is controversial. In a recent sociological reassessment, Abram de Swaan resuscitates the long-standing charge, dating back to Saul Bellow's novel *Mr. Sammler's Planet* (1970), that Arendt's "catchy phrase" is not only an inaccurate description of Eichmann, whom Bellow and de Swaan alike see as diabolical, but also a contributor to morally pernicious worldviews. "The isolation, deportation, extreme exploitation, and final extermination of millions of people is not banal," de Swaan writes. "Calling it that is frivolous."[15]

While the novel of human rights has focused with greatest frequency upon the interior states of witnesses and survivors, it has also struggled to take up Arendt's implicit challenge: namely, to understand the worst of perpetrators not as demonic others who will perpetually remain psychologically opaque, but rather as people who are like us, or could be like us, or, at least, could be understood by us. Perpetrators have appeared as central characters in a range of rights novels, including novels about state tyrants, like Mario Vargas Llosa's *The Feast of the Goat* (2000) and Anchee Min's *Becoming Madame Mao* (2000); novels featuring career torturers, like Elvira Orphée's *El Angel's Last Conquest* (1984), Jonathan Dee's *The Liberty Campaign* (1993), Adam Johnson's *The Orphan Master's Son*, Edwidge Danticat's *The Dew Breaker*, and Viet Thanh Nguyen's *The Sympathizer*; and novels about children and young men turned by war into killers, like

Héctor Tobar's *The Tattooed Soldier* (1998), Uzodinma's Iweala's *Beasts of No Nation* (2006), Abani's *Song for Night* (2007), and Laleh Khadivi's *The Age of Orphans* (2009).

Part of the special fascination of perpetrator novels is the shock we experience when those who can take or grant life with a word, who seem to embody the power of gods—like the torturer from Thomas Glave's "The Torturer's Wife," who is only ever referred to by the capitalized "He" or "Him"—are revealed to be as frail as we are. As Harold Rosenberg writes of the Nuremberg trials, it is disorienting to see perpetrators reduced from monstrous grandiosity to people "just like other people":

> The real criminals have been carried off by history and will never return. In their place has been left a group of aging stand-ins, sick and trembling with fear. Judgment will be pronounced on a round-up of impersonators, a collection of dummies borrowed from the waxworks museum . . . "But, ah!" cried a voice from the balcony at the Eichmann trial in Jerusalem, "you should have seen him in his colonel's uniform." Yes, the trial is about that other, the creature empowered to dispatch millions to destruction, not this pathetic organism anxiously following the proceedings through his earphones.[16]

Regimes that seem to transcend law and time and perpetrators who can act without limits—we believe that this is the very stuff of power. But as Arendt counterintuitively explains, violence is the opposite of power, and this is precisely the point of the perpetrator novel. "Rule by sheer violence comes into play where power is being lost," she writes. "Power and violence are opposites; where the one rules absolutely, the other is absent. Violence appears where power is in jeopardy, but left to its own course it ends in power's disappearance . . . Violence can destroy power; it is utterly incapable of creating it."[17] Part of the satisfaction of perpetrator novels, then, is the narrative satisfaction of seeing what happens to those who feel so powerful that they believe they will never have to face the consequences of their actions; that they will never have to account for, explain, or hide their names; that they can forever reject the justice plot. Using the case study of Trujillo fiction, Richard Patterson explains that the satisfaction that comes from demystifying tyrants (Vargas Llosa depicting Trujillo's inability to control his bladder, for instance) isn't just part of an individual reading experience. It is part of a deliberate, even ritualistic, social act. "Danticat, Alvarez, and Vargas Llosa all knew that to kill him was not enough," Patterson writes. "He *had* to be brought back to life, so that he could be unwritten and rewritten, unmasked and definitively disempowered through the strength and integrity of their art."[18]

Perpetrator portraits span a wide range, from young to old, misguided to sociopathic, sympathetic to repugnant. But if there is a single idea that unites the conception of perpetrators throughout the genre, it is this: there is nothing we hate more than our own shame embodied in others. At the macroscopic level, this principle manifests itself across perpetrator novels as a recurring concern with interior enemies: the anti-Communist "enemy within" that must be eliminated from the social body in *Becoming Madame Mao* (166), or the traitorous "germs" (70) inside the "organism" of Special Section in *El Angel's Last Conquest*. At the level of individual psychology, such perpetrator violence is typically modeled as fear of ethnic or gender contamination. *The Age of Orphans* tells the story of Reza, a Kurdish boy conscripted into the Shah's army. Reza is uniquely brutal to Kurdish villagers, outdoing even his most violent peers, because he is ashamed of the "dirty" Kurdish boy he sees hidden inside himself. "He *has* kicked and killed his first Kurd and that is right as it *was* the Kurd boy in himself that he kicked and killed to die and be dead and now *that* is clean and in order and erased." Reza's crimes against women are depicted as following the same logic. In one of the novel's more appalling scenes, Reza breast-feeds while raping a young Kurdish mother. In so doing, he symbolically murders his own mother—from whom he breast-fed into early adolescence—proving that he is "the son of a yet undefined nation of Iran" and not of a contaminating woman.[19] The perpetrator of *The Tattooed Soldier* has a similarly self-hating relationship to his Mayan heritage.[20] And in *The Kindly Ones*, Jonathan Littell uses this psychic model to account even for the collective genocidal violence of Nazi Germany. "By killing the Jews," one character declares, "we wanted to kill ourselves, kill the Jew within us, kill that which in us resembles the idea we have of the Jew."[21]

Arguably, *The Kindly Ones* is the contemporary novel that has committed itself most comprehensively to examining the interior state of perpetrators, and it is with this novel that I shall conclude. *The Kindly Ones* is an ambitious and wildly uneven book, sprawling toward 1,000 pages with paragraph breaks as infrequent as water stations at a marathon. It tells the story of SS officer Maximilian Aue from the early days of the war through the Battle of Stalingrad and the fall of Berlin, with extended reflections upon Aue's childhood and young adulthood.

While the novel's controversial content merits extended discussion, its reception is also a topic of interest in its own right. Published originally in French, the novel won that nation's most prestigious literary award, the Prix Goncourt, and sold over one million copies across Europe. Littell, a US citizen who grew up in the United States, had previously been rejected twice when applying to become a citizen of France. After the book's success, France offered Littell citizenship based upon a clause in the national code allowing citizenship for those whose "meritorious actions contribute to the glory of France"—easily one of the best book reviews an author could hope for. In Anglophone nations and Germany, however, *The Kindly Ones* was met with outright derision by prominent literary reviewers. The *New Yorker* called it an "unintentionally comic" caricature. The *New York Times* described it as "a middlebrow historical epic gone willfully weird" and "a sheer test of endurance." And the *Literary Review* gave it the "Bad Sex in Fiction Award," declaring that its sex scenes were "pretentious," "like much of the whole" novel.[22]

Recasting the Holocaust as part bildungsroman, part picaresque— and, within the genre, as part justice plot and part escape plot—*The Kindly Ones* nearly bursts at the seams with all of its conceptually interlocked, even palimpsestic parts. It begins by presenting itself as an Arendtian study of the banality of evil. "I am a man like other men," Aue insists at the opening. "I am a man like you. I tell you I am just like you!" (24). He works hard at his job, worries over career ambition and office politics, struggles in his love life, feels lonely, happy, empathetic, frightened. But overlaid onto this model of banal evil is an alternative model of refined evil. *The Kindly Ones*, in other words, presents two challenges to moral common sense. First, it claims that evils that seem mysteriously, demonically transcendent are committed by the most ordinary, least imaginative, least *distinct* of people. And second, it claims that evils that seem ugly, animalistic, and ignorant are committed by the most sophisticated and thoughtful of people.

Max is a highly educated lawyer. He enjoys classical music, especially Bach. He reads Stendhal as he invades France, discusses Kant with Eichmann, and carries his Flaubert along even as he drops everything else during a panicked retreat from advancing Russian forces. His conversations are peppered with references to exemplars of classical and enlightened Germany, including Friedrich Schiller, Friedrich Nietzsche, and Bach, all of whom lived at one point in Weimar—a city nestled up against Buchenwald concentration camp, which Aue visits as part of his job to "rationalize" the management of Jewish slave labor. "How was such a horror possible?" Zygmunt Bauman asks, ventriloquizing the shock that many experience trying to reconcile intellectual refinement with grave moral stupidity. "How could it happen in the heart of the most civilized part of the world?"[23] *The Kindly Ones* takes this question seriously. The novel invokes, and subjects to intense pressure, a loosely circulating model of personhood that sees unity in the desires for aesthetic and moral beauty. This model has its loose origins in Wordsworthian Romantic ethics, which connected aesthetic pleasure to universal sympathy, and in the ancient Greek view that dramatic poetry and philosophical inquiry were, in Martha Nussbaum's words, "framed by, seen as ways of pursuing, a single and general question: namely, how human beings should live."[24]

Littell reconciles the seeming paradoxes above through what might best be described as a bureaucratic narrative. Evil, in this conceptual model, is not only *not* mysterious; it is not even personal. It is a matter of role morality and bureaucratic rationality. As an account of evil, *The Kindly Ones* offers a grindingly realistic memoir of life in a complex organization. While the world burns around them, Nazi administrators engage in petty office politics, write reports, work through interdepartmental rivalries, and seek advancement in their suborganizations. They are negative exemplars of Max Weber's pre–World War I organizational sociology, which characterizes the state as a monopoly over violence that, through increasing bureaucratization, creates an "iron cage" of rationalized coercion, reducing human imagination to goal-oriented calculation, efficiency, and control. Indeed, Aue seems to derive self-esteem from his reduction to naked instrumentalism. In the second half of the novel, he is tasked with finding the optimal balance between the political goal of eliminating European Jews and the economic goal of maximizing industrial output from Jewish slave labor. As a man dedicated to rational organizational planning, Aue takes pride in not allowing himself to be distracted by the nonrational concerns of, on the one hand, anti-Semitism, and, on the other hand, empathy. "With well-trained Aryan supervisors, and a rational, modern division and organization of labor," he explains repeatedly, "we could have very good results" (583).

Importantly, morality is not excluded from the iron cage. Any bureaucracy that attempted such a coercive reworking of daily, lived personality would be unsustainable. Morality is, instead, integrated into the primary organizational method of bureaucracies: specialization. Much like the Fordist factory assembly line, complex organizations work best when individuals limit their focus to particular tasks. While division of labor is a matter of efficiency in generating a product—repetition and focus are, effectively, the equivalent of expertise—it is also a matter of reinforcing behavioral control over workers. All bureaucracies—but especially bureaucracies that manage violence—seek to minimize internal resistance to larger organizational goals. Role specialization eliminates ethical frictions by insulating individuals from responsibility for anything outside the narrow compass of their prescribed actions.

In its most common manifestation, such role morality is a matter of passing the buck. Aue is tasked with improving the effectiveness of slave labor by decreasing the Jewish death rate. Whenever he discovers an especially lethal form of neglect, he is rebuffed with the same morally self-comforting excuse: "Not my job" (618, 856). In its more extreme, interiorized manifestations, role morality amounts to moral blindness. Sturmbannführer Dr. Morgen is tasked with investigating "diversions of food, medicine, or property" (603) in the concentration camps. He, with Aue, is morally outraged to discover widespread evidence that prisoners are being robbed and murdered. But the outrage is a matter of a very specific *role* morality:

> "I suspect that must give rise to colossal misappropriations and thefts. We were alerted by a package sent from the KL by military post: because of its unusual weight, it was opened; inside, they found three chunks of dental gold, big as fists, sent by a camp nurse to his wife. I calculated that such a quantity of gold represents more than a hundred thousand dead." I let out an exclamation. "And imagine!" He went on. "That's what a single man could divert. When we've finished here, I'll go set up a commission in Auschwitz." (603)

The Jews must be killed, he concedes, but not to cover up embezzlement. That would be "a crime" (597).

Role morality excuses you from considering moral violations outside your purview. It is not your responsibility when it is not your job. But as Aue explains, it is also not your responsibility when it *is* your job:

> Just as, according to Marx, the worker is alienated from the product of his labor, in genocide or total war in its modern form the perpetrator is alienated from the product of his actions. This holds true even for the man who places a gun to the head of another man and pulls the trigger. For the victim was led there by other men, his death was decided on by yet others, and the shooter knows that he is only the last link in a very long chain, and that he doesn't have to ask himself any more questions than does a member of a firing squad who in civilian life executes a man duly sentenced under the law. The shooter knows that it's chance that has appointed him to shoot, his comrade to guard the cordon, and a third man to drive the truck; at most he could try to change places with the guard or driver. (18–19)

Discussing early Nazi euthanasia programs, he continues:

The nurse didn't kill anyone, she only undressed and calmed the patients, ordinary tasks in her profession. The doctor didn't kill anyone, either, he merely confirmed a diagnosis according to criteria established by higher authorities. The worker who opened the gas spigot, the man closest to the actual act of murder in both time and space, was fulfilling a technical function under the supervision of his superiors and doctors . . . Why should the worker assigned to the gas chamber be guiltier than the worker assigned to the boilers, the garden, the vehicles? The same goes for every facet of this immense enterprise. (19)

Thus a soldier posted to a concentration camp rather than the front understands that "chance alone makes him a killer rather than a hero" (592). Thus it is a matter of moral luck that Rudolf Höss became commandant of Auschwitz rather than, as his father had planned, a priest. And thus the citizens of Rawa Ruska and Lemberg, "through the horrible smell and the smoke," "chatted, argued, wrote letters, spread rumors, told jokes" (587).

Perversely, the further you swerve away from your principles in upholding the system, the more powerful the ethical claim you can make. As Aue repeatedly explains, he and other Nazis must continually exemplify loyalty and moral strength by transcending their normal human empathy, their inescapably human aversion to witnessing suffering. Aue stays awake, troubled, "thinking of the Jews." But as a servant of the Reich he cannot allow himself the easy escape of succumbing to his more human, empathic inclinations. "It was a question of rigor," he declares (43). Robert Jay Lifton finds a similar, grandiose self-pity in the Nazi doctors at Auschwitz, who experienced the burden of their task as an "ordeal" of self-sacrifice for "the immortal Germanic people."[25]

Through Aue's evil-as-heroic-burden, Littell offers a plausible vision of the interior experience of role morality. In the character of Eichmann, Littell provides a flip side psychological model, substituting pettiness for grandiloquence. Eichmann is neither malevolent nor grandiose. He is, instead, defined by the very common, basic human need for recognition. "It was the same to him whether or not the Jews were killed, the only thing that counted, for him, was to show what he could do, to prove his worth, and also to use the abilities he had developed" (782). Eichmann is entirely self-focused, as if the shrinking of moral horizons that role morality enables finds its logical end point in the mere self as full compass of concern. In a typical moment, Eichmann displays his envy for Aue's combat decorations, noting with self-pity that he was given an Iron Cross "really just so I'd have something" (555). Littell's Eichmann is Arendt's Eichmann, a man whose stultifying "lack of imagination" meant that he *"never realized what he was doing,"* in Arendt's controversial characterization (287).

Chester Barnard, an organizational theorist prominent over the war years, held the view that bureaucracies are "cooperative systems where the organizational and individual objective must coincide."[26] But as Littell reveals through Eichmann, the incentive system designed to bring about this synchronization can in complex organizations lead to terrifying myopia. How else to explain, Littell asks, the "delirium of murder" at war's end, when "functionaries and specialists" like Eichmann remained self-destructively focused upon mobilizing resources not for the war effort but rather for "massacring Jews" (780)? Eichmann is intent upon performing well in his appointed job because, as Littell depicts it, he simply cannot envision anything else. As one of his comrades criticizes: "He's good at what he does, within the limits of his specialization . . . But he has no imagination. He is incapable of reacting to events outside his field, of evolving. He built his career on Jews, on the destruction of Jews, and for that he is very efficient. But once we've done with the Jews—or else if the wind shifts, if the time comes no longer to destroy Jews—then he'll be unable to adapt, he'll be lost" (770, 793).

For Arendt, Eichmann's moral vacuity is linked to damaged language. Eichmann's testimony during his trial was, as the Israeli judges characterized it, "empty talk." "Officialese," he said in inauthentic self-deprecation, "is my only language." Arendt expands:

> Eichmann, despite his rather bad memory, repeated word for word the same stock phrases and self-invented clichés (when he did succeed in constructing a sentence of his own, he repeated

it until it became a cliché) each time he referred to an incident or event of importance to him. Whether writing his memoirs in Argentina or in Jerusalem, whether speaking to the police examiner or the court, what he said was always the same, expressed in the same words. The longer one listened to him, the more obvious it became that his inability to speak was closely connected with an inability to *think*, namely, to think from the standpoint of somebody else. No communication was possible with him, not because he lied but because he was surrounded by the most reliable of all safeguards against the words and the presence of others, and hence against reality as such.[27]

Importantly, Arendt's Eichmann—like Littell's, who is drawn from Arendt—is neither an aberration nor a symptom of bureaucratic dysfunction. Eichmanns are what bureaucracies require; Eichmanns are what bureaucracies regularly create. "He wasn't the only one, this man, everyone was like him," Aue says. "I too was like him, and you too, in his place, you would have been like him" (783). The monsters of the Reich, *The Kindly Ones* argues, are institutionally created. And while their institution represents a historic, pathological extreme, it nonetheless reveals moral hazards inherent to all complex organizations. Most dangerously, because bureaucracies control lexical frames and channels of communication, they can also control behavior, and can do so without the appearance of coercion. "*Man lebt in seiner Sprache*," Aue explains. "You live in your language" (632). Thus the crimes he and others committed felt not like actions but rather like "brute realities, either already present or waiting for their inevitable accomplishment" (631).

Part of what makes *The Kindly Ones* as long as it is—indeed, at times, "a sheer test of endurance"—is that Littell is painstaking in revealing the particular and sometimes minute procedures behind this abstraction: *Man lebt in seiner Sprache*. "Tall" organizations like the Nazi military, for instance, are capable of functioning effectively only because they actively filter out information as it passes upward through the chain of command, converting the fog of war into concise, actionable packages of data. Sociologists James March and Herbert Simon call this process, which they find in all complex organizations, "uncertainty absorption." They note that such filtering can lead to informational dysfunction, emphasizing that in bureaucracies "the recipient of a communication is severely limited in his ability to judge its correctness."[28] Charles Perrow expands upon their field-defining work by explaining that this bureaucratic disciplining of language not only streamlines decision making but also expands domination over individuals by limiting thought. Discussing uncertainty absorption, as well as the development of organizational vocabularies and the sedimentation of communication channels, Perrow writes:

> Such mechanisms affect organizational behavior in the following ways: they limit information content and flow, thus controlling the premises available for decisions; they set up expectations so as to highlight some aspects of the situation and play down others; they limit the search for alternatives when problems are confronted, thus ensuring more predictable and consistent solutions; they indicate the threshold levels as to when a danger signal is being emitted (thus reducing the occasions for decision making and promoting satisficing rather than optimizing behavior); they achieve coordination of effort by selecting certain kinds of work techniques and schedules. Note the extent to which behavior is shaped, or controlled, without reference to conventional items of rules and commands. In most organizational theory, the discussion of such "latent" or unobtrusive means of control of behavior applies primarily to professional roles and the reliance on professional training, standards, and expectations and to informal group pressures.[29]

The Kindly Ones catalogs example after example of cognitive premise setting through language control. As an information gatherer—negatively modeled as a "snitch" through the *Sicherheitsdienst* (207, 614)—Aue is a conduit connecting the field of war to various access points on the decision tree. He sees what kind of information is generated, how it is processed, and where it might be blocked. In most cases, he draws attention to the way bureaucratization of information leads to inefficiencies. Detail-obscuring practices of uncertainty absorption mean that, for instance, German troops are given boots that fit them, even though those on the front report that it would be better to give troops boots two sizes too large, as the Russians do, so as to accommodate swelling from frost and allow room for insulating straw and newspaper. What is most important to note in this example is that the resulting dysfunction—when winter comes, countless German soldiers have their toes amputated—is neither an anomaly nor a contradiction of organizational goals. Rather, the dysfunction follows necessarily from the organization's primary aim, like collateral damage. In this case, the Nazi bureaucracy's primary aim is the aim of controlling thought, which here requires filtering out any information that might raise questions about the Führer's vision of a quick conquest of Russia, completed well before the onset of a winter that would require oversized boots.

Early in the novel, Aue learns the lesson of restricting information that challenges established decision-making premises. He is tasked with anticipating the French reaction to the Führer's planned invasion of Poland. The information he gathers is "pessimistic, but lucid." France, he concludes, will perceive such expansionism as a threat to its vital interests and will go to war. Meanwhile, his friend Thomas writes a contrary report, telling his superiors "what they want to hear": that French industrialists and the military will oppose the war and successfully persuade the government to "bow before the fait accompli" (58). Thomas turns out to be wrong but is promoted; Aue turns out to be right but is "left to vegetate in Berlin" (58). Littell thus presents the Nazi bureaucracy as a case study in organizational inertia, in which previously established goals set the frame for interpreting and describing new information, which then further reinforces the previously established goals.

Example after example accumulates in the novel. Aue finds evidence that field commanders are inflating the numbers of eliminated Jewish civilians, for instance, both because they wish to give command the kind of information it wants to hear and because "bureaucratic habits" cause agencies to "get fixated on some number, no one really knows why, and then this number is taken up and repeated as fact, without any criticism or modification in time" (463). As Littell reveals, the overarching effect of these thousands of instances of organizational inertia can be disastrous. It inhibits independent thought, radicalizes organizations by disconnecting them from external perspectives and moral reference points, and renders them vulnerable to moral catastrophe by transforming goals into, effectively, fates. As Aue puts it when describing Eichmann's crimes against humanity, "Once the decision was made, it had to be seen through to the end" (570).

The Nazi bureaucracy's assault on language is most clearly revealed in the practice of refusing to name. Trying to explain how he and others became what they became—"there was a lot of talk, after the war, in trying to explain what had happened, about inhumanity" (589)—Aue draws frequent attention to silence and euphemism. He points to the power of Nazi *Spachregelungen*—which translates roughly to "convention of speech," in the sense of a language regime with message discipline—by listing key redescriptors of genocide: "*Sonderbehandlung* (special treatment), *abtransportiert* (transported onward), *entsprechend behandelt* (treated appropriately), *Wohnsitzverlegung* (change of domicile), or *Executivmassnahmen* (executive measures)" (631). Aue notes that he does not discuss his work with his intimate companion, Helene, citing the importance of "tact" (762). Elsewhere, he refuses to explain directly that women and children are executed in "work" camps, saying only, "We don't keep the women, the elderly, or the children" (653). Just so, his colleague Döll avoids directly naming his task—euthanizing their own wounded troops—describing it as "special operations" and "special measures." "Between us, we say T-four" (588), Döll says. Aue writes:

> This tendency spread to all our bureaucratic language, our *bürokratisches Amtsdeutsch*, as my colleague Eichmann would say: in correspondence, in speeches too, passive constructions dominated: "it has been decided that . . . ," "The Jews have been conveyed to the special treatment," "this difficult task has been carried out," and so things were done all by themselves, no one ever did anything, no one acted, they were actions without actors, which is always reassuring. (631)

Passive constructions, misdirection, clichés, and euphemism— these are all silences achieved through words. They are, so to speak, the lexical equivalent of role morality. They radically reduce the scope of language's responsibilities and deliberately strip away moral context, unburdening language of the requirement to bear clear and full meaning. Language pathologized thus becomes, in the end, sound, as physiologically quieting as a melody and as coercive as a shout. Acquiescence replaces interpretation. Ruminating over the "streaming beauty" of the German word for the "Final Solution," Endlösung, Aue asks: "How could one resist the seduction of such a word? It would have been as inconceivable as resisting the word *obey*, the word *serve*, the word *law*" (631).

One of the reasons *The Kindly Ones* was lambasted by US critics is that everything I have just analyzed—the hundreds of pages that develop a persuasive portrait of Arendtian evil—is undone by several hundred other pages that build a different, even incompatible, model. For however often Aue depicts himself as an ordinary man, and however often Littell maps out the structural conditions that promote terrifyingly banal evil, Aue is also, to be blunt, the caricature of an evil Nazi villain—that is, "evil" pronounced with a long, drawn-out "e." Aue is decidedly not ordinary. Independently of his participation in genocide, he is a serial killer, murdering a random pianist, a casual lover, and his closest friend. When he murders his mother in a psychotic break, it is depicted not as a result of war trauma but rather as the natural end point of his lifelong emotional dysregulation. He has an incestuous affair with his sister when they are children, engaging almost exclusively in anal sex so as to avoid pregnancy. Ever after (with schoolmates, priests, strangers), Aue prefers to be penetrated as a way of bringing himself closer to his sister, whom he continues to love with Humbert Humbert–like devotion. He sleeps in his own feces, dresses as a woman, sodomizes himself with a tree stump, a lit candle, and a sausage—the last of which he, afterwards, sneakily and gleefully feeds to his stepfather and stepmother. As an adult, Aue anally rapes his sister while tying her up under a guillotine in a torture museum—or he thinks he does, but he cannot be sure if it was reality or a dream. And he is overcome with images of his mother when he orgasms during anal sex because, of course, Nazis hate their mothers.

In sharp dismissal, the *Times* writes: "Novelists love those kinky, stinky Nazis . . . Without anality and sexual dysfunction, the rationale seems to be, how could you make them credible?"[30] Is it that genocidal acts can be demoted even further down the moral hierarchy if tainted by sexual "deviance"? Is it that nonconformist sexual practices are meant to be a signal of psychosis for the reader? Is it that a straight, cisgendered villain just doesn't seem villainous enough? Or is it that Littell believes this character portrait will inspire a complicating sympathy—that is, we feel for this tortured soul who has been marginalized his entire life because his sexual appetites do not fit neatly into socially acceptable patterns? I am frankly not sure what Littell is up to. But I'm certain that evil in this model is not structural, it is individual; it is not systemic, it is psychological. And more important, it is not threatening, because moral outliers like Aue—or Eugene, or Brewster—are easy to dismiss as exceptions to the rule of commonsense morality and its comforting, daily guarantee of group safety. If I were to be as generous as possible, I would say that highlighting this sharp structure/individual distinction might just be the point of Littell's decision to layer Aue-deviant over Aue-bureaucrat. The former blinds us to ourselves, the latter holds up a mirror. Both have a significant cultural function. Obsessively encyclopedic, Littell wants to represent it all.

Littell's banal evil requires a realistic bureaucratic narrative. His fantastic evil, by contrast, calls into being the style of an absurdist fugue. Nightmare dream sequences are predictably disorienting, and, despite the efforts of film director Tom DiCillo to kill the trope in *Living in Oblivion*, center around a dwarf. German soldiers have what even Aue sees as depraved orgies, complete with women hired to use their bare hands to wipe soldiers clean after defecating. And the plot as a whole arcs toward a deliberately ridiculous conclusion, in which Aue finally meets Hitler and, for no reason that he can explain, bites him on the nose—hard. In more effective narrative efforts, bands of child soldiers commit unspeakably vicious war crimes in the senseless, apocalyptic landscape of collapsing Germany, and occupied towns descend into horrifying pageants of confused brutality:

> In the center of the crowd, in a large cleared circle, a few men were strutting about in costumes stolen from a theater or a museum—extravagant outfits, a Regency wig with a hussar's jacket from 1812, a magistrate's gown bordered with ermine,

Mongolian armor and Scottish tartans, a half-Roman, half-Renaissance operetta costume, with a ruff; one man was wearing Budyenny's red cavalry uniform, but with a top hat and a fur collar, and was waving a long Mauser pistol; all of them were armed with clubs or rifles. At their feet several men on their knees were licking the pavement; from time to time, one of the men in costume kicked them or hit them with the butt of his rifle; most of them were bleeding profusely; the crowd was screaming louder than ever. Behind me, someone started up a lively tune on the accordion; immediately, dozens of voices struck up the words, while the man in a kilt whipped out a violin on which, since he had no bow, he scraped out chords as on the guitar. A spectator pulled me by the sleeve and shouted at me excitedly, *"Yid, yid, kaputt!"* (46)

On top of all this, *The Kindly Ones* is also a murder mystery/detective story. Here, sadly, the plot goes seriously awry. The *New Yorker* barb that the novel is "unintentionally comic" will shortly come to mind. After Aue murders his mother, two Nazi detectives—Clemens and Weser—begin to pursue him with the bulldog tenacity of the best *Law & Order* cops. They reappear every so often in the novel with new evidence pinning him to the crime scene, only to be stiff-armed by authorities like Himmler who wish to protect Aue. At the end of the novel, however, they get their chance for closure. When the Russians invade Berlin and begin shooting everyone in sight, there is no need to worry about the people protecting Aue. Clemens and Weser miraculously track him down and confront him. They have finally solved the mystery, and proceed to tell him in detailed, TV-series monologue how they cracked the case. As they prattle on, the Russians noisily advance. Eventually, the Russians interrupt the cop-criminal showdown by shooting Weser in the face. Aue escapes. But bereaved Clemens is no quitter. Turning his focus to the Russians for now, he yells over his shoulder at the fleeing Aue: "I'll get you!" And unbelievably, he does, only a few pages later.

Clemens barred my path, his feet in a puddle at the end of the footbridge, his wet hat still dripping with rainwater, his automatic in his hand. I raised my hands, as in the movies. "You

made me run," Clemens panted. "Weser is dead. But I got you."
"Kriminalkommissar Clemens," I hissed, out of breath from
running, "don't be ridiculous. The Russians are a hundred me-
ters away. They'll hear your gunshot."—"I should drown you
in a pool, you piece of shit," he belched, "sew you in a bag and
drown you. But I don't have time." (974)

But Clemens only gets this single moment of noir verbal sparring
with Aue before he, also, is shot dead.

Earlier in the novel, Aue describes Clemens and Wester as "idiotic
cops" (737). The line is, I think, a sign of authorial anxiety bubbling
up through the narrative, just as on the exhausting 913th page, when
Aue declares to his readers: "You must be thinking: Ah, finally this
story is over. But no, it still goes on." So why weave this murder mystery into an already complicated, sometimes self-contradicting, even
bloated novel? What narrative or moral need does the detective plot
fulfill? On this, I am fairly certain I know what Littell is up to. He is
trying to balance two competing moral demands: the conflicting demands, as we saw in a different way in Chapter 1, of individuality and
collectivity. Littell wants to explore the idea of macroscopic crimi-
nality and collective responsibility through genocide. That is, he
seeks to contextualize moral actions, to show how the individual perpetrator is the product of a system. But in doing so, Littell risks
excusing the individual, risks losing focus on the inescapable responsibility of each moral agent. As the narrator of Bernhard Schlink's
The Reader characterizes the problem, describing his struggle to
come to terms with the revelation that a woman he loved is also a
Nazi war criminal: "I wanted simultaneously to understand Han-
na's crime and to condemn it. But it was too terrible for that. When
I tried to understand it, I had the feeling I was failing to condemn it as
it must be condemned. When I condemned it as it must be condemned,
there was no room for understanding. I wanted to pose myself both
tasks—understanding and condemnation. But it was impossible to
do both."[31]

Littell, however, is determined to do both—hence the felt necessity of the murder mystery / detective plot, which is the contemporary
world's primary narrative for mapping out, step by step, individual

responsibility for individual actions. Aue is a bureaucratic cog, an example of a general cultural condition, a result rather than a cause. But as the detective plot reminds us, he is also a single man who committed a single crime for which he is solely and fully responsible. Context is no excuse. It is relevant only as a matter of idle curiosity. Arguing with the detectives, Aue asks:

> "Why would I have done that? What would be the motive? You have to have a motive."—"We don't know," Weser said calmly. "But actually it's all the same to us. Maybe you wanted Moreau's money. Maybe you're a sex fiend. Maybe your wound messed up your head. Maybe it was just an old family hatred, that's pretty common, and you wanted to take advantage of the war to settle your accounts on the sly, thinking it would hardly be noticed among so many other deaths. Maybe you simply went mad." (968)

Susan Rubin Suleiman has written in strong praise of *The Kindly Ones*, describing Aue as a new creation in fiction because he is a "reliable historical witness—that is, one who functions as a witness informed by retrospective historical knowledge." However, she is also aware that her admiration for the novel requires a strong argument. *The Kindly Ones*, she admits, is balanced precariously between several competing narrative demands: between realist and postmodern technique, between moral "belonging" to Nazi monstrosity and moral "distance" from it, and between the novel's authority as a "public history" and its subversion of its own authority with its bizarre "family tragedy."[32] Philip Watts describes Littell's "aesthetics of heterogeneity" also by way of nervously balanced oppositions. He points to the contradiction between the novel's moral poles of epochal tragedy and aesthetic junkyard. The former frames the Holocaust with relentless allegories of Greek myth, principally the *Oresteia*; the latter uses "comedy, pulp fiction, kitsch, slasher films, 1970s pornography, zoo animals, statistics, *mode rétro* movies, slapstick, and *Tintin*." Watts is sensitive to the ethical tension of such "temporal and ideological scrambling." On the one hand, it forces us to the salutary task of thinking "about the legacy of violence from Athens to Auschwitz and to our own times." On the other hand, it runs the risk of mini-mizing the historically unique crime of the Holocaust.[33]

In the end, Suleiman and Watts believe Littell pulls it off. I think both critics are spot on in their identification of the novel's surplus of contradictions. But in my view, the totality is closer to a grand failure than a masterpiece. *The Kindly Ones* is a magisterially ambitious work that falls apart under its own weight. But it is precisely because the book is so internally conflicted that I see it as an emblematic text with which to conclude. *The Kindly Ones'* inclusive ambitions lead inevitably to contradiction: banality, exception; system, individual; historical generality, historical specificity. As we have seen throughout this study, much the same can be said for the novel of human rights as a genre. In the texts we have seen, privacy is both privative and the source of dignity. Norms function as protective inclusion but also blinding exclusion. Addressing gender-based violence can in-volve reproducing it. Focusing on the local in all its particularity can mean losing sight of the whole, while focusing on the whole can obscure the realities of the local. Focusing on crimes in one part of the world can involve ignoring crimes in another. Focusing on first-generation rights can come at the expense of second-generation rights, just as third-generation rights can undermine both. The list could go on.

The conflicts explored throughout these novels reflect real tensions in the contemporary human rights movement. For rights are, at their most basic, simply claims made against other claims. Contradiction is inherent to their nature; they are not, to borrow a term from Leibniz, compossible. Claims made on the basis of eco-nomic rights can conflict with claims made on the basis of property rights. Claims made on the basis of freedom of expression can con-flict with claims made on the basis of religious freedom or protection from discrimination. And claims made on the basis of the right to self-defense can conflict with claims made on the basis of rights to liberty, mobility, and privacy.[34] To make matters more complicated, rights claims have proliferated over time, increasing the probability of such rights conflicts.

For some the historical expansion of rights is an unfolding uto-pian horizon of promise. The great project of universal emancipation is advancing almost as a matter of rational necessity. As Elaine Scarry might argue, the experience of coming to awareness of injustice in one part of our world can open our awareness and heighten our sensitivity to injustices previously ignored elsewhere—a process that is multiplicative rather than additive. To many others, however, this accelerating rights expansion is a threat best understood through economic models of inflation. As Amy Gutmann characterizes the position, "Proliferation of human rights to include rights that are not clearly necessary to protect the basic agency or needs or dignity of persons cheapens the purpose of human rights and correspondingly weakens the resolve of potential enforcers."[35] Michael Ignatieff has advocated a "thin" theory of rights, protecting only those norms that could command near-universal consent, as a way of minimizing the possibility that rights claims will be used as mutually negating trump cards. And Mchangama and Verdirame—emphasizing that rights claims function not only as tools to help the violated but also as propaganda for violators—have explicitly called for the demotion of second- and especially third-generation rights in favor of more narrowly focused first-generation rights.[36]

I began this book by describing how human rights has become one of the dominant moral languages in the United States and, arguably, much of the world. As the writers and theorists I have discussed demonstrate, however, the movement is a matter of cacophony rather than harmony. Some find this concerning. But as one who has committed many years to thinking about promoting dignity through human rights, I am heartened rather than troubled by this discord. The contradictions and anxieties of the texts I have discussed seem to me a sign of human rights' vitality of thought rather than its philosophical or political implausibility. Part of this, I must confess, comes from my training. As a literary scholar, I have an Emersonian discomfort with insistent, strict consistency. And I am untroubled by the problem of compossibility, the mess of language, and the sometimes bewildering and conflictual plenitude of our imagination and ideals. Those I know involved in the human rights movement, like the literature about them, are self-conscious and self-critical in a way that is rarely acknowledged in academic theorizing—and these are qualities I love not only as a matter of personal politics but also of aesthetics. I have puzzled for decades over what I perceive to be the historical failure of politicized art and am encouraged by the way human rights literature, through its wonderful muddle, has transcended so much that has preceded it.

I do not mean by all of this, however, to endorse an aesthetically pleased, detached stance that ignores what's at stake in the many conflicting views of human rights raised by the texts we have considered. And so I want, here, to return to a handful of questions I left open in the Introduction by summarizing three final stories—stories that together, I believe, formulate most directly and urgently the crisis of the modern human rights movement.

According to one dominant narrative, human rights is essentially a history of documents, beginning with the Magna Carta (1215) and moving with ever greater inclusiveness through the French Declaration of the Rights of Man and of the Citizen (1789), the US Bill of Rights (1791), Britain's Abolition of the Slave Trade Act (1807), the 1864 Geneva Convention, and interwar documents like the International Convention for the Suppression of the Traffic in Women and Children (1921) and the Protocol for the Prohibition of the Use in War of Asphyxiating or Poisonous or Other Gases (1925). These and other treaties, protocols, and conventions all culminate teleologically in the Nuremberg Trials (1945–1946), the post–World War II Geneva Conventions (1949), and, most dramatically, the UN Universal Declaration of Human Rights (1948). In this narrative, the legal instruments that proliferated after the Universal Declaration, from the 1951 Genocide Convention to the 1989 Indigenous and Tribal Peoples Convention, become minor characters, extensions of and corrections to the UN's foundational document of modern human rights. This progress narrative imagines us advancing, through the accumulating interlock of international treaties, toward a system of robust global governance. Sovereign nation-states will cede a minimally acceptable portion of their power such that cooperative enforcement of rights becomes a background reality rather than a utopian hope, a regular result of established norms rather than an exceptional buckling to nongovernmental agitation and indirect international pressures.

This narrative of linear progress through treaties, however, tends to frame human rights as a predominantly Western invention. In response, many have argued that a better story of human rights progress involves transcultural synthesis. Scholars like Micheline Ishay and Paul Gordon Lauren, for instance, have tracked the emergence of human rights in the common principles of Hinduism, Judaism, Christianity, Buddhism, Islam, and Confucianism, and in the diverse cultural and philosophical traditions found in Babylon, Greece, Rome, India, China, Africa, Europe, and the Americas. The ICRC's 1999 *People on War Report*, a worldwide consultation with 12,860 civilians and combatants in twelve countries from Afghanistan to South Africa, makes equally strong claims about the basic universal features of human morality. It argues that humanitarian law's "unconditional principle" that behavior in war has limits is consistent with and, indeed, is perhaps the most basic expression of a common "notion of human dignity" found in seemingly incompatible religions, traditions, and personal codes.[37] Here, the narrative is neither one of progress nor of evolution—it is one of inevitability. Rights is not an invention. It is a name we use for an aspect of the human condition.

Against both of the stories above, however, there is a counter-story, a redescription that points not to a more robust future for the regime of human rights but rather to irresolvable conflict and likely decay. The insistent discovery of common foundational principles, for instance, only reveals the depth of our concern over the profound legitimacy crisis of human rights. Scholars now emphasize shared traditions because they are increasingly anxious over the still unresolved conflict between the universalizing ambitions of human rights and the particularist claims of cultural relativism. They fear that if human rights is characterized as a Western invention rather than a cooperative human project, its utility as an organizing global narrative will be finished.

Moreover, conventions and protocols have proliferated not as any sort of justice cascade but rather because they have proved not to matter very much. Countries can enjoy the esteem due to signatories while only rarely, if ever, having to face consequences for noncompliance. *Why not sign?* one might ask. *It's great PR, and costs nothing.*[38] Just as bad, nations can promote themselves as human rights defenders by hewing to a minimalist conception of negative rights and civil liberties that works hand in glove with free-market capitalism and the principles of neoliberal globalization. These principles have, according to critics, effectively disenfranchised populations throughout the globe. If human rights cannot help us here, the disaffected say, then human rights cannot help us. Finally, and perhaps most disheartening, states can do more than just ignore human rights. They can also use its principles and rhetoric to justify acts of aggression.

Are human rights our best available instruments for promoting human dignity? Whether or not the human rights movement continues to inspire our devotion and efforts, whether or not we turn to alternative vocabularies, institutions, and tactics to realize visions of social justice—all of this will depend quite literally upon a competition among stories. Which ones do we remember? Which ones do we believe? Which ones continue to move us? Which ones will we choose to tell, and are we ready for the consequences of our choice?

It is my hope that continued attention to the burgeoning genre of the novel of human rights will help illuminate these and other questions. As the first of such studies, however, the aims of this book have been more modest. Let me use this closing moment to restate what those have been. Given that a number of novels and issues have been considered in this book, a clarifying synopsis might be useful.

I began by describing the rise of the popular culture of human rights in the United States, along with the concomitant rise of literature and human rights as a scholarly subfield. I then made the case for thinking of the novel of human rights as a specifically US genre, in large part because of the unique history of the relationship between human rights and civil rights in the United States. Ultimately, I hope that this nation-reifying argument will be dismantled. It seems clear to me that the genre, like the deep political and cultural forces that produce it, is not defined by or restricted to nation-state boundaries. But for now it's useful to work within limits.

The first half of the book emphasized form, making the case for and mapping out the basic features of the novel of human rights. I began by arguing that two key plot lines dominate the genre: the justice plot and the escape plot. Offering a handful of case studies, I showed how authors work with these patterns to explore key issues in human rights. Here, I focused primarily on the consequences of the ideological split in the United States between the "generations" of rights. I then identified a core group of three concepts that unify the genre: the heteronormative family, physical and political mobility, and privacy (which comprises residence, secrecy, and naming). I emphasized that while many authors write to complicate or challenge US-centric, liberal conceptions of human rights, the pervasiveness of these three concepts, each of which encodes a set of unspoken liberal assumptions about citizenship and personhood, often undermines their efforts.

The second half of the book focused upon modes of representing the two most basic figures in human rights discourse: the "victim" and the "perpetrator." Looking at the former, I argued that human rights produces the idea of "subjects to be saved." This idea has especially troubling and even openly dangerous implications when women are used as the epitome of victimhood (as they so frequently are in the novel of human rights, often with the best of intentions). I showed how the genre's use of voyeuristic, sensationalizing violence against women has its ideological counterpart in the use of safe, heterosexual union with women as a device for closure. This "international allegory" maps triumphant cross-border romances onto a vision of utopic global possibilities. The most interesting novels, I concluded, are the ones that are self-conscious about these narrative patterns. Such novels subvert the expectations they generate in readers, interrogate the idea of "subjects to be saved," and thoughtfully analyze the cultural function of categories like childhood and disability.

I concluded, finally, with consideration of the perpetrator, arguably the least analyzed figure in the "savages-victims-saviors" triptych of human rights. Framing the discussion by suggesting that the perpetrator might not be so ethically distant from us as we might imagine, I compared and contrasted psychological and organizational answers to one of the most important questions in human rights work: What makes men into monsters? In this chapter I emphasized that the novel of human rights is defined by aesthetic contradictions and wrenching moral paradoxes. This has been my primary claim throughout, starting with my consideration of the competing conceptions of rights in US political culture. We live in a world of compromised options and unforeseen consequences. Nonetheless, justice urgently calls us to decisive action.

NOTES

ACKNOWLEDGMENTS

INDEX

Notes

Introduction

    1. Paul Gordon Lauren, *The Evolution of International Human Rights: Visions Seen* (Philadelphia: University of Pennsylvania Press, 2011), 139.

    2. Mark Philip Bradley, "American Vernaculars: The United States and the Global Human Rights Imagination," *Diplomatic History* 38.1 (2014): 13, 15.

    3. See for instance Cynthia Soohoo, "Human Rights and the Transformation of the 'Civil Rights' and 'Civil Liberties' Lawyer," in *Bringing Human Rights Home: A History of Human Rights in the United States*, ed. Cynthia Soohoo, Catherine Albisa, and Martha Davis (Philadelphia: University Pennsylvania Press, 2007), 198–234.

    4. Elizabeth Swanson Goldberg and Alexandra Schultheis Moore, "Introduction: Human Rights and Literature: The Development of an Interdiscipline," in *Theoretical Perspectives on Human Rights and Literature*, ed. Swanson Goldberg and Moore (New York: Routledge, 2012), 3–18.

    5. Among the welcome exceptions to this general trend is Crystal Parikh, whose monograph on literature and human rights, *Writing Human Rights: The Political Imaginaries of Writers of Color*, came out as this book was being copyedited. While the timing means I cannot engage substantially with Parikh's arguments, I can say that her writing is powerful and important, and promises to help reshape the field. See Crystal Parikh, *Writing Human Rights: The Political*

Imaginaries of Writers of Color (Minneapolis: University of Minnesota Press, 2017).

6. Greg Mullins, "Atrocity, Literature, and Criticism," *American Literary History* 23.1 (Spring 2011): 226.

7. For recent examples of each that draw upon an explicit human rights framework, see, respectively, Jodi Melamed, *Represent and Destroy: Rationalizing Violence in the New Racial Capitalism* (Minneapolis: University of Minnesota Press, 2011); April Shemak, *Asylum Speakers: Caribbean Refugees and Testimonial Discourse* (New York: Fordham University Press, 2011); Mark Greif, *The Age of the Crisis of Man* (Princeton, NJ: Princeton University Press, 2015); and Colin Dayan, *The Law Is a White Dog: How Legal Rituals Make and Unmake Persons* (Princeton, NJ: Princeton University Press, 2011).

8. Claudio Guillén *Literature as System*, quoted in *Theory of the Novel: A Historical Approach*, ed. Michael McKeon (Baltimore: Johns Hopkins University Press, 2000), 35.

9. For literary criticism focusing on form and human rights, see Parikh, *Writing Human Rights;* Sophia McClennen and Joseph Slaughter, eds., "Introducing Human Rights and Literary Forms; or, The Vehicles and Vocabularies of Human Rights," special issue, *Comparative Literature Studies* 46.1 (2009); Kay Schaffer and Sidonie Smith, *Human Rights and Narrated Lives: The Ethics of Recognition* (New York: Palgrave Macmillan, 2004); and Joseph Slaughter, *Human Rights, Inc.: The World Novel, Narrative Form, and International Law* (New York: Fordham University Press, 2007).

10. See Samuel Moyn, *The Last Utopia* (Cambridge, MA: Harvard University Press, 2010); Barbara Keys, *Reclaiming American Virtue: The Human Rights Revolution of the 1970s* (Cambridge, MA: Harvard University Press, 2014); Micheline Ishay, *The History of Human Rights: From Ancient Times to the Globalization Era* (Berkeley: University of California Press, 2004); Paul Gordon Lauren, *The Evolution of International Human Rights: Visions Seen* (Philadelphia: University of Pennsylvania Press, 2011); Lynn Hunt, *Inventing Human Rights: A History* (New York: Norton, 2007); Jenny Martínez, *The Slave Trade and the Origins of International Human Rights Law* (Oxford: Oxford University Press, 2012).

11. On the concept of America and the "hemispheric turn," see Ralph Bauer, "Hemispheric Studies," *PMLA* 124.1 (2009): 234–250; Heinz Ickstadt, "American Studies in an Age of Globalization," *American Quarterly* 54.4 (2002): 543–562; Rodrigo Lazo, "The Invention of America Again: On the Impossibility of an Archive," *American Literary History* 25.4 (Winter 2013): 751–771; and Claire Fox and Claudia Sadowski-Smith, "Theorizing the Hemispheric: Inter-Americas Work at the Intersection of American, Canadian, and Latin American Studies," *Comparative American Studies* 2.1 (2004): 5–38.

12. Cited in Carolyn Porter, "What We Know That We Don't Know: Remapping American Literary Studies," *American Literary History* 6.3 (1994): 472.

13. Cited in Shemak, *Asylum Speakers*, 39.

14. Porter, "What We Know That We Don't Know," 510. Separate from the question of how academics choose to frame literature according to nation and

region is the question of how writers themselves do. For authors included in this study on what it means to be called an "American" writer, see Lucia M. Suarez, "Julia Alvarez and the Anxiety of Latina Representation," *Meridians: Feminism, Race, Transnationalism* 5.1 (2004): 117–145; and Marisel Moreno and Thomas F. Anderson, "'I Am an American Writer': An Interview with Daniel Alarcón," *MELUS* 39.4 (Winter 2014): 186–206.

15. Sophia McClennen, "Inter-American Studies or Imperial American Studies?," *Comparative American Studies* 3.4 (2005): 402.

16. On the nationalism / internationalism debate in human rights, see Elaine Scarry, "The Difficulty of Imagining Other People," in *For Love of Country?*, ed. Martha Nussbaum (Boston: Beacon Press, 2002), 98–110. Addressing a parallel dialectic in American studies, Carolyn Levander writes: "The Americas are distinctive in that they all experienced a revolutionary rupture with the colonizing power; that they are a stage of varying degrees of hybrid culture; and that their histories of slavery, indigenous cultures, national formation, and economic development interconnect as well as distinguish them from other geo-political areas of the globe . . . [But there are also] important distinctions between the Americas. Be it the asymmetrical formation of nations, unparallel history of slavery and emancipation, or divergent emergence of a national literature, the Americas are a myriad combination of forces that constantly complicate and destabilize any coherent commentary on the area's literary history." See Levander, "Reinventing American Literary History," *American Literary History* 20.3 (2008): 450. For more on the tension between "the need to rethink the presumed integrity and impenetrability of national borders" and the continued salience of "the category of the national . . . for the study of modern literature," see Paula Moya and Ramon Saldivar, "Fictions of the Trans-American Imaginary," *Modern Fiction Studies* 49.1 (Spring 2003): 1–18.

17. See Eleni Coundouriotis, *The People's Right to the Novel: War Fiction in the Postcolony* (New York: Fordham University Press, 2014). It is possible, for instance, to read Gabriel García Márquez's *One Hundred Years of Solitude* as a Colombian text, a Latin American text, and / or a world text, but, as Diana Sorensen demonstrates, each different audience-as-prism yields significantly different readings. See *A Turbulent Decade Remembered: Scenes from the Latin American Sixties* (Stanford: Stanford University Press, 2007), 177–186.

18. Elizabeth Anker, *Fictions of Dignity: Embodying Human Rights in World Literature* (Ithaca, NY: Cornell University Press, 2012), 45–46.

19. On the way Eggers uses depictions of US racism to foreground the "limitations of humanitarian narrative and activism," see Michelle Peek, "Humanitarian Narrative and Posthumanist Critique: Dave Eggers's *What Is the What*," *Biography* 35.1 (Winter 2012): 115–136.

20. Dorothy Q. Thomas, "Against American Supremacy: Rebuilding Human Rights Culture in the United States," in Soohoo, Albisa, and Davis, *Bringing Human Rights Home*, 155.

21. See Carol Anderson, "'A Hollow Mockery': African Americans, White Supremacy, and the Development of Human Rights in the United States," in Soohoo, Albisa, and Davis, *Bringing Human Rights Home*, 84–86.

22. See Carol Anderson, "'A Hollow Mockery': African Americans, White Supremacy, and the Development of Human Rights in the United States," in Soohoo, Albisa, and Davis, *Bringing Human Rights Home*, 86–88.

23. Domna Stanton, "Top-Down, Bottom-Up, Horizontally: Resignifying the Universal in Human Rights Discourse," in Swanson Goldberg and Moore, *Theoretical Perspectives on Human Rights and Literature*, 65–86.

24. Soohoo, "Human Rights and the Transformation of the 'Civil Rights' and 'Civil Liberties' Lawyer," in Soohoo, Albisa, and Davis, *Bringing Human Rights Home*, 198, 206.

25. These core instruments include the International Convention on the Elimination of All Forms of Racial Discrimination (1965), the International Covenant on Civil and Political Rights (1966), the International Covenant on Economic, Social and Cultural Rights (1966), the Convention on the Elimination of All Forms of Discrimination against Women (1979), the Convention against Torture and Other Cruel, Inhuman or Degrading Treatment or Punishment (1984), the Convention on the Rights of the Child (1989), the International Convention on the Protection of the Rights of All Migrant Workers and Members of Their Families (1990), the International Convention for the Protection of All Persons from Enforced Disappearance (2006), and the Convention on the Rights of Persons with Disabilities (2006).

26. See Human Rights Watch, "Declaration in Support of Access to Guantánamo for UN Torture Expert," May 12, 2016, https://www.hrw.org/news /2016/05/12/declaration-support-access-guantanamo-un-torture-expert# _ftn1.

27. Michael Barnett, "Human Rights and Humanitarianism: Distinctions with or without a Difference?," Arizona State University, April 4, 2016.

28. See "MSF Pulls Out of World Humanitarian Summit," IRIN, May 5, 2016, http://www.irinnews.org/news/2016/05/05/msf-pulls-out-world-humanitarian -summit.

29. See his website, http://corbanaddison.com/bio/.

30. See her website, http://patriciamccormick.com/frequently-asked -questions/.

31. On the influence of African American slave narratives on modern human rights narratives, see Yogita Goyal, "African Atrocity, American Humanity: Slavery and Its Transnational Afterlives," *Research in African Literatures* 45.3 (Fall 2014): 48–71.

CHAPTER 1 · The US Novel of Human Rights

1. Shoshana Felman and Dori Laub, *Testimony: Crises of Witnessing in Literature, Psychoanalysis, and History* (New York: Routledge, 1992), 111.

2. Viet Thanh Nguyen, *Race and Resistance: Literature and Politics in Asian America* (Oxford: Oxford University Press, 2002), 112.

3. Rony Brauman, "When Suffering Makes a Good Story," in *Life, Death and Aid: The Médecins sans Frontières Report on World Crisis Intervention*, ed. Jean François (London: Routledge, 1993), 150.

4. Junot Díaz, *The Brief Wondrous Life of Oscar Wao* (New York: Riverhead, 2007), 97.

5. Julia Alvarez, *In the Time of the Butterflies* (Chapel Hill, NC: Algonquin Books, 1994), 199.

6. This insight has been developed brilliantly in Elizabeth Swanson Goldberg, "Intimations of What Was to Come: Edwidge Danticat's *The Farming of Bones* and the Indivisibility of Human Rights," in Goldberg and Moore, *Theoretical Perspectives on Human Rights and Literature*, 103–119.

7. Mary Ann Glendon, *A World Made New: Eleanor Roosevelt and the Universal Declaration of Human Rights* (New York: Random House, 2002), 116.

8. Cited in Stephen Hopgood, *Keepers of the Flame* (Ithaca, NY: Cornell University Press, 2013), 55–56.

9. Mark Philip Bradley, "American Vernaculars: The United States and the Global Human Rights Imagination," *Diplomatic History* 38.1 (2014): 19.

10. John Edgar Wideman, *Philadelphia Fire* (Boston: Mariner Books, 2005), 19.

11. John Edgar Wideman, *Brothers and Keepers: A Memoir* (New York: Mariner Books, 2005), 77.

12. For analysis of the way Wideman layers historical atrocities upon one another for complex political and aesthetic effect, with particular emphasis on the Holocaust, see Eric Sundquist, *Strangers in the Land: Blacks, Jews, Post-Holocaust America* (Cambridge, MA: Harvard University Press, 2009), 465–473; and Jeffrey Severs, "'Playing Father Son and Holocaust': The Imagination of Totalitarian Oppression in the Works of John Edgar Wideman," *MELUS* 41.1 (2016): 72–92.

13. Ulrich Eschborn, "'To Democratize the Elements of the Historical Record': An Interview with John Edgar Wideman about History in His Work," *Callaloo* 33.4 (Fall 2010): 993.

14. Madhu Dubey, "Literature and Urban Crisis: John Edgar Wideman's *Philadelphia Fire*," *African American Review* 32.4 (Winter 1998): 591.

15. Jan Clausen, "Native Fathers," *Kenyon Review* 14.2 (Spring 1992): 53–54.

16. Susan Pearsall, "'Narratives of Self' and the Abdication of Authority in Wideman's *Philadelphia Fire*," *MELUS* 26.2 (Summer 2001): 24.

17. Wideman, *Brothers and Keepers*, xvii.

18. Francisco Goldman, *The Long Night of White Chickens* (New York: Grove Press, 1992), 101.

19. James Dunkerley, *The Pacification of Central America: Political Change in the Isthmus, 1987–1993* (London: Verso, 1994), 79.

20. Francisco Goldman, "State of the Art: Latino Writers," *Washington Post*, February 28, 1999, X01.

21. Flanders cited and discussed in Bruce Robbins, *Feeling Global: Internationalism in Distress* (New York: New York University Press, 1999), 141.

22. Stephen Hopgood, *The Endtimes of Human Rights* (Ithaca, NY: Cornell University Press, 2013), x. For an interesting literary critical take on the need to move beyond the universal/particular binary, see Mitchum Huehls, "Referring to the Human in Contemporary Human Rights Literature," *Modern Fiction Studies* 58.1 (Spring 2012): 1–21.

23. American Anthropological Association, "Statement on Human Rights," *American Anthropologist* 49.4 (1947).

24. Alan Cheuse, *Chicago Tribune*, http://www.chicagotribune.com/lifestyles /books/chi-books-review-i-hotel-yamashita-story.html.

25. On third-generation rights, see Jan Eckel, "Human Rights and Decolonization: New Perspectives and Open Questions," *Humanity* 1.1 (Fall 2010): 111–135; and Carl Wellman, "Solidarity, the Individual and Human Rights," *Human Rights Quarterly* 22.3 (August 2000): 639–657.

26. Karen Tei Yamashita, *I Hotel* (Minneapolis: Coffee House Press, 2010), 15.

27. United Nations Environment Programme, "Declaration of the United Nations Conference on the Human Environment," June 16, 1972, http://www .unep.org/documents.multilingual/default.asp?documentid=97&articleid =1503.

28. Interview with Brett Anthony Johnston, National Book Foundation, http://www.nationalbook.org/nba2010_f_yamashita_interv.html#.V5Yi1EvkrK9I.

29. Roland Burke, *Decolonization and the Evolution of International Human Rights* (Philadelphia: University of Pennsylvania Press, 2010), 13, 2.

30. "Final Communiqué of the Asian-African Conference of Bandung," April 24, 1955, http://franke.uchicago.edu/Final_Communique_Bandung _1955.pdf.

31. Burke, *Decolonization and the Evolution of International Human Rights*, 40.

32. For more on Bandung, see also Crystal Parikh, *Writing Human Rights: The Political Imaginaries of Writers of Color* (Minneapolis: University of Minnesota Press, 2017), 45, 57–58.

33. Jacob Mchangama and Guglielmo Verdirame, "The Danger of Human Rights Proliferation," *Foreign Affairs*, July 24, 2013, https://www.foreignaffairs .com/articles/europe/2013–07–24/danger-human-rights-proliferation.

34. For related analysis of the tensions and overlaps between nationalist and internationalist struggles in *I Hotel*, see Jinqi Ling, *Across Meridians: History and Figuration in Karen Tei Yamashita's Transnational Novels* (Stanford: Stanford University Press, 2002), 147–188; and Nathan Ragain, "A Revolutionary Romance: Particularity and Universality in Karen Tei Yamashita's *I Hotel*," *MELUS* 38.1 (Spring 2013): 137–154.

35. For an insightful related analysis of power asymmetries in transnationalized Chicana/Latina struggles, see Ana Patricia Rodríguez, "The Fiction of Solidarity: Transfronterista Feminisms and Anti-Imperialist Struggles in Central American Transnational Narratives," *Feminist Studies* 34.1/2 (Spring/Summer 2008): 199–226.

36. Bruce Robbins, "The Worlding of the American Novel," in *The Cambridge History of the American Novel*, ed. Leonard Cassuto, Claire Virginia Eby, and Benjamin Reiss (Cambridge: Cambridge University Press, 2011), 1100.

37. Anticipating but also mischaracterizing the readings of defector memoirs that I and others provide, John Cussen heatedly charges that such work is wrongheaded but to be expected from the "'feminist' camp" along with "the Critical Theory and Postcolonial groups that reject paradigmatic, essentialist representations of non-Western societies, of alterities, as they say." He con-

tinues: "Premonitory of this imminent interrogation is the work of Shine Choi—currently a visiting professor in Korean studies at the University of Mississippi's Croft Institute. Grounded in deconstructive and post-colonial theories headlined by names like Spivak and Bhabba, she begins her book *Re-Imagining North Korea in International Politics: Problems and Alternatives* this way: 'The international problem of North Korea is that North Korea is a work of fiction.' No, for their insistence that North Korea is one kind of place and no other—repressive, dystopian, nightmarish—, the defector memoirists are not likely to get a friendly reading in Choi's heady quarter of academia when their books eventually arrive there." "On the Call to Dismiss North Korean Defectors' Memoirs and on Their Dark American Alternative," *Korean Studies* 40 (2016): 146.

38. Nguyen, *Race and Resistance*, 107–124.

39. Viet Thanh Nguyen, *The Sympathizer* (New York: Grove, 2015), 163.

40. Francisco Goldman, *The Ordinary Seaman* (New York: Grove, 1997), 58.

41. For brilliant analysis on this and other matters in *The Ordinary Seaman*, see Kirsten Silva Gruesz, "Utopía Latina: *The Ordinary Seaman* in Extraordinary Times," *Modern Fiction Studies* 49.1 (2003): 54–83.

42. Hannah Arendt, *The Origins of Totalitarianism* (New York: Harvest, 1976), 299. I am indebted to April Shemak's extended analysis of *The Ordinary Seaman* in her *Asylum Speakers: Caribbean Refugees and Testimonial Discourse* (New York: Fordham University Press, 2011), 177–212.

43. Alexander Coleman, "Reconciliation among the Ruins," *New York Times*, May 12, 1985, http://www.nytimes.com/1985/05/12/books/reconciliation -among-the-ruins.html?pagewanted=all.

44. John Rodden, "'The Responsibility to Tell You': An Interview with Isabel Allende," *Kenyon Review* 13.1 (Winter 1991): 114–115.

45. Isabel Allende, "Writing as an Act of Hope," in *Paths of Resistance: The Art and Craft of the Political Novel*, ed. William Zinsser (Boston: Houghton Mifflin, 1989), 59.

46. Isabel Allende, interview with Lawrence Donegan, "This Much I Know," *The Observer*, July 12, 2008.

47. Rodden, "'The Responsibility to Tell You,'" 117.

48. Angel Island Immigration Station Foundation, Interview Archives, http://aiisf.org/immigrant-voices/stories-by-author/608-isabel-allende-the -unexpected-immigrant/.

49. Allende, "Writing as an Act of Hope," 50–51.

50. Helon Habila, *Measuring Time* (New York: Norton, 2007), 178.

51. Cited in James Dawes, *That the World May Know: Bearing Witness to Atrocity* (Cambridge, MA: Harvard University Press, 2007), 209.

CHAPTER 2 · The Central Features of the Novel of Human Rights

1. Johannes Morsink, *The Universal Declaration of Human Rights: Origins, Drafting, and Intent* (Philadelphia: University Pennsylvania Press, 1999), 134. See also Lars Adam Rehof, "Article 12," in *The Universal Declaration of Human*

Rights: A Commentary, ed. Asbjørn Edie et al. (London: Scandinavian University Press, 1992), 188.

2. Morsink explains that the article "was put in the Declaration to prevent governments from placing people in ghettos and thus segregating them as being of a lower status than the rest of the population, as Hitler had done." See his *The Universal Declaration of Human Rights*, 27, 73.

3. Elaine Scarry, *Thermonuclear Monarchy: Choosing between Democracy and Doom* (New York: Norton, 2014), 288.

4. Franco Moretti, "Conjectures on World Literature," *New Left Review* 1 (January-February 2000): 57.

5. Todd Presner, "The Ethics of the Algorithm: Close and Distant Listening to the Shoah Foundation Visual History Archive," in *History Unlimited: Probing the Ethics of the Holocaust* (Cambridge, MA: Harvard University Press, 2015).

6. Rey Chow, *The Age of the World Target: Self-Referentiality in War, Theory, and Comparative Work* (Durham, NC: Duke University Press, 2006), 31. Drawing upon Paul Virilio's work on war and vision and Heidegger's concept of the "world picture," Chow writes of war in the nuclear age: "To conceive of the world as a target is to conceive of it as an object to be destroyed" (31). She argues that "the dominance of the modern technological attitude—namely an exploitative, ordering attitude that sees human beings as the center of the universe for whose use everything else exists," collaborates with war technology to birth a new "politics of vision" (12).

7. Lawrence Thornton, *Imagining Argentina* (New York: Bantam, 1991), 98.

8. Dinaw Mengestu, *The Beautiful Things That Heaven Bears* (New York: Riverhead, 2007), 189.

9. For an interesting related analysis of the novel's fixation with residence in urban space that draws heavily upon David Harvey's Marxist geography, see Dayo Olopade, "Go West, Young Men: Conspicuous Consumption in Dinaw Mengestu's *The Beautiful Things That Heaven Bears*, as Prefigured by V. S. Naipaul's *A Bend in the River*," *Transition* 100 (2009): 107–118.

10. Dinaw Mengestu, *How to Read the Air* (New York: Riverhead, 2010), 129–130.

11. Elaine Scarry, *The Body in Pain: The Making and Unmaking of the World* (Oxford: Oxford University Press, 1985), 38–41.

12. Nathan Englander, *The Ministry of Special Cases* (New York: Knopf, 2007), 18, 25.

13. Anthony Marra, *A Constellation of Vital Phenomena* (London: Hogarth, 2013), 35, 39.

14. Ann Patchett, *Bel Canto* (New York: Perennial, 2001), 283.

15. Paolo Bacigalupi, *The Windup Girl* (San Francisco: Night Shade Books, 2010), 325.

16. James Ridgeway, "The Secret History of Hurricane Katrina," *Mother Jones*, August 18, 2009, http://www.motherjones.com/environment/2009/08/secret-history-hurricane-katrina.

17. Dave Eggers, *Zeitoun* (New York: Vintage, 2009), 212, 222, 227.

18. Joy Kogawa, *Obasan* (New York: Anchor, 1994), 216.

19. Vyvyane Loh, *Breaking the Tongue* (New York: Norton, 2004), 22.

20. Elizabeth Walcott-Hackshaw, "Home Is Where the Heart Is: Danticat's Landscapes of Return," *Small Axe*, no. 27 (October 2008): 74.

21. Héctor Tobar, *The Tattooed Soldier* (New York: Penguin, 2000), 17.

22. Elizabeth Anker, *Fictions of Dignity: Embodying Human Rights in World Literature* (Ithaca, NY: Cornell University Press, 2012), 146.

23. Madeleine Thien, *Do Not Say We Have Nothing* (New York: Norton, 2016), 82.

24. Chris Abani, *The Secret History of Las Vegas* (New York: Penguin, 2014), 151.

25. Susan Choi, *The Foreign Student* (New York: Perennial, 2004), 14.

26. For more, see Crystal Parikh's analysis of *The Foreign Student* in her *Writing Human Rights: The Political Imaginaries of Writers of Color* (Minneapolis: University of Minnesota Press, 2017), 119–156.

27. Susan Choi, *A Person of Interest* (New York: Penguin, 2008), 221, 217.

28. Adam Johnson, *The Orphan Master's Son* (New York: Random House, 2012), 369.

29. Edwidge Danticat, *The Farming of Bones* (New York: Penguin, 1999), 35. For more on exposure in *The Farming of Bones*, see April Shemak, *Asylum Speakers: Caribbean Refugees and Testimonial Discourse* (New York: Fordham University Press, 2011), 161. Relatedly, on shame and privacy in Danticat, see Elina Valovirta, "Reading the Intimacies of Shame in Edwidge Danticat's *Breath, Eyes, Memory*," in *Scenes of Intimacy: Reading, Writing and Theorizing Contemporary Literature*, ed. Jennifer Cooke (London: Bloomsbury, 2013), 37–54.

30. Shemak, *Asylum Speakers*, 73.

31. Jerry A. Varsava, "An Interview with Ha Jin," *Contemporary Literature* 51.1 (Spring 2010): 13.

32. Ha Jin, *War Trash* (New York: Vintage, 2005), 312.

33. Mark Greif, *The Age of the Crisis of Man* (Princeton, NJ: Princeton University Press, 2015), 178.

34. Stona Fitch, *Senseless* (New York: Soho, 2001), 150.

35. Dave Eggers, *What Is the What: The Autobiography of Valentino Achak Deng* (San Francisco: McSweeney's, 2006), 340.

36. Demetria Martínez, *Mother Tongue* (New York: One World, 1994), 13.

37. See Marta Caminero-Santangelo, *On Latinidad: US Latino Literature and the Construction of Ethnicity* (Gainesville: University Press of Florida, 2007), 198; and Ariana Vigil, "Transnational Community in Demetria Martínez's *Mother Tongue*," *Meridians: Feminism, Race, Trans-Nationalism* 10.1 (2009): 59, 60. Ana Patricia Rodríguez summarizes deftly: "Ultimately, *Mother Tongue* shows that, although we may attempt to build communal ground or solidarity based on identifying with others' pain and injury, in the end we must recognize the limits of those forms of identification . . . In writing about her relationship with a Salvadoran refugee man, Mary sets out to write a solidarity fiction, only to discover the fiction of her own solidarity . . . In solidarity, Mary appropriates José Luis's pain and attempts to fill the gaps of his incomplete story, but, in doing so, she exposes the limits, transgressions, and mishaps of solidarity." See Rodríguez, *Dividing the Isthmus: Central American Transnational Histories, Literatures, and Cultures* (Austin: University of Texas Press, 2009), 157, 161.

38. International Covenant on Civil and Political Rights, December 16, 1966, available at Office of the High Commissioner for Human Rights, http://www .ohchr.org/en/professionalinterest/pages/ccpr.aspx.

39. International Covenant on Civil and Political Rights, art. 24.

40. Thornton, *Imagining Argentina*, 43, 45, 99.

41. Ariel Dorfman, *Death and the Maiden* (New York: Penguin, 1994), 7.

42. Daniel Alarcón, *Lost City Radio* (New York: HarperPerennial, 2007), 9.

43. "About the Author," in Alarcón, *Lost City Radio*, 10.

44. Edwidge Danticat, *The Dew Breaker* (New York: Knopf, 2004), 241.

45. Walter Mosley, *The Man in My Basement* (New York: Little, Brown, 2004), 134.

46. Johnson, *The Orphan Master's Son*, 350.

47. Hannah Arendt, *The Human Condition* (Chicago: University of Chicago Press, 1989), 38, 41, 72, 119, 223.

48. Judith Herman, *Trauma and Recovery* (New York: Basic Books, 1992), 3.

49. Elaine Scarry, *Thermonuclear Monarchy*, 286–289. See also Scarry, "Consent and the Body: Injury, Departure, and Desire," *New Literary History* 21.4 (1990): 867–896.

50. Corban Addison, *The Tears of Dark Water* (Nashville: Regulus, 2015), 235.

51. On translation as a key thematic of the novel, see "'Bled In, Letter by Letter': Translation, Post Memory, and the Subject of the Korean War: History in *The Foreign Student*," *American Literary History* 21.3 (Fall 2009): 550–583.

52. Valorie Thomas, "'Dust to Cleanse Themselves,' a Survivor's Ethos: Diasporic Disidentifications in *Zeitoun*," *Biography* 35.2 (Spring 2012): 280.

53. Edwidge Danticat, *Breath, Eyes, Memory* (New York: Vintage, 1994), 139.

54. Sandy Alexandre and Ravi Y. Howard, "My Turn in the Fire: A Conversation with Edwidge Danticat," *Transition* 12.3 (2002): 113, http://www.worldcat .org/title/my-turn-in-the-fire-a-conversation-with-edwidge-danticat/oclc /58025326&referer=brief_results.

55. See Paul Gilroy on the image of the ship as entangling both slavery and redemption. Discussing J. M. W. Turner's *The Slave Ship*, Gilroy writes: Ships "need to be thought of as cultural and political units rather than abstract embodiments of the triangular trade. They were something more—a means to conduct political dissent and possibly a distinct mode of cultural production. The ship provides a chance to explore the articulations between the discontinuous histories of England's ports, its interfaces with the wider world. Ships also refer us back to the middle passage, to the half-remembered micro-politics of the slave trade and its relationship to both industrialization and modernization. As it were, getting on board promises a means to reconceptualise the orthodox relationship between modernity and what passes for its prehistory." *The Black Atlantic: Modernity and Double Consciousness* (London: Verso, 1993), 17.

56. Alexandre and Howard, "My Turn in the Fire," 113.

57. Louise Erdrich, *The Round House* (New York: HarperPerennial, 2013), 161.

58. Dianna Shandy, *Nuer-American Passages: Globalizing Sudanese Migration* (Gainesville: University Press of Florida, 2009), 65. See also Viet Thanh Nguyen, *The Sympathizer* (New York: Grove, 2015), 69.

59. See E. Valentine Daniel and John Chr. Knudsen, introduction to *Mistrusting Refugees*, ed. E. Valentine Daniel and John Chr. Knudsen (Berkeley: University of California Press, 1996), 3.

60. Gillian Whitlock, *Postcolonial Life Narratives: Testimonial Transactions* (Oxford: Oxford University Press, 2015), 182.

61. On Eggers's resistance of empathy and teleology, see Sean Bex and Stef Craps, "Humanitarianism, Testimony, and the White Savior Industrial Complex: *What Is the What* versus *Kony 2012*," *Cultural Critique* 92 (Winter 2016): 32–56.

62. Jacqueline Bhabha, "The Child: What Sort of Human?," *PMLA* 121.5 (October 2006): 1526–1535.

63. Julia Alvarez, *In the Time of the Butterflies* (Chapel Hill, NC: Algonquin Books, 1994), 52.

64. Alexandre and Howard, "My Turn in the Fire," 118.

65. On the River Massacre as both death and "generative potential," see Elizabeth Swanson Goldberg, *Beyond Terror: Gender, Narrative, Human Rights* (New Brunswick, NJ: Rutgers University Press, 2007), 162–164.

66. Chandan Reddy, *Freedom with Violence: Race, Sexuality, and the US State* (Durham, NC: Duke University Press, 2011), 160. For more detailed analysis, see Greg Mullins, "Seeking Asylum: Literary Reflections on Sexuality, Ethnicity, and Human Rights," *MELUS* 28.1 (Spring 2003): 145–171.

67. Kate Chopin, *The Awakening* (Boston: Bedford, 2000), 138.

68. Taylor Antrim, *Daily Beast*, January 6, 2012, http://www.thedailybeast.com/articles/2012/01/06/the-orphan-master-s-son-by-adam-johnson-review.html.

69. Wyatt Mason, "*Dear Leader:* A Novel of Life in North Korea," *New Yorker*, February 6, 2002, http://www.newyorker.com/magazine/2012/02/06/dear-leader.

70. "Zeitoun: How a Hero in New Orleans after Hurricane Katrina Was Arrested, Labeled a Terrorist & Jailed," *Democracy Now*, August 27, 2010, http://www.democracynow.org/2010/8/27/exclusivezeitoun_how_a_hero_in_new.

71. Victoria Patterson, "Did Dave Eggers Get 'Zeitoun' Wrong?," *Salon*, December 9, 2012, http://www.salon.com/2012/12/09/did_dave_eggers_get_zeitoun_wrong/.

72. Nancy Raquel Mirabal, "Diasporic Appetites and Longings: An Interview with Edwidge Danticat," *Calaloo* 30.1 (Winter 2007): 29.

73. Thomas Glave, *The Torturer's Wife* (San Francisco: City Lights, 2008), 69.

74. Wole Soyinka, *The Burden of Memory, the Muse of Forgiveness* (Oxford: Oxford University Press, 1999), 38–39.

75. Fiona Wright, *The Israeli Radical Left: An Ethics of Complicity* (Philadelphia: University of Pennsylvania Press, 2018), 46.

CHAPTER 3 · Ethical Concerns in the Novel of Human Rights

1. Thomas Laquer cited in Rachel Ablow, "Tortured Sympathies: Victorian Literature and the Ticking Time-Bomb Scenario," *ELH* 80.4 (Winter 2013): 1150.

2. Ibid., 1152.

3. See Lauren Wilcox, *Bodies of Violence: Theorizing Embodied Subjects in International Relations* (Oxford: Oxford University Press, 2015), 184, 30–31.

4. Lynn Chun Ink, "Remaking Identity, Unmaking Nation: Historical Recovery and the Reconstruction of Community in *In the Time of the Butterflies* and *The Farming of Bones*," *Callaloo* 27.3 (Summer 2004): 794. For a response to Ink, see Crystal Parikh's analysis of *In the Time of the Butterflies* in her *Writing Human Rights: The Political Imaginaries of Writers of Color* (Minneapolis: University of Minnesota Press, 2017), 181–183.

5. See W. Lawrence Hogue, "Radical Democracy, African-American (Male) Subjectivity, and John Edgar Wideman's *Philadelphia Fire*," *MELUS* 33.3 (Fall 2008): 46, 55, 65–67; see also Jan Clausen, "Native Fathers," *Kenyon Review* 14.2 (Spring 1992): 52–53.

6. Adam Roberts, review of *The Windup Girl* by Paolo Bacipaguli, December 17, 2010, http://www.theguardian.com/books/2010/dec/18/windup-girl-paolo-bacigalupi-review.

7. See for instance "Feminist Fiction," http://feministfiction.com/2012/08/13/the-windup-girl/; and "Asking the Wrong Questions," http://wrongquestions.blogspot.com/2009/12/windup-girl-by-paolo-bacigalupi.html.

8. See Brooklyn Public Library, "Brooklyn by the Book Series: Laurie Muchnick in Conversation with Chang-rae Lee," January 19, 2014, https://www.youtube.com/watch?v=BCYRbQgO-ao, and his talk at the Chautauqua Institution, "Chang-rae Lee—On Such a Full Sea," July 4, 2014, https://www.youtube.com/watch?v=j84OAG7mZQ4. Relatedly, see Joanna Biggs, "We: Chang-rae Lee's *On Such a Full Sea*," *New Yorker*, January 27, 2014, http://www.newyorker.com/magazine/2014/01/27/we-4.

9. Ron Charles, "Bob Shacochis Wins Dayton Literary Peace Prize for Fiction," *Washington Post*, September 24, 2014, https://www.washingtonpost.com/news/arts-and-entertainment/wp/2014/09/24/bob-shacochis-wins-dayton-literary-peace-prize-for-fiction/.

10. Bob Shacochis, *The Woman Who Lost Her Soul* (New York: Grove, 2013), 17, 9.

11. Amy Wilentz, "The Unquiet Americans," September 20, 2013, http://www.nytimes.com/2013/09/22/books/review/bob-shacochiss-woman-who-lost-her-soul.html.

12. Wendy Hesford, *Spectacular Rhetorics: Human Rights Visions, Recognitions, Feminisms* (Durham, NC: Duke University Press, 2011), 94–96.

13. Charles, "Bob Shacochis Wins Dayton Literary Peace Prize for Fiction."

14. Ruth Seifert, "War and Rape: A Preliminary Analysis," in *Mass Rape: The War against Women in Bosnia-Herzegovina*, ed. Alexandra Stiglmayer (Lincoln: University of Nebraska Press, 1994), 63–64.

15. See Tamsin Paige, "Piracy and Universal Jurisdiction," *Macquarie Law Journal* 12 (2013): 131–154.

16. See Kelly Dawn Askin, *War Crimes against Women: Prosecution in International War Crimes Tribunals* (The Hague: Martinus Nijhoff, 1997), 48, 13–14, 248, xiv, 226.

17. Corban Addison, *A Walk across the Sun* (New York: Quercus, 2012), 272.

18. See my *That the World May Know: Bearing Witness to Atrocity* (Cambridge, MA: Harvard University Press, 2007), 164–229.

19. Patty Rhule, review of *A Walk across the Sun* by Corban Addison, *USA Today*, February 19, 2012, https://www.usatoday.com/story/life/books/2013/06/28/sun-explores-child-sex-trafficking/2470401/.

20. Corban Addison, "A Prism, Not a Peep Show: Exposing Child Trafficking in Fiction," *Huffington Post*, March 5, 2012, http://www.huffingtonpost.com/corban-addison/a-prism-not-a-peep-show-e_b_1313728.html.

21. Makau Mutua, "Savages, Victims, and Savers: The Metaphor of Human Rights," *Harvard International Law Journal* 42.1 (2001): 201.

22. Corban Addison, *The Garden of Burning Sand* (New York: Quercus, 2013), 27.

23. See Addison, *Garden of Burning Sand*, 361, 360, 382, 384, 398.

24. Gillian Whitlock, *Postcolonial Life Narratives: Testimonial Transactions* (Oxford: Oxford University Press, 2015), 110.

25. Fredric Jameson, "Third World Literature in the Era of Multinational Capitalism," *Social Text* 15 (1986): 69.

26. Imre Szeman, "Who's Afraid of National Allegory? Jameson, Literary Criticism, Globalization," *South Atlantic Quarterly* 100.3 (Summer 2001): 806.

27. Caren Irr, *Toward the Geopolitical Novel: U.S. Fiction in the Twenty-First Century* (New York: Columbia University Press, 2013), 117. Unfortunately I came to the work of Caren Irr only at the end of this project. Her work on geopolitical novels is deeply interesting, and this book would have been better had I encountered her work earlier.

28. Jean-Jacques Rousseau, *Politics and the Arts: Letter to M. D'Alembert on the Theater* (Glencoe, IL: Free Press, 1960), 25.

29. Ibid., 24.

30. See Paul Bloom, *Against Empathy: The Case for Rational Compassion* (New York: HarperCollins, 2016).

31. I have taken language here from my essay "Is Empathy Bad?," Harvard University Press Blog, June 3, 2013, http://harvardpress.typepad.com/hup_publicity/2013/06/james-dawes-on-empathy.html.

32. James Dawes, *Evil Men* (Cambridge, MA: Harvard University Press, 2013), 197–202, 208–213.

33. Chang-rae Lee, Dayton Literary Peace Prize speech, 2011, http://www.daytonliterarypeaceprize.org/2011_files/videos/Chang-rae_Lee.htm.

34. Dayton Literary Peace Prize, http://daytonliterarypeaceprize.org/2011-fiction_winner.htm.

35. See Dawes, *That the World May Know*, 203–205, 210.

36. Chang-rae Lee, *The Surrendered* (New York: Riverhead, 2010), 323.

37. Richard Powers, *Operation Wandering Soul* (New York: Perennial, 2002), 107.

38. Thomas Palaima, personal conversation, April 9, 2016, and "Courage and Prowess Afoot in Homer and the Vietnam of Tim O'Brien," *Classical and Modern Literature* 20.3 (2000): 1.

39. On refusal of closure in the novel, see Richard Hardack, "'Militant Expectations': Childhood's End and Millenarianism in Richard Powers' *Operation Wandering Soul*," *Studies in American Fiction* 36.2 (Autumn 2008): 221–238.

40. For more on narrative as healing and harm, see April Lindner, "Narrative as Necessary Evil in Richard Powers's *Operation Wandering Soul*," *Critique* 38.1 (Fall 1996): 68–79.

41. Rebecca Skloot, *The Immortal Life of Henrietta Lacks* (New York: Crown, 2010), 2.

42. See Mikhail Bakhtin, *Rabelais and His World*, trans. Helene Iswolsky (Bloomington: Indiana University Press, 1984), 1–58, 303–367.

43. Ibid., e.g., 273–277, esp. 276.

44. *USA Today* cited from Richard Powers's homepage, http://www.richard powers.net/operation-wandering-soul/.

45. John Rawls, *A Theory of Justice* (Cambridge, MA: Belknap Press of Harvard University Press, 1971), 27.

46. David T. Mitchell and Sharon L. Snyder, *Narrative Prosthesis: Disability and the Dependencies of Discourse* (Ann Arbor: University of Michigan Press, 2000), 49, 47, 48.

47. Stephanie Hsu, "The Ontology of Disability in Chang-rae Lee's *The Surrendered*," *Journal of Literary and Cultural Disability Studies* 7.1 (213): 23–24, 32, 22.

48. Ruth Hubbard, "Abortion and Disability: Who Should and Should Not Inhabit the World?," in *The Disability Studies Reader*, 4th ed., ed. Lennard J. Davis (New York: Routledge, 2013), 84.

49. See for instance Jon E. Lewis, *A Documentary History of Human Rights: A Record of the Events, Documents and Speeches That Shaped Our World* (New York: Carroll Graf, 2003).

50. Elizabeth Anker, *Fictions of Dignity: Embodying Human Rights in World Literature* (Ithaca, NY: Cornell University Press, 2012), 15.

51. Arlene Kanter, *The Development of Disability Rights under International Law: From Charity to Human Rights* (New York: Routledge, 2015), 6.

52. *Documents on the Laws of War*, 2nd ed., ed. Adam Roberts and Richard Guelff (Oxford: Oxford University Press, 1989), 468.

53. Richard Rhodes, "Absolute Power," *New York Times*, March 21, 2014, http://www.nytimes.com/2014/03/23/books/review/thermonuclear-monarchy -by-elaine-scarry.html.

54. Lauren Wilcox, *Bodies of Violence: Theorizing Embodied Subjects in International Relations* (Oxford: Oxford University Press, 2015), 184, 30–31.

CHAPTER 4 · Perpetrators in the Novel of Human Rights

1. See openDemocracy.net, "Engaging with Perpetrators for Human Rights: When, How and at What Cost?," https://www.opendemocracy.net /openglobalrights/engaging-with-perpetrators-for-human-rights.

2. See Elaine Scarry, *On Beauty and Being Just* (Princeton, NJ: Princeton University Press, 1999).

3. Gillian Whitlock, *Postcolonial Life Narratives: Testimonial Transactions* (Oxford: Oxford University Press, 2015), 164.

4. Quoted in Katja Kurz, *Narrating Contested Lives: The Aesthetics of Life Writing in Human Rights Campaigns* (Heidelberg: Universitätsverlag Winter, 2015), 134.

5. Belinda Luscombe, "Pop Culture Finds Lost Boys," *Time*, February 12, 2007, 62–64.

6. Kurz, *Narrating Contested Lives*, 159.

7. See Timothy Williams, "Suicides Outpacing War Deaths for Troops," *New York Times*, June 8, 2012, http://www.nytimes.com/2012/06/09/us/suicides -eclipse-war-deaths-for-us-troops.html; and Gregg Zoroya, "VA study: 22 Vets Commit Suicide Every Day," *USA Today*, February 1, 2013, http://www .usatoday.com/story/news/nation/2013/02/01/veterans-suicide/1883329/.

8. Roy Scranton, "The Trauma Hero: From Wilfred Own to *Redeployment* and *American Sniper*," *Los Angeles Review of Books*, January 25, 2015, https:// lareviewofbooks.org/article/trauma-hero-wilfred-owen-redeployment -american-sniper/.

9. For more on the way the novel presents the white US soldier as "the foremost victim of an event in which Iraqi civilians died at the hands of American soldiers," see Joseph Darda, "The Ethnicization of Veteran America: Larry Heinemann, Toni Morrison, and Military Whiteness after Vietnam," *Contemporary Literature* 57.3 (Fall 2016): 436.

10. Michael Richardson, *Gestures of Testimony: Torture, Trauma, and Affect in Literature* (New York: Bloomsbury, 2016), 7–8.

11. Quoted in Bron Sibree, "To Listen and Learn," *New Zealand Herald*, August 6, 2007, http://www.nzherald.co.nz/terrorism/news/article.cfm?c_id =340&objectid=10455525.

12. Hannah Arendt, *Eichmann in Jerusalem: A Report on the Banality of Evil* (New York: Penguin, 1994), 279.

13. Mark Athitakis, review of *The Secret History of Las Vegas* by Chris Abani, *Washington Post*, February 7, 2014, https://www.washingtonpost.com /entertainment/books/the-secret-history-of-las-vegas-by-chris-abani/2014 /02/07/73f67826-8785-11e3-916e-e01534b1e132_story.html?utm_term= .6d2fe8b6d505.

14. Arendt, *Eichmann in Jerusalem*, 46, 252, 288, 276.

15. Abram de Swaan, *The Killing Compartments: The Mentality of Mass Murder* (New Haven, CT: Yale University Press, 2015), 23.

16. Harold Rosenberg, "The Shadow of the Furies," *New York Review of Books*, January 20, 1977, 47–48.

17. Hannah Arendt, *On Violence* (New York: Harvest, 1970), 53, 56.

18. Richard F. Patterson, "Resurrecting Rafael: Fictional Incarnations of a Dominican Dictator," *Callaloo* 29.1 (Winter 2006): 234.

19. Laleh Khadivi, *The Age of Orphans* (New York: Bloomsbury, 2009), 201, 129, 132.

20. Ana Patricia Rodríguez, *Dividing the Isthmus: Central American Transnational Histories, Literatures, and Cultures* (Austin: University of Texas Press, 2009), 122, 125.

21. Jonathan Littell, *The Kindly Ones* (New York: HarperPerennial, 2010), 874.

22. See Marie-Laure Combes, "American Novelist Becomes French Citizen," The Associated Press, March 9, 2007, http://www.washingtonpost.com/wp-dyn /content/article/2007/03/09/AR2007030901337_pf.html; "Briefly Noted," *New Yorker*, March 23, 2009, http://www.newyorker.com/magazine/2009/03/23/the

-kindly-ones; and David Gates, "The Monster in the Mirror," *New York Times*, March 5, 2009, http://www.nytimes.com/2009/03/08/books/review/Gates-t .html?_r=0.

23. Zygmunt Bauman, *Modernity and the Holocaust* (Ithaca, NY: Cornell University Press, 1990), xi.

24. Martha C. Nussbaum, *Love's Knowledge: Essays on Philosophy and Literature* (New York: Oxford University Press, 1990), 15.

25. Robert Jay Lifton, *The Nazi Doctors: Medical Killing and the Psychology of Genocide* (New York: Basic Books, 1986), 435–436. See also Arendt, *Eichmann in Jerusalem*, 106.

26. Charles Perrow, *Complex Organizations: A Critical Essay*, 3rd ed. (New York: McGraw-Hill, 1986), 121.

27. Arendt, *Eichmann in Jerusalem*, 49.

28. James March and Herbert Simon, *Organizations*, 2nd ed. (New York: Wiley-Blackwell, 1993), 186.

29. Perrow, *Complex Organizations*, 128. Satisficing involves finding adequate solutions given limited information and time constraints; optimizing involves developing strategies to find the best solutions.

30. David Gates, "The Monster in the Mirror," *New York Times*, March 5, 2009, http://www.nytimes.com/2009/03/08/books/review/Gates-t.html?_r=0.

31. Bernhard Schlink, *The Reader* (New York: Vintage, 1998), 157.

32. Susan Rubin Suleiman, "When the Perpetrator Becomes a Reliable Witness of the Holocaust: On Jonathan Littell's *Les Bienveillantes*," *New German Critique* 106 (Winter 2009): 8–9, 15, 18.

33. Philip Watts, "Literature and History: Around *Suite Française* and *Les Bienveillantes*," *Yale French Studies* 121 (2012): 164–165, 167–168.

34. See James Griffin, *On Human Rights* (Oxford: Oxford University Press, 2008), 63. See also Peter Jones, *Rights* (New York: St. Martin's Press, 1994), 201.

35. Amy Gutmann, introduction to Michael Ignatieff, *Human Rights as Politics and Idolatry*, ed. Amy Gutmann (Princeton, NJ: Princeton University Press, 2001), x.

36. Ignatieff, *Human Rights as Politics and Idolatry*, 56; Jacob Mchangama and Guglielmo Verdirame, "The Danger of Human Rights Proliferation," *Foreign Affairs*, July 24, 2013.

37. *The People on War Report: ICRC Worldwide Consultation on the Rules of War*, prepared by Greenberg Research, Inc. (Geneva: ICRC, 1999), x.

38. The question of enforcement and the plausibility of international rule of law is, of course, much debated. Hannah Arendt cites sociologists representing the "realist" tradition: "'All politics is a struggle for power; the ultimate kind of power is violence,' said C. Wright Mills, echoing, as it were, Max Weber's definition of the state as 'the rule of men over men based on the means of legitimate, that is allegedly legitimate, violence.'" Arendt, *On Violence*, 35. As one military thinker writes: "In the last analysis the action of States is regulated by nothing but power and expediency." Samuel P. Huntington, *The Soldier and the State* (Cambridge, MA: Harvard University Press, 1985), 66. For commentary on the ineffectiveness of both the United Nations and the collective nonvio-

lent pressure of the international community, see Adam Roberts, "The Laws of War: Problems of Implementation in Contemporary Conflicts," *Duke Journal of Comparative and International Law* 6 (Fall 1995): 11, 47. Arendt attacks this realist view by reformulating power as an expression of consent that both includes moral norms and excludes violence: "It is the people's support that lends power to the institutions of a country, and this support is but the continuation of the consent that brought the laws into existence to begin with" (41).

H. L. A. Hart offers an argument that extends Arendt's explanation of domestic power to the international arena. "To argue that international law is not binding because of a lack of organized sanctions," he writes, "is tacitly to accept the analysis of obligation contained in the theory that law is essentially a matter of orders backed by threats." As Hart explains:

> This theory . . . identifies "having an obligation" or "being bound" with "likely to suffer the sanction or punishment threatened for disobedience." Yet . . . this identification distorts the role played in all legal thought and discourse of the ideas of obligation and duty. Even in municipal law, where there are effective organized sanctions, we must distinguish . . . the meaning of the external predictive statement "I (you) are likely to suffer for disobedience," from the internal normative statement "I (you) have an obligation to act thus" which assesses a particular person's situation from the point of view of rules accepted as guiding standards of behavior. It is true that not all rules give rise to obligations or duties; and it is also true that the rules which do so generally call for some sacrifice of private interests, and are generally supported by serious demands for conformity and insistent criticism of deviations. Yet once we free ourselves from the predictive analysis and its parent conception of law as essentially an order backed by threats, there seems no good reason for limiting the normative idea of obligation to rules supported by organized sanctions.

H. L. A. Hart, *The Concept of Law* (Oxford: Clarendon Press, 1961), 212–213.

Immanuel Kant, indeed, argues not for the possibility but the inevitability of the development of binding international obligations. He begins by asserting that "peoples who have grouped themselves into nation states may be judged in the same way as individual men living in a state of nature, independent of external laws; for they are a standing offence to one another by the very fact that they are neighbours. Each nation, for the sake of its own security, can and ought to demand of the others that they should enter along with it into a constitution, similar to the civil one, within which the rights of each could be secured. This would mean establishing a *federation of peoples*." Such a federation, he is quick to explain, would not be equivalent to a global state:

> This federation does not aim to acquire any power like that of a state, but merely to preserve and secure the *freedom* of each state in itself, along with that of the other confederated states, although this does not mean that they need to submit to public laws and to a coercive power which enforces them, as do men in a state of nature. It can be shown that this idea of *federalism*,

extending gradually to encompass all states and thus leading to perpetual peace, is practicable and has objective reality.

He goes on to argue that the development of republicanism and an increasing economic interdependence will generate this federalism. Immanuel Kant, *Kant: Political Writings*, ed. Hans Reiss, trans. H. B. Nisbet (Cambridge: Cambridge University Press, 1991), 102, 104.

Acknowledgments

Sᴏᴍᴇ ᴀʀɢᴜᴍᴇɴᴛꜱ ᴘʀᴇꜱᴇɴᴛᴇᴅ in this book rest on my previous writings. The Introduction and a section of Chapter 1 incorporate my essay "The Novel of Human Rights," *American Literature* 88.1 (March 2016): 127–157, republished by permission of the copyright holder, Duke University Press. A short passage from "Human Rights, Literature, and Empathy," in *The Routledge Companion to Literature and Human Rights*, ed. Sophia McClennen and Alexandra Schultheis (New York: Routledge, 2016): 427–432, appears in the Introduction. Elements of Chapter 2 are examined in "Afterword: Human Rights Formalism," in *Teaching Human Rights in Literary and Cultural Studies*, ed. Alexandra Schultheis Moore and Elizabeth Swanson Goldberg (New York: MLA, 2015): 321–326.

I owe a special debt of gratitude to Alexandra Schultheis Moore and Elizabeth Swanson for their intellectual generosity and rigor.

And to Barış, Michael, and Christopher: my forevers.

Index

Abani, Chris: *Song for Night*, 68; *The Secret History of Las Vegas*, 70, 97, 109, 162–168, 175–177
Ablow, Rachel, 117, 118
Addison, Corban: human-rights orientation of novels of, 18; *The Tears of Dark Water*, 95, 128, 130, 135–136, 139–141; *The Garden of Burning Sand*, 110, 128, 133–135, 139; *A Walk across the Sun*, 110, 127–128, 131–133, 134, 135, 138–139
Age of Orphans, The (Khadivi), 180
Alarcón, Daniel: *Lost City Radio*, 86–88, 96, 171; *At Night We Walk in Circles*, 171
Allende, Isabel: *Of Love and Shadows*, 24, 51; *Maya's Notebook*, 49–51, 77, 93–94, 96
Alvarez, Julia, *In the Time of the Butterflies*, 26–27, 109, 119
Amnesty International, 28–29
Anil's Ghost (Ondaatje), 26
Anker, Elizabeth, 10, 69
Apartheid, 70, 123–124, 163–165, 176, 177

Appeal to the World, An, 11–12
Arendt, Hannah: on human rights, 47, 57; on household and patriarchy, 92; on Eichmann, 175, 178, 186–187; on power and violence, 179, 220n38, 221n38
Askin, Kelly Dawn, 129–130
At Night We Walk in Circles (Alarcón), 171
Awakening, The (Chopin), 111–112

Bacigalupi, Paolo, *The Windup Girl*, 65, 120–121
Bakhtin, Mikhail, 153–154
Bandung Conference (1955), 41–42
Barnard, Chester, 186
Barnett, Michael, 15
Beah, Ishmael, *A Long Way Gone*, 170–171
Beautiful Things That Heaven Bears, The (Mengestu), 58
Bel Canto (Patchett), 18, 63–64, 95
Benenson, Peter, 28
Bercovitch, Sacvan, 8
Bhabha, Jacqueline, 108
Bloom, Paul, 142

225